Ethics for the Public Service Professional

Second Edition

To:

An inspiring
of virtuous pr...

Ethics for the Public Service Professional

Second Edition

Aric W. Dutelle
Randy S. Taylor

CRC Press
Taylor & Francis Group
Boca Raton London New York

CRC Press is an imprint of the
Taylor & Francis Group, an **informa** business

CRC Press
Taylor & Francis Group
6000 Broken Sound Parkway NW, Suite 300
Boca Raton, FL 33487-2742

First issued in paperback 2020

ISBN-13: 978-1-138-03504-1 (hbk)
ISBN-13: 978-0-367-78162-0 (pbk)

Library of Congress Cataloging-in-Publication Data

Names: Dutelle, Aric W., author. | Taylor, Randy S., author.
Title: Ethics for the public service professional / Aric W. Dutelle and Randy S. Taylor.
Description: Second edition. | Boca Raton, FL : CRC Press, [2018] | Revised edition of: Ethics for the public service professional / Aric W. Dutelle. 2011. | Includes bibliographical references and index.
Identifiers: LCCN 2017033719| ISBN 9781138035041 (hardback : alk. paper) | ISBN 9781315269658 (ebook)
Subjects: LCSH: Civil service ethics--United States. | Law enforcement--United States. | United States--Officials and employees.
Classification: LCC KF4568 .D88 2018 | DDC 172/.2--dc23
LC record available at https://lccn.loc.gov/2017033719

Visit the Taylor & Francis Web site at
http://www.taylorandfrancis.com

and the CRC Press Web site at
http://www.crcpress.com

This book is dedicated to those who have chosen a life of public service. Although you may not often hear it, you are very much appreciated.

Aric W. Dutelle

Over my career, I have assimilated many memories where unethical behavior has damaged the lives of good, innocent people. This book is dedicated to my children and all who take the opportunity to be a voice of virtuous principles.

Randy S. Taylor

It is not the critic who counts, not the man who points out how the strong man stumbled, or where the doer of deeds could have done better. The credit belongs to the man who is actually in the arena, whose face is marred by the dust and sweat and blood, who strives valiantly, who errs and comes up short again and again, who knows the great enthusiasms, the great devotions and spends himself in a worthy course, who at the best, knows in the end the triumph of high achievement, and who, at worst, if he fails, at least fails while daring greatly, so that his place shall never be with those cold and timid souls who know neither victory [n]or defeat.

Theodore Roosevelt
Paris Sorbonne, 1910

Contents

Preface

While there are several noteworthy texts within the academic market which have been written on the topic of ethics, unfortunately they tend to be written from a philosophical point of view, written for a business/management audience, or written strictly for a police audience (with limited applicability and in-depth study of the topic of ethics). The market remains thin relating to a text written for those individuals currently involved within the field of public service, to include not just those in law enforcement, but also those in other areas of emergency public service at the local, county, state, and federal levels. This should include not only those at the "street" level, but also those within administrative positions. With news headlines almost weekly showing instances where individuals, departments, and organizations have been involved in unethical situations or scenarios, it is more important than ever to impress upon those preparing for a career in public service the importance of ethics within their actions and decision-making processes.

Building upon the success of the first edition, "Ethics for the Public Service Professional, Second Edition" has further evolved, with the addition of a very experienced and appropriate co-author, Randy Taylor. His dissertation, *A Qualitative Phenomenological Examination of Ethics Based Training in Law Enforcement*, was integrated throughout the first edition and it just made good sense to add him to the writing team! Hopefully, the reader will find that having the additional insight and research adds another level to the text and gives the reader a more diverse, while also more in-depth, view of the need for ethical training within public service.

It is our hope that *Ethics for the Public Service Professional, Second Edition*, will be a single-source reference for the topic of ethics and ethical decision making as it relates to government service, and service within the areas of homeland security and emergency services at the local, county, state, and federal levels. This text will discuss the challenges faced by today's public service professionals and administrators with regard to incorporating ethics within daily decisions, discretion, and duties. This in-depth reference will help to eliminate the warped impressions created by modern dramas as to what is ethical and what is discretionary within the confines of a public servant's job. The text has been infused with current and historical events in an effort to provide a proper examination of the history of ethics, codes, and legislation relating to public service. This text will be essential for the foundational development and explanation of protocols used within a successful organization for those persons new to the realm of emergency services and will serve as a reference for those already involved within the field.

Acknowledgments

There are a number of people who the authors would like to thank for their selfless assistance with this text, without whose assistance this work would fall incredibly short of hitting the mark.

We wish to thank:

Tom Caywood. Your mentorship and insight, as well as your friendship and professional advice over the years are much appreciated.

Carrie Holberg. You are a truly amazing person with a vast array of possibilities in front of you. I appreciate you taking time out of your busy schedule to contribute to this text. Your friendship and work ethic are deeply appreciated.

Ed Ross. Your insight regarding the more personal side of the criminal justice system has been greatly appreciated. Thank you for taking time out to contribute your knowledge and experience in helping to make this text a well-rounded one.

Elicia Blazer. Your continued support of the visual elements of this text are very much appreciated. Your vision and professionalism are once again on display.

Laura Dutelle. Your assistance at crunch time was amazing. We are blessed to have had you on our side.

The authors also wish to thank: Jay Margolis, Mark Listewnik, Misha Kydd, and Jonathan Achorn, and the entire editorial, production, and marketing staff at Taylor & Francis Group for giving us the opportunity, assisting us with the production, and helping to create what we hope will be a work that will fill a much-needed void in professional education.

Lastly, we wish to thank our families and friends for their love and support. We are grateful for your patience and understanding throughout this endeavor.

About the Authors

Aric W. Dutelle has been involved in law enforcement since 1999. During this time, he has held positions as a police officer, deputy sheriff, crime scene technician, and reserve medico-legal investigator. He has a Master of Forensic Sciences (MFS) degree, with a specialty in impression evidence and is the author of over 20 articles, as well as author and co-author of seven texts, to include *An Introduction to Crime Scene Investigation* (three editions) and *Criminal Investigation* (4th and 5th editions) by Jones and Bartlett Learning. The author continues to be actively involved in training, consulting, and assisting law enforcement agencies with criminal investigations and crime scene processing around the United States and internationally. The author also calls upon his 14 years of university-level instruction to assemble this text into a pedagogical friendly text to those within the education and training community.

Randy S. Taylor, D.M. is currently the Chief of Police for the town of Clarkdale, Arizona. Prior to working for Clarkdale, he was the chief of police for a community in Kansas. These appointments followed his retirement from a career of police work in Colorado, marking over 40 years in law enforcement. His education consists of a bachelor's of science degree in Criminal Justice, a master's in business, and a doctorate of management in organizational leadership. His dissertation was conducted in the area of ethics ("A Qualitative Phenomenological Examination of Ethics-Based Training in Law Enforcement"). Simultaneous to his career in law enforcement, he developed management experience through owning a variety of businesses to include title insurance companies in Kansas and Colorado, a construction company, a football equipment specialty corporation, an idiosyncratic coffee service, a commercial and residential rental company, and fire and water restoration business. These experiences have afforded him the opportunity to evaluate ethics in their application for both the public and private sectors. As an adjunct professor at Fort Hays State University the past three years, he has challenged students to evaluate the multifaceted philosophical challenges these sectors face in their application of ethics.

Introduction

Law and punishment are coercive forms of social control linked to the community moral code. Contemporary emergency personnel, bearing common oaths of office, navigate an ethical minefield, made increasingly public due to modern media. The individuals employed in these positions are sometimes confronted with decisions that must weigh personal values against peer demands for group cohesion, in frustrating environments where challenging peacekeeping responsibilities pit them against the unethical underbelly of criminal America. Sometimes at odds within their own ranks, ethical issues abound.

Frank Kardasz

Hoping that this text will serve those not only new to the field, but those already employed within it, it must be realized that public service corruption scandals are painful reminders of the need for continuing education in the subjects of ethics and integrity. In a statement by the International Association of Chiefs of Police, the topic of ethics education was made intuitively obvious:

Ethics is our greatest training and leadership need today and into the next century. In addition to the fact that most departments do not conduct ethics training, nothing is more devastating to individual departments and our entire profession than uncovered scandals or discovered acts of officer misconduct and unethical behavior.

The United States Department of Justice has since echoed this sentiment:

Creating a culture of integrity is an integral part of fostering an environment conducive to problem solving and community engagement.

What will set this text apart is the manner and direction in which it is prepared.

- The text will examine timely and up-to-date coverage of current police and public service controversies, revised since the first edition.
- It will discuss important new mechanisms of accountability, such as comprehensive use of force reporting, citizen complaint procedures, and early intervention systems. It also will include a helpful list of websites for further research on the topics covered within this book.

- The study of ethics is best addressed through the analysis of real-life situations confronted by those within public service. There will be news story reviews incorporated throughout the text to challenge the reader and educate them on the diverse scope of ethics within the public work place.
- Ethical scenarios will be included to instigate healthy debate and educated discussion regarding the topics being covered.

Pedagogical Features

- **Learning Objectives.** The learning objectives are listed at the beginning of each chapter. Emphasis is placed on active learning rather than passive learning. It is hoped that the reader gains knowledge of how to apply the concepts and material, and not simply retain it temporarily with plans to regurgitate. The learning objectives concentrate on the acquisition of knowledge and foundations needed to understand, compare, contrast, define, explain, predict, estimate, evaluate, plan, and apply.
- **Key Terms.** If one is to study the topic of ethics, it is necessary that he/she become familiar with the terminology and associated vocabulary. To assist with this, key terms are listed at the beginning of each chapter to alert the readers to specific terms that they should key in on in order to best grasp an understanding of the subject matter.
- **"Ripped from the Headlines" current event examples.** In an effort to apply the theory and guidelines addressed within the book, the reader is provided with examples of real-world incidents involving the content discussed within the chapter. It is hoped that this application to real-world situations will enable the reader to better grasp the concepts presented.
- **"A Question of Ethics" boxes.** These boxes are ethical dilemmas that are posed to the reader and seek personal weigh-in and insight from the reader as to the "correctness" of the answer.
- **"Reflections."** These boxes are examples, insights, or questions that are posed to the reader, and challenge them to consider a scenario, situation, or event for themselves.
- **"View from an Expert" insights.** As a way to further the real-world information that the reader is exposed to within the text, many chapters also include insight from a public servant within the chapter content field.
- **Questions for Review.** At the end of each chapter, the reader is confronted with eight to ten questions that are directly related to the

learning objectives stated at the beginning of the chapter. A thorough review of the provided questions will enable the reader (and instructor) to gauge meaningful learning and attainment of the stated learning objectives.

- **References.** In addition to that which is cited within each chapter, an exhaustive reference list is also given at the end of the text, to assist the reader and educator with providing additional depth and insight into the topical area.

Reference

Kardasz, F. 2008. *Ethics training for law enforcement: Practices and trends.* Saarbrücken, Germany: VDM Verlag.

Ethics

A Look at the Basics

1

Always do right—this will gratify some and astonish the rest.

Mark Twain

Key Terms

Descriptive ethics
Ethics
Meta-ethics

Morals
Normative ethics values

Learning Objectives

1. Define **ethics**.
2. Define and distinguish between **morals, values,** and **ethics**.
3. Define and differentiate among the three types of ethical subdivisions.
4. Differentiate between personal and political ethics.
5. Understand how ethics and morals are separate from law.

What Are "Ethics"?

History credits Theodore Roosevelt with saying that "to educate a man in mind, but not in morals is to create a menace to society." It is for precisely this reason that the topic of ethics is discussed within this text as a vital component of public service. Public servants must not only do technical things correctly and professional things in a professional manner, but they also must do ethically correct things. Everyone encounters ethical dilemmas in his or her personal and professional lives; the question is whether they are ready for them when they do. There has historically been a lack of training and education associated with ethics and with ethical decision making, which often sets the individual up for failure, or at the very least uncertainty, when confronted with an ethical dilemma. But what does it mean to have an ethical dilemma, and what are ethics? Perhaps exploring the origin of the word, and its historical usage, will assist in providing the answers necessary to evaluate ones choices and responses pertaining to a challenging event.

The term **ethics** means the study of moral standards and how they affect conduct. The Greek root for ethics is *ethos*, which emphasizes the perfection of the individual and the community in which he or she is defined (Foster, 2003).

There is great debate as to whether or not ethics should, or even can, be taught to adults. The two most common juxtaposition sides pertaining to this debate are that by the time one has reached adulthood, understanding of values and ethics is fixed, while others believe that lifelong education can influence and modify behavior, and thus ethics should be taught. Chapter 13 discusses the topic of ethical training and education. For now, let us concentrate on defining what ethics is and is not.

Revisiting the Basics

Nearly all educated people acknowledge the importance of ethics. However, relatively few understand ethics as well as they think that they do, or as well as they should. Ethics can best be meaningfully discussed and applied only when it is fully understood. This understanding requires that one revisit the philosophical and moral basics associated with that which encompasses the study of ethics. So, what then is ethics about?

Right and Wrong: "We do not call anything wrong, unless we mean to imply that a person ought to be punished in some way or other for doing it; if not by law, by the opinion of his fellow creatures; if not by opinion, by the reproaches of his own conscience" (Mill, 1861).

Virtue and Vice: "Vice, the opposite of virtue, shows us more clearly what virtue is. Justice becomes more obvious when we have injustice to compare it to" (Quintilian, 2006).

Benefit and Harm: "The two essential ingredients in the sentiment of justice are the desire to punish a person who has done harm, and the knowledge or belief that there is some definite individual or individuals to whom harm has been done" (Mill, 1869).

Universal Rules of Conduct: "Ethics encompasses fixed, universal rules of right conduct that are contingent on neither time nor culture nor circumstance" (Foster, 2003).

Character: Ethics is entwined within ones character, "the traits, qualities, and established reputation that define who one is and what one stands for in the eyes of others" (Foster, 2003).

Providing an Example: Ethics is founded upon "an established pattern of conduct worthy of emulation" (Foster, 2003).

Morals, Values, and Ethics

If one were to analyze the often-used interchangeable words of **morals** and **ethics**, he or she might encounter a great deal of confusion, as it often appears that many do not know that they are in fact entirely separate matters. While the delineation between the two is perhaps not as elementary as will be made within the text, it is not nearly as complex nor commingled as is found in common media and human interaction. While overly simplified, perhaps it is most easily summarized by Charles Colson (2000), "Morality describes what is. Ethics describes what ought to be."

The word **morality** originates from the Latin word *moralis*, which means "traditional customs or proper behavior." Therefore, fundamentally, morals refer to a set of rules defining what is considered to be right or wrong. These rules are defined by (although not typically written down or "defined" by writing) and accepted by a group or society. The group or society can include peers, educators, religion, media, and the family unit. If someone within the group or society breaks one of the rules, then they are typically considered to have been "bad" or "immoral."

Values, on the other hand, provide direction in the determination of right versus wrong or good versus bad. Values are what an individual believes to have worth and importance, or to be valuable. As such, morals are values that an individual attributes to a system of beliefs that assist the individual in defining right from wrong or good from bad.

Ethics, which has as its core the Greek word *ethos* (Merriam-Webster.com), refers to the "moral character of an individual." The Greeks believed that *ethos* included an emphasis on an individual's character as well as including the citizen as a component of a greater community. At the core, this seems an easy beginning; that ethics begins with the individual (**Figure 1.1**).

Ethics Versus Morals

Morals	Ethics
Derived from Latin word *moralis*, meaning "traditional customs"	Derived from the Greek word, *ethos*, meaning moral character
Typically associated with personal behavior	Typically refers to professional practices and behavior
Customs or manners practiced in any given community or culture	Conveys sense of stability/permanence
May be different from culture to culture	An absolute standard of behavior
May change as acceptable social behavior as the culture(s) change	Standard is universal and immutable (not subject to change)

Figure 1.1 Greek cardinal virtues. (Courtesy of Ellie Blazer. Adapted from Dreisbach, C. 2009. *Ethics in criminal justice*, New York: McGraw-Hill.)

ETHICAL SUBDIVISIONS

- **Normative ethics:** How moral values should be determined. (What do individuals think is right?)
- **Descriptive ethics:** What morals are actually followed or adhered to. (How should individuals act?)
- **Meta-ethics:** The fundamental nature of ethics, including whether it has an objective justification, how individuals determine for themselves what societal norms to follow. (What does it mean to be "right"?)

Ethics involves attempting to address questions as to how a moral outcome can be achieved. This is sometimes referred to as "applied ethics." For our purposes, we will divide the study of ethics into three areas: normative, descriptive, and meta-ethics.

Ethical Subdivisions

Normative Ethics

The field of **normative ethics** is concerned with investigating the questions that arise when one asks, "How should one act, ethically speaking?" It seeks to examine the standards for the rightness or wrongness of one's actions. Sociologically speaking, *normative* is derived from the term *norm*. As such, norms are concerned with those attributes of a culture that compose the largely unspoken, yet almost universally shared expectations as to what constitutes appropriate or inappropriate behavior. Norms are pointed to as defining the boundaries of what is considered conformity and what is considered deviance within a society. They are expectations not behaviors.

There are a number of areas that relate to the theoretical study of normative ethics. Although a philosophical approach is not the intent of this text, it is worth mentioning or directing the reader to the various theories.

Virtue Ethics

This theoretical approach to ethics was first advocated by Aristotle. Its focus was on the inherent character of an individual rather than on specific actions performed by them. In recent times, there has been a significant resurgence of virtue ethics. The reader is directed to the work of such philosophers as Alasdair Macintyre, Rosalind Hursthouse, Philippa Foot, and G. E. M. Anscombe.

Deontology

Those subscribing to deontological theories argue that ethical decisions should be made through the consideration of one's duties and obligations along with other individual's rights.

Contractarianism: Foundation surrounds the concept that moral acts are those that all individuals would agree with if they were to be unbiased. The reader is directed to the works of John Rawls and Thomas Hobbes for examples.

Natural rights theory: Foundation is that human beings have absolute, natural rights. The reader is directed to the works of Thomas Aquinas and John Locke.

Categorical imperative: Foundation is that morality is rooted in the capacity of individuals to be rational, and it also asserts that there are certain inviolable moral laws within society. The reader is directed to the works of Immanuel Kant as they pertain to this theory.

Consequentialism

These theories argue that the morality associated with an action is related to the outcome or result of the action. They differ by the value associated with the action or decision.

Utilitarianism: Best action/decision is one that results in the most happiness for the greatest number of individuals.

Egoism: Best action/decision is one that maximizes good for oneself.

Hedonism: Best action/decision is one that will maximize pleasure.

Intellectualism: Best action/decision is one that best promotes knowledge.

Consequentialist libertarianism: Liberty should be maximized.

Welfarism: Best action/decision is one that best increases economic well-being.

Situation ethics: Best action/decision is one that results in the most love.

Descriptive Ethics

Sometimes referred to as **comparative ethics**, **descriptive ethics** involves the study of an individual's beliefs relating to morality. The goal of descriptive ethics is to attempt to define individual beliefs relating to values and what actions are deemed right and wrong. It may also include researching what actions society condemns or punishes with regards to law and/or politics. It is important that the reader recognize that the attempt is to describe morality and not customs, etiquette, or laws of a group of people or society.

REFLECTIONS

Differentiating between ethics and morals

Consider a defense attorney: A lawyer may find murder immoral, according to their personal moral code; however, ethics require that lawyers defend their accused client to the best of their ability, even knowing their client is most likely guilty and that his/her acquittal or release could potentially result in additional crime.

If lawyers begin to question their ability to adhere to these ethical principles, then they must remove themselves from the practice or risk damaging the ethics of their profession. This is a fundamental concept within our public service system, that ethics must trump personal morals for the greater good of maintaining the integrity of a system.

This area is largely empirical as to research and, thus, typically involves the areas of biology, anthropology, sociology, and psychology, but also may carry over to the area of philosophy at times.

Meta-Ethics

Meta-ethics refer to the fundamental nature of ethics, including whether or not such ethics have an objective justification. More specifically, it refers to how individuals determine for themselves what societal norms to follow. For instance, "What does it mean to be 'right'"?

Therefore, if someone is to question a rule, he/she becomes engaged in an ethical discussion or argument because ethics is concerned with the justification for a rule or set of rules. Morals are a property of a society or an individual, while society or individuals can argue about ethics. This is a more flexible and adaptable field of ethics with less foundation to draw from and more "gut driven."

Differentiating Ethics and Morals from Law

Morals and ethics should be distinguished from law as well. Simply because something is legally permissible does not mean that it is morally and ethically permissible. This is the fundamental argument around the debates surrounding abortion, medical marijuana, child labor, capital punishment, and many others. And, just as legality does not suggest morality, illegality does not imply immorality. **Figure 1.2** shows a Venn diagram that displays an example of the relationship among ethics, morality, and law.

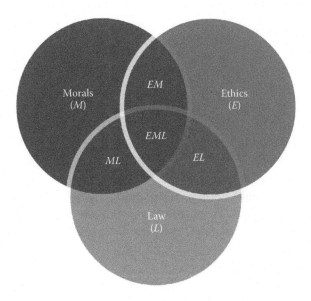

Figure 1.2 The relationship among ethics, morality, and law. (Courtesy of Laura Rider Dutelle.)

As can be seen in the diagram, the intersection of the three circles, representing the three distinct areas, results in seven classification areas. These areas reflect that there are decisions, choices, and considerations that may be moral, ethical, or legal, or that may be combinations of them. In fact, any action or decision made by an individual will ultimately fall within one of these seven classifications. Recognition of where one's decision or choice would fall is important, so as to know whether it is an appropriate one for the given scenario. Where the choice or decision is placed, within the figure, will determine whether it is acceptable, unacceptable, rejectable, or neutral.

M: Moral. This decision or choice would be based on individual or groupthink, typically influenced by peers, religion, family, friends, society, and other environmental factors. Some may view this as a "more right" choice, made based upon unwritten laws or views.

E: Ethical. A decision or choice that is viewed as "right" and that is not impacted by environmental factors. It is a universal truth and "right" choice.

L: Legal. A decision or choice that conforms to the written law of the land or society. This is typically a foundational requirement for all decisions made within public service.

EM: Ethical and moral. This combination may appease the individual or individuals but may not likely be able to be implemented due to not having a legal foundation.

QUESTION OF ETHICS

Consider some of the following examples, based on **Figure 1.2**:

- Where would choosing to solicit a prostitute (in the majority of the United States) fall within? What if the location was changed to Las Vegas?
- Where would capital punishment fall?
- What about murder?
- Where would abortion be placed?
- Where would a policy based upon tattoos be placed?
- Where would a theft made in a life or death decision be placed?
- Where would physical fitness requirements for a job be placed?
- Where would accepting a gratuity fall? What about accepting a bribe?

EL: Ethical and legal. This is where the vast majority of public service actions and decisions should land, resulting in decisions and actions that are "right" and "legal."

ML: Moral and legal. An action or decision that lands here is typically made for a religious or social reason, versus a strictly "right" versus "wrong" reason.

EML: Ethical, moral, and legal. Actions and decisions that fall into this area are able to satisfy the requirements of "right" and "legal" while also being acceptable to the individual or group making them.

An action or decision can be ethically right, morally wrong, and legally neutral. An example of this would be the following: Mike likes to eat red meat. The location where Mike lives frowns on its citizens eating red meat. It is not illegal, just socially unacceptable. Since there is a moral tenet in place, which essentially forbids eating red meat, doing so is thus viewed as immoral ("wrong"). However, since the behavior of Mike does not affect any other person directly, it is viewed as ethically neutral by others, but as "right" by Mike. Since there is no law that exists making the eating of red meat illegal, doing so is legally neutral.

But what about homicide? There are various categories of homicide: excusable homicide, justifiable homicide, murder, etc. The use of this figure and guidance for navigating ethical dilemmas will be further discussed in Chapter 3. What is important to remember is that this text is one on ETHICS for public service professionals. It is not a text regarding laws for public service professionals, nor one for morals. Legal codes and moral codes are not addressed in the remainder of this text. Once the reader feels comfortable with what ethics are (and are not), they are ready to move on to the remainder of the text to explore the manners in which ethics and ethical decision making are incorporated within the field of public service.

What Ethics Involves

"There is more to ethics than simply knowing what it is about" (Foster, 2003). It is just as important to know what is involved in its makeup. Ethics is the way values are practiced. As such, it is both a process of inquiry (deciding how to decide) and a code of conduct (a set of standards governing behavior).

"To think well is to think critically. Critical thinking, the conscious use of reason, stands clearly apart from other ways of grasping truth or confronting choice: impulse, habit, etc. Impulse is nothing more than an unreflective spontaneity, a mind on autopilot. Habit on the other hand is programmed repetition" (Foster, 2003). This is akin to muscle memory, except as applies to behavior. Repetition is habitual.

Therefore, "the object of critical thinking is to achieve a measure of objectivity to counteract or diminish the subjective bias that experience and socialization bestow on us all" (Foster, 2003). This is imperative because "when we are dealing with matters of ethical concern, the well-being of someone or something beyond ourselves is always at stake" (Foster, 2003).

Ethical foundation begins with the individual. While simplistic in nature, it is this issue that also is the starting point for the complications and travesties relating to ethics in public service, the fact that it all begins with an individual. An agency or organization cannot have ethics; it is its employees who have ethics. It is the administration that makes ethical decisions. The upside is that the majority of people desire to be ethical, most organizations desire to act ethically, and the majority of employees and organizations desire to be treated ethically. The downside to this is that a great many individuals and organizations simply are not proficient at the application of shared values, or group ethics, to the process of decision making. "The glory of the human story is that the capacity for good news makes ethics possible; the tragedy is that the propensity for evil makes ethics necessary" (Preston, 2001).

If we are to look at the simplicity and difficulty relating to the topic of ethics in public service, we must first differentiate between personal and political ethics.

First, the purpose of personal ethics is to make individuals morally better, or rather to ensure that the relationships between individuals are morally tolerable. Political ethics, on the other hand, while also serving to guide the actions of individuals, does so only with respect to their institutional roles and only to the degree necessary for the greater good of the institution or society (West and German, 2006).

Although these may appear to be two different areas of ethics, they have as their foundation a commonality. That is, regardless of either private or political (public) ethics, there is the common theme of a desire and expectation for respecting other's rights, fulfillment of obligations, fair treatment, and truthful words and actions.

Ethical decision making and implementation requires an individual to have both critical thinking and communication skills (Johnson, 2005). This would seem simplistic enough, but it is in passing along the decisions that the waters are muddied and the message blurred. It requires that the decision maker have a fundamental knowledge of leadership and of the leader–follower relationship (Ciulla, 2004).

In public service, there is hierarchy that relates to the various levels of ethics, each having its own set of responsibilities and own possibilities for complexities. At the first step is personal morality, or an individual's concept of right and wrong. This is formed as a basis of upbringing and environment. Second is professional ethics. These are typically codified within an organization or professional association relating to the organization or position. The third level is organizational. These can include written policies and procedures that dictate organizational expectations relating to ethical decision making and behavior. Lastly, there are social ethics. These are typically enacted as societal laws and also can be part of an individual's personal social conscience (Shafritz, Russell, and Borick, 2007).

Further Defining Ethical Makeup

This text does not intend to aide unethical people in becoming ethical. There is no such recipe for that. Rather, the intent is for the contents within this text to build upon the moral strength of the reader. As such, it is necessary to define several additional terms relating to those tools that the reader possesses in aiding them in the challenges confronted by an ethical dilemma.

> **Accountability** refers to public service professionals being liable or answerable to someone. It is a measure of their demonstration in fulfilling their promises. It is an external test.
> **Integrity** is the adherence to moral and ethical principles and integration of moral virtues into one's decisions and actions. It is an internal test.
> **Responsibility** is the act of being reliable or dependable, or the burden of accountability for having done something.

Causal and Moral Responsibility

In discussing the aforementioned, we must distinguish between what is referred to as **causal** responsibility and **moral** responsibility. A blind individual who knocks something over while attempting to negotiate his/her way through a congested shopping mall that is not adhering to compliancy for those who are handicapped is causally responsible for the damage that occurred, but he/she is not morally responsible. The individual had no way of controlling or foreseeing his/her actions, and therefore he/she deserves no moral blame for his/her actions. However, if a nonhandicapped person were to traverse the same location and decide to knock something over, causing it to break, then he/she would be both causally and morally responsible for the damage.

Therefore, there are four basic conditions that must be present in order to decide moral responsibility:

1. The individual must be aware of the facts pertaining to the situation or decision.
2. The individual must be cognizant of the difference between right and wrong.
3. The individual must have had intent to have done what he/she did.
4. The individual must have been able to do otherwise than what he/she did.

Infants and those with severe mental or physical impairments fail to meet the conditions set forth to determine moral responsibility and, therefore, require no excuse for their acts. However, those who are capable have no excuses beyond there being no other alternative to the actions taken, which would thusly result in the conditions not being met. If there is no excuse, then the only acceptable action is to take responsibility for one's actions. This is the basis for integrity and virtue.

The ancient Greeks recognized four basic virtues associated with ethics: courage, justice, temperance, and prudence (**Figure 1.3**). Aristotle believed that virtue was "the ability habitually to know the good and to do the good" (Dreisbach, 2009). This definition aids in reminding us that no person is morally good simply based on a single act or moment. Rather, "morality is a matter of character, and character is a matter of habit. The more one is in the habit of knowing and doing the good, the more one is virtuous" (Dreisbach, 2009).

Anyone who has ever used a firearm knows that hitting the bull's eye 100% of the time is not a realistic expectation. However, proper training, muscle memory, repetition, and development of positive habits certainly assist in improving the accuracy with which one shoots. However, just as a great marksman will on a rare occasion miss his or her mark, a poor marksman will sometimes hit the target. This is not as a result of habit, but is similar to the adage that "even a broken clock is correct twice a day." This anomaly does not make the poor marksman suddenly good, just as it does not make the excellent marksman suddenly bad when he or she is to finally

The Greek Cardinal Virtues

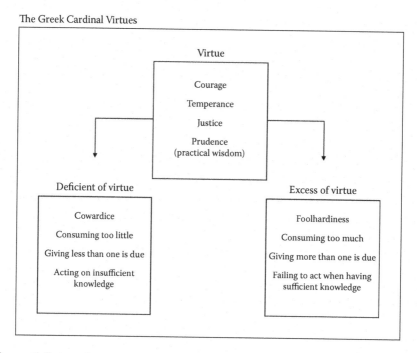

Figure 1.3 Morals versus ethics. (Adapted from http//courses.washington.edu /cee440/NotesWP.htm.)

miss the mark. As such, a random good deed or act does not result in a virtuous person, just as a scathing or misguided deed does not make a virtuous individual suddenly without virtue. Virtue, as with marksmanship, is about habit. It is about developing good muscle memory. Practice does not make perfect; perfect practice makes perfect. Although this is only an adage, because perfection is an actual impossibility... and really, what would "ethical perfection" be?

Guilt and fear play a vital role in ethical development and adherence. There are many who maintain their actions within accepted ethical norms simply due to the fear associated with being caught if they were to stray from normal. Some will violate any ethical norm and do whatever they feel they can get away with without being caught. Others are much too paranoid to stray from norms and regulate their actions based on fear.

On the other hand, guilt is sometimes the motivator under which honest people operate. Decisions about whether or not to comply with ethical norms is not founded upon the fear of being caught, but rather on the knowledge that they will know that they did something that they believe to be wrong. Perhaps those who discover guilt as children decide to be good and honest people simply because they do not want to feel the burden of guilt. As a person matures into adulthood, this honesty and goodness becomes a habit, and guilt is a continual burden to bear for straying from "good." Sociopaths, on the other hand, do not have the capacity to feel guilt, because they do not believe their actions to be wrong.

Conclusion

As is readily apparent, there are as many ethical definitions as there are people, or subsets of people. However, as pertains to the study of ethics, these ethical perspectives can be roughly grouped so as to allow the reader to gain some insight into ethical decision making. Chapter 2 will discuss these ethical perspectives, while Chapter 3 will incorporate these perspectives into the decision-making process. The remainder of the text is dedicated to ethical issues, challenges, perspectives, and decision making as it pertains to various areas of public service. As with all areas of ethics, the reader is wise to view such information and discussions as "framework" and "guidelines" rather than foundational or as strict rules to be adhered to.

Questions for Review

1. _____ is the study of moral standards and how they affect conduct.
2. Experts debate on whether or not ethics should or can be taught to adults. What are the two opposing sides to this debate?
3. Ethics is about _____ and wrong, virtue and _____, benefit and _____.
4. _____ describes what is and _____ describes what ought to be.
5. Morals are _____ that an individual attributes to a system of beliefs that assist the individual in defining right from wrong or good from bad.
6. Define and differentiate between the three types of ethical subdivisions.
7. _____ involves the study of an individual's beliefs relating to morality.
8. What does meta-ethics refer to?
9. True or false: Morals and ethics should not be distinguished from law.
10. True or false: Ethics is the way values are practiced.
11. What is the difference between personal ethics and political ethics?
12. An individual's concept of right and wrong is known as _____.
13. In public service, the three levels of ethics include _____, _____, and _____.
14. True or false: Guilt can be a motivator under which honest people operate.

References

Ciulla, J. B., ed. 2004. *Ethics, the heart of leadership*, 2nd ed. Westport, CT: Praeger.

Colson, C. W. 2000. The problem of ethics. *Christian Ethics Today: Journal of Christian Ethics* 031, 6 (6). http://www.christianethicstoday.com/Issue/031/The%20Problem%20of%20Ethics%20By%20Charles%20W%20Colson_031_6_.htm (accessed March 21, 2017).

Dreisbach, C. 2009. *Ethics in criminal justice*, New York: McGraw-Hill.

Foster, G. D. 2003. Ethics: Time to revisit the basics. In *The ethics edge*, 2nd ed., eds. J. P. West and E. M. Berman. Washington, D.C: International City/County Management Association. (Originally published in *The Humanist*, March–April 63(2).)

Johnson, C. 2005. *Meeting the ethical challenges of leadership*, 2nd ed. Thousand Oaks, CA: Sage.

Mill, J. S. 1861. *Utilitarianism. Fraser's Magazine.* Reprinted in book form in 1963, London: Parker, Son, and Bourn. From http://www.utilitarianism.com/mill1.htm (accessed May 20, 2017).

Mill, J. S. 1869. *On Liberty.* London: Longman, Roberts, and Green; New York: Bartleby.com, 1999. www.bartleby.com/130/.

Preston, N. 2001. *Understanding ethics*, 2nd ed. Annandale, NSW, Australia: Federation Press.

Quintilian, M. F. 2006. *Institutio oratoria.* From http://penelope.uchicago.edu?Thayer/E/Roman/Texts/Quintilian/Institutio_Oratoria/home.html (accessed July 20, 2009).

Shafritz, J. M., E. W. Russell and C. P. Borick. 2007. *Introducing public administration*, 5th ed. New York: Pearson Longman, Inc.

West, J. P., and E. M. German, eds. 2006. *The ethics edge*, 2nd ed. Washington, DC: International City/County Management Association. www.merriam-webster.com (accessed June 10, 2017).

Ethical Perspectives

2

In any ethical situation, the thing you want least to do is probably the right action.

Jerry Pournelle

Key Terms

Altruism
Categorical imperative
Ethical culture

Sanctions
Utilitarianism

Learning Objectives

1. Define **altruism**.
2. Define **utilitarianism**.
3. Identify types of and definition for **sanctions**.
4. Define **categorical imperative**.
5. Define **ethical culture**.

Introduction

As was addressed in Chapter 1, there is often intense confusion with regards to the topics of ethics, morals, and values. When one begins to delve deeper into the study of such matters, the water often becomes murkier before it ever begins to clear. After briefly differentiating between what morals, values, and ethics typically are recognized as consisting of, let us take the time to look at some ethical perspectives. That is, the manner in which one looks at or perceives a given situation and, thus, forms decisions based upon his or her perceptions and beliefs associated with the situation at hand. The decision-making process is discussed within Chapter 3; however, before decisions can be made, or the decision-making process can be discussed, we must consider the direction from which one is looking at a given situation.

While there are a myriad of ethical perspectives, discussed within thousands of research materials on the topic, there are several basic ethical perspectives that will be covered within this book. As with many concepts presented here, it is not possible to be all-inclusive. Each topic could itself have a book written entirely on it, and many do. Therefore, with that said, the categories of ethical perspectives presented here may not coincide exactly with those found elsewhere; however, they are sufficient and general enough to facilitate our discussion.

There are four ethical perspectives that will be covered: altruism, utilitarianism, categorical imperative, and ethical culture. Each of these identifies a different standard or view of decision making, and each refers to some interest that is preferred or valued above others. Of importance, and worth taking note of, is that most ethical decisions benefit someone or, at the very least, satisfy some interest that the decision maker has. As a result, because not all share the same interests or preferences, there can be a temptation to judge others choices as "unethical" or "wrong." So, as one looks at the presented ethical perspectives, it is useful to understand how individuals discriminate between what is "right" and what is "wrong."

Altruism

Altruism is possessing unselfish concern for the welfare of others. It is recognized as being the opposite of selfishness. This ethical perspective is a traditionally held virtue in many cultures and is a core component of most traditional religious beliefs, such as Christianity, Islam, Judaism, Hinduism, Buddhism, and others. As such, it is sometimes referred to as the "love your neighbor" perspective, due to the perspective representing the concepts behind the biblical (and others) instructions to "love thy neighbor as thyself."

Altruism is quite different than possessing loyalty or having a sense of duty toward something or someone. The perspective of altruism is focused on a motivation to help others or a want to do good without reward, while duty or loyalty is focused primarily on a moral obligation toward a specific organization (employer, government, country), an individual (person, deity), or even an abstract concept (such as patriotism). It is possible that an individual would feel both altruistic and duty-bound/loyal, while it is also possible that some may not feel either. The perspective of pure altruism is grounded in giving without regard to the receipt of reward, benefits, need, or recognition of the giving.

The concept of altruism has a lengthy history within philosophical and ethical teaching. The term was first used by Auguste Comte (1798–1857), a French sociologist and philosopher of science. Since then, it has become a major topic of study for psychologists, evolutionary biologists, and ethologists.

INTERNATIONAL ETHICAL PERSPECTIVE

The website, www.ethical-perspectives.be/ is home to "Ethical Perspectives," an international collaboration among ethicists and specialists from diverse sciences. According to the site, it "primarily intends to be an international forum for the promotion of dialog between fundamental and applied ethics."

It is a worthwhile trip to venture to this online forum and peruse the varying insights into the complex world of ethics. In ancient times, a "forum" was a marketplace, typically in the center of town, where people would mass to exchange goods, services, and also knowledge. "The forum has always been the place for political oratory, religious celebrations, and jurisprudence. To witness events through the forum is to feel the heartbeat of community life."

www.ethical-perspectives.be

Utilitarianism

Utilitarianism is the perspective that actions that produce the greatest good for the greatest number of persons are "good" actions. It also is known as the "consequentialist" or "teleological ethical theory." "The basic principle is that human beings judge morality of actions in terms of the consequences or results of those actions. Moral acts elicit good consequences—those that create happiness and are justifiable. Immoral acts elicit bad consequences—those that induce pain and suffering and are unjustifiable. In this approach, actions may be moral or immoral based on the capacity to achieve the greatest good for the greatest number of people" (Bowen, 2010, p. 4). This perspective is one of the easiest to subscribe to and has the most intuitive appeal for most people. This is because a "good" result or acquiring/maintaining well-being is such a natural ambition of everyday human endeavor. The sticking point with this perspective typically revolves around one's concept of what is "good" or "successful"? For some it may revolve around material items or pleasures, for others it may include financial or professional success. Therefore, "the greatest common good," in fact, may not be so common.

Under utilitarianism, at least two conditions must be met if an individual is to pursue his or her own well-being. First, the individual must possess a maximum degree of personal freedom. Secondly, he or she must be capable of realizing well-being within the basic conditions of his or her own existence, however well-being is defined. For instance, it would not be possible for an individual to pursue his or her well-being if he or she was sick and unable to obtain proper medical care, or if he or she was exposed to unsafe working conditions. There may be other conditions that also would be required for a person to realize his or her well-being, such as education and companionship.

While the utilitarian perspective is very influential and popular, there are two major concerns with the utilitarian perspective on ethical decisions.

1. If one is to implement the utilitarian perspective, they must possess extensive knowledge of data and facts, and sometimes this information is simply not available. This is especially present in instances of cost/benefit and risk/benefit analysis. In order to balance the cost or negative utility of a decision, it is necessary to calculate the long-term effects of the decision on all affected members of the audience. Such long-term positive and negative consequences of an action or policy may not be identifiable or measureable. In these instances, utilitarianistic decisions are reduced to a "best guess" approach, which may not be equitable or satisfactory.

2. The second concern with utilitarianism is that utilizing this ethical perspective may lead to injustice for individuals, while attempting to make a decision that is "best" for the masses. This is represented in military decisions, for example, where a decision is made based on the benefit of many, based on the sacrifice of a few. For instance, in Stephen Spielberg's movie, *Saving Private Ryan*, the character Captain Miller is seen discussing the application of utilitarian perspective as relates to military missions, "When you end up killing one of your men, you tell yourself it happened so that you could save the lives of two or three or ten others. Maybe a hundred others.... That's how simple it is. That's how you rationalize making the choice between the mission and the man." However, utility maximization at the expense of the individual presents serious ethical issues, which the utilitarian perspective is not well-suited to address.

The history of utilitarianism is traced by some as far back as Epicurus, the Greek philosopher. However, with regards to it being viewed as a specific school of thought, it is typically credited to Jeremy Bentham. It was Bentham who surmised that "nature has placed mankind under the governance of two sovereign masters, pain and pleasure" (Bentham, 1789). Bentham's view of utilitarianism incorporated the principle of utility into decision making.

Bentham felt that man and society could co-exist based on common motivations he referred to as **sanctions**: (1) physical sanctions, or the natural sensation of happiness and pain; (2) political sanctions, the legal acts that can counteract immoral acts; (3) moral sanctions, approval, or disapproval from those around a person; and (4) religious sanctions, the blessing or condemnation by a supreme being, consistent with one's faith (Bentham, 1789). The weakness of his theory was that the core principle was vague and did not account for individual rights.

THE PRINCIPLE OF UTILITY

1. Recognition of the role of pain and pleasure as fundamental influences on human life, especially as concerns decision making.
2. Approves or disapproves of an action or decision based on the basis of the amount of pain or pleasure brought about by the action or decision (otherwise known as "consequences").
3. Equates good with pleasure and evil with pain, as to consequentialism.
4. Pleasure and pain are capable of quantification and, thus, are measurable.

Belief in hedonism was the basis for Bentham's work, as it was the most famous version of the utilitarian theory where the fundamental good is happiness. Whichever action produces the greatest amount of happiness for the most people is considered the most moral act. Although this seems straightforward, many problems make the concept of happiness hard to employ. First, the greatest happiness is achieved at the expense of the fewest people. Consider this: It is not always possible to predict consequences for everyone involved. While we do make decisions based on consequences, this philosophy may lead to situations with no set of rules or standards. Finally, happiness could appear to condone some actions with which most people would not agree, such as a person gaining happiness through child pornography, creating potential conflicts with individual human rights.

Although the concept is typically credited as being articulated first by Bentham, it is John Stuart Mill who, as a proponent of utilitarianism, wrote *Utilitarianism* in 1861, which was an interpretation and an attempt at more effectively explaining Bentham's earlier theories. Although entitled *Utilitarianism*, his conception of it was quite different from Bentham's. Mill's perspective has been known as "the greatest happiness principle," in that it too formulated that one must always act so as to produce the greatest happiness for the greatest number of people, but the key was that such a decision must be made within reason. Bentham treated all forms of happiness as being equal, whereas Mill believed that intellectual and moral pleasures were superior to more physical forms of pleasure. Mill distinguished between and establishes the importance of each of these through a witty statement made within his work *Utilitarianism*, "[i]t is better to be a human being dissatisfied than a pig satisfied; better to be Socrates dissatisfied than a fool satisfied. And if the fool, or the pig, are of a different opinion, it is because they only know their own side of the question" (Mill, 1861).

Categorical Imperative

Immanual Kant was an eighteenth-century German philosopher who believed that individuals have certain obligations regardless of the consequences they evoke. His theory was based on the premise that moral actions occur out of obligation and are judged based on the intention and motivation for the action. Kant believed that those who choose to follow the utilitarian approach are omitting a large part of ethics by neglecting their duty and the intention to do what is right. Kant summed up his feelings by stating, "It is impossible to conceive anything at all in the world, or even out of it, which can be taken as good without qualification, except *good will*" (Kant 1964, p. 61).

Kant's philosophy is sometimes referred to as "The Golden Rule" perspective. It may be defined as the standard of rationality from which all moral requirements are derived. While the concept of a golden rule (Do unto others as you would have them do unto you) has historically been found in one form or another within most major religious traditions, the concept of "**categorical imperative**" was the central philosophical concept developed by Immanuel Kant, introduced in *Groundwork for the Metaphysics of Morals* in 1785. To many, this theory may sound religious or "theological," but as an ethical perspective within the deontological field of ethics, it attempts to identify a concept of "right," which is more universal than religion. For instance, telling the truth is a moral obligation, not simply because it is instructed within almost all religions, but because it is almost universally understood what it is like to be lied to.

"Moral actions are guided by duty and are based on 'dutiful principles' or laws. The rules of conduct or laws to which Kant refers are *maxims*, such as 'honesty is the best policy' or 'innocent until proven guilty.' Maxims should be universally accepted and commanding so people cannot make up rules as they go and so everyone will act the same way without exception. There are two types of maxims: hypothetical and categorical. Hypothetical maxims are conditional instructions that stress what ought to be done, such as, 'If I want to get a job in criminal justice, then I ought to stay out of trouble.' Categorical maxims are unconditional orders to state principles that need to be done, for example, 'Tell the truth.' In comparison, the hypothetical maxim would state, 'If you want to stay out of trouble, tell the truth.' In the study of ethics, categorical maxims provide a foundation for ethical decision making" (Bowen, 2010, p. 8).

"Kant developed the *categorical imperative*, which is a fundamental principle that allows people to act consistently from situation to situation. The categorical imperative is divided into two formulations. The first formulation is *universalizability*, which states that a justifiable action is when another person faces the same circumstances and acts in the same way. If a person makes a decision that he or she feels is morally justifiable, he or she knows 99 of 100 people would make the same decision. The idea of universalizability also may be described as a person treating everyone the same way as he or she would want to be treated" (Bowen, 2010, p. 8).

There are three premises that make up the categorical imperative. The first premise is that an individual acts ethically if their conduct would, without condition, be the "right" conduct for any individual in a similar circumstance. The second premise is that an individual's conduct is "right" if others are treated as ends in themselves rather than as means to an end. The final premise is that an individual acts ethically when he acts as if his conduct was establishing a universal law governing others on how to act in a similar circumstance.

Hypothetical imperatives instruct an individual on which means best achieves his ends. They do not tell an individual which ends he or she should choose. The struggle in choosing ends is typically between ends that are "right" (i.e., charity) and those that are "good" (i.e., educating oneself). Kant taught that the "right" was superior to the "good." Kant believed that "good" was morally irrelevant.

While this theory of ethical perspective is often referred to as The Golden Rule perspective, Kant stated in his work, *Groundwork for the Metaphysics of Morals*, that what he was attempting to teach was not the same as the Golden Rule

MODERN ETHICAL CULTURE

While Ethical Culture has adapted and remained dynamic since its inception, there are a number of focal points that remain important. These include:

- *Human Worth and Uniqueness*: Each individual is believed to have inherent worth that is not dependent on the value of what it is that they do. Each is deserving of dignity and respect, and their individual gifts are to be celebrated and encouraged.
- *Eliciting the Best*: "Always act so as to elicit the best in others, and thereby yourself" is as close as ethical culture comes to having a Golden Rule.
- *Interrelatedness*: In his formation of the concept, Adler used the term *The Ethical Manifold* to refer to how he believed "the universe to be composed of unique and indispensable moral agents (individual human beings), each of which has an influence on each of the others, which is unable to be measured or estimated, but which is inherently present nonetheless. This interrelatedness is at the heart of ethics. ... Each has an effect on the whole."

because, under the Golden Rule, many things cannot be universal. He believed that the Golden Rule was instead the categorical imperative with limitations.

Ethical Culture

The Ethical Culture Movement was started in 1876 by Felix Adler. **Ethical culture** has its foundation on the premise that living with and honoring ethical principles is at the heart of what it takes to live a fulfilling and meaningful life, while helping to create a world that is good and positive for all individuals. A fundamental key to the foundation of ethical culture was the observation that oftentimes disputes regarding religious or philosophical doctrines were distracting individuals from following through on living ethically and doing good. This is why, consequentially, "deed before creed" has developed into an informal motto of the movement (www.newworldencyclopedia.org).

Although those subscribing to ethical culture perspectives generally share common beliefs as to what constitutes ethical or unethical behavior, individuals are encouraged to recognize the complexities inherent in such matters, and, thus, remain open to continued exploration, education, and dialog rather than remain inflexible or unable to adapt.

The movement had the original aim of attempting to uphold through example the highest ideals of living, while attempting to support the weaker in attaining such ideals. The original aims were the following:

- To teach the supremacy of the moral ends above all human ends and interests.
- To teach that the moral law has an immediate authority not contingent on the truths of religious beliefs or of philosophical theories.
- To advance the science and art of right living.

Members of the society were encouraged to adhere to whatever religious doctrine they saw most fit, choosing to confine societal attention to moral problems within life rather than religious ones. A central concept was the encouragement of the individual to always act so as to elicit the best in others and, thereby, in themselves.

Conclusion

Although not every decision that one is presented with is an ethical one, it is helpful to have a foundation in the varying categories of ethical perspectives. Each category of ethical perspective identifies a different standard or view of decision making and each refers to some interest that is preferred or valued above others. However, because not all individuals share the same interest or preferences, there is a temptation to judge other's choices and decisions as "unethical" or "wrong." Chapter 3 will apply these ethical perspectives into the decision-making process.

Questions for Review

1. _____ is possessing unselfish concern for the welfare of others.
2. True or false: The perspective of pure altruism is grounded in giving without regard to the receipt of reward, benefits, need, or recognition of giving.
3. What do moral acts elicit? Immoral?
4. Under utilitarianism, what two conditions must be met if an individual is to pursue his own well-being?
5. What are the two concerns with the utilitarian perspective?
6. Identify and define the four types of sanctions.
7. The _____ perspective may be defined as the standard of rationality from which all moral requirements are derived.
8. True or false: Categorical imperative is a fundamental principle that allows people to act inconsistently from situation to situation.
9. _____ has its foundation on the premise that living with and honoring ethical principles is at the heart of what is takes to live a fulfilling and meaningful life, while helping to create a world that is good and positive for all individuals.
10. When looking at the ethical culture, individuals are encouraged to remain open to continued _____, _____, and _____ rather than remain _____ or unable to _____.

References

Bentham, J. 1789. *An introduction to the principles of morals and legislation.* Chap. 1. London: B. Hensley.

Bowen, R. T. 2010. *Ethics and the practice of forensic science.* Boca Raton, FL: Taylor & Francis Group.

Kant, I. 1964. *The metaphysical principles of virtue: Part II of the metaphysics of morals.* University of Michigan: Bobbs-Merrill Co.

Kant, I. 1785. *Groundwork on the metaphysics of morals.* (Trans. in 1964 by H.J. Paton. New York: Harper & Row.)

Mill, J. S. 1861. *Utilitarianism. Fraser's Magazine.* Reprinted in book form in 1863, London: Parker, Son, and Bourn.

www.ethical-perspectives.be/page.php?LAN=E&FILE=subject&ID=119&PAGE=1 (accessed February 15, 2017).

www.newworldencyclopedia.org/entry/Ethical_Culture (accessed December 21, 2016).

Further Reading

Ciulla, J. B., ed. 2004. *Ethics, the heart of leadership*, 2nd ed. Westport, CT: Praeger.

Colson, C. W. 2000. The problem of ethics. *Christian Ethics Today: Journal of Christian Ethics* 031, 6 (6). http://www.christianethicstoday.com/Issue/031/The%20 Problem%20of%20Ethics%20By%20Charles%20W%20Colson_031_6_.htm (accessed February 21, 2017).

Dreisbach, C. 2009. *Ethics in criminal justice*, New York: McGraw-Hill.

Johnson, C. 2005. *Meeting the ethical challenges of leadership*, 2nd ed. Thousand Oaks, CA: Sage.

Shafritz, J. M., E. W. Russell, and C. P. Borick. 2007. *Introducing public administration*, 5th ed. New York: Pearson Longman, Inc.

West, J. P., and E. M. German, eds. 2006. *The ethics edge*, 2nd ed. Washington, DC: International City/County Management Association.

Ethical Decision Making

3

You cannot make yourself feel something you do not feel, but you can make yourself do right in spite of your feelings.

Pearl S. Buck

Key Terms

Argument
Bad argument
Conclusion
Determinism
Ethical dilemma
Ethics triangle
Existentialism

Good argument
Intentionalism
Invalid
Premises
Scientific determinism
Sound
Unsound

Learning Objectives

1. Understand the components of a proper ethics-based decision process.
2. Define and understand the four levels of moral thinking that occur.
3. Distinguish between good and bad arguments.
4. Distinguish between deductive and inductive arguments.
5. Understand how to properly evaluate the results of a decision.

Introduction

Not all choices that one makes are ethical ones. For instance, the choice of "2" or "3" in deciding the correct answer to the problem of "what is 1 + 1?" is not at all an ethical one. Nor is deciding the answer to: "How far away is the Earth from the sun?" A great many decisions are made as a result of testing, through a logical, methodological system, such as mathematics and science. Other times, math and science are of no use in the decision-making process and one must delve deeper in order to come up with the "right" solution to the problem at hand.

Having previously covered what ethics are and are not, and individual views or perspectives relating to ethics, how then does an individual translate these theories into real-world decision making?

When the choice to be made is between what is clearly right and clearly wrong, a decision as to what to do is essentially one of moral courage, rather than an ethical dilemma. An ethical man knows he should not steal, whereas a moral man would not steal.

However, there are additional factors that may serve as an impetus for ethical decision making. These factors may include, but are not limited to, family, friends, profession, religion, community, culture, and law. It is these factors, combined with one's personal bias, that impact an individual's concept of right and wrong, and, thus, impact the ethical decision-making process.

A determination of what to do in a given situation is more difficult when the choices are closer to shades of gray as to right and wrong or between competing rights (virtues). Such a quandary would be what is referred to as an **ethical dilemma**. An ethical dilemma is a situation in which one is faced with choosing between competing virtues that are considered equally important, but which cannot be simultaneously honored (Roetzel, 2003).

So, if one is truly confronted with an ethical dilemma, rather than a decision between what is ethical and what is moral, then perhaps an ethical dilemma is best described as a decision between two competing rights, or a "right versus right" conflict. In "How Good People Make Tough Choices," Rushworth M. Kidder suggests that there are commonly four "right versus right" dilemmas that must be chosen between:

1. Truth versus loyalty
2. Individual versus community
3. Short term versus long term
4. Justice versus mercy

Before one can set about making a decision, one must define the problem as either a moral versus ethical one or as an ethical dilemma (right versus right). Once the ethical dilemma has been identified, an analysis as to ones course of action can be undertaken.

Making a Decision

When one is confronted with an ethical dilemma, necessitating a decision, one should attempt to work through a decision-making process. A sample process is outlined below:

1. When attempting to make a decision, analyzing the issue or problem is typically the best place to begin.
2. The next step is to consider the facts involved. For instance, one should ask what is beneficial? What is necessary?

3. At this point, it is helpful to consider perspectives that others might hold regarding the issue at hand. If time and place allows for it, it is suggested that opening the issue or decision up for debate might help. Asking questions of others and receiving feedback from those outside of the decision process may aid an individual to discover novel solutions or enable unique perspectives to present themselves. It is not uncommon for decisions to be made without adequate time to stop, ask for input, analyze the information, and think about the repercussions of the decision. It is in these situations that individuals should rely on their personal character as a guide for the decision-making process.

After the initial process, there may be multiple decisions that may emerge. Each decision-making scenario that an individual is confronted with is unique and, thus, requires a thorough look at the options that present themselves.

1. At this point, an individual would be wise to weigh the pros and the cons of each potential decision outcome.
2. What are the values of each action compared with the consequences that may occur from each option presented?
3. The application of situational ethics may assist an individual in rationalizing decisions or actions and, thus, assist in the decision-making process. However, the application of situational ethics may create a double standard or a subjective decision with relation to ethical principles because each person is unique and what may work for one individual or group in one situation, may not work for another in another situation.

Although not all-encompassing or correct in all situations, the previously discussed outline represents an example of a decision-making process. It serves as a guideline rather than as a standard operating procedure for the decision-making processes, which will be discussed throughout this text.

Typically, when ethical decisions are made in routine situations, they are simple because there is consistency of choice, most often based on established rules and regulations. While each situation is unique, particularly unusual situations often pose a more difficult challenge to an individual because of conflicting views of religion, values associated with culture, or variations in law that are foreign to the individual.

Alternate Views of Decision Making

Going back to the "right versus right" approach, there is yet another school of thought to the decision-making process. If one is faced with a right versus right scenario, one should test the possible courses of action against three

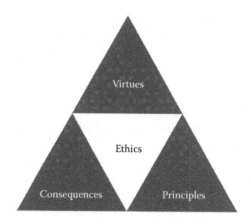

Figure 3.1 Ethics triangle. (Courtesy of Laura Rider Dutelle.)

completely different criteria, before arriving at a decision. These criteria encompass three very different approaches to the answer. They are the following:

1. Rules or principles-based approach
2. Utilitarian or consequences-based approach
3. Virtues-based approach

These also each happen to be the basic schools of thought for the topic of ethics, and encompass what is commonly referred to as the "**ethics triangle**" (Kem, 2006).

The **ethics triangle** (**Figure 3.1**) considers three different approaches to ethical reasoning. One perspective is from the view that desirable virtues such as justice and benevolence define ethical outcomes (virtues). A second perspective derives from a set of agreed-upon values or rules, such as a code of ethics or ones constitutional rights (principles). Lastly, the third perspective considers the consequences of the decision on whatever produces the greatest good for the greatest number (consequences).

Principles-Based Decision

When considering an ethical dilemma from a principles-based (or rule-based) point of view, one should ask the following questions:

- What rules exist (or should exist)?
- What are my moral obligations?

Virtues-Based Decision

When considering an ethical dilemma from a virtues-based (or Golden Rule-based) point of view, one should ask the following questions:

- What would my family think?
- What if it ended up on the news?

Consequences-Based Decision

When considering an ethical dilemma from a consequences-based (or utilitarianism) point of view, one should ask the following questions:

- Which decision results in the greatest good for the greatest number?
- Who wins and loses?

Applying the Ethical Triangle to Decision Making

Considering the different ethical perspectives, allowed for within the ethical triangle, and accepting that an ethical dilemma involves a decision between two choices of "right," it is perhaps time to discuss a model for ethical decision making associated with the ethical triangle.

A guideline for such decision making could most logically be broken down into six steps:

1. Define the ethical dilemma (in terms of "right versus right").
   a. Truth versus loyalty
   b. Individual versus community
   c. Short-term versus long-term
   d. Justice versus mercy
2. Consider courses of action.
3. Test the courses of action against the "ethics triangle" (testing).
   a. Principles-based ethics
   b. Consequences-based ethics
   c. Virtues-based ethics
4. Revisit courses of action and see if an alternative course of action has been revealed (reassess).
5. Choose a course of action (make a decision).
6. Implement the course of action (implementation).

Guidelines for Ethical Decision Making

There are many guidelines one encounters for ethical decision making, as evidenced by those earlier stated. Using such guidelines are useful to an individual in organizing one's thoughts and in assessing moral thinking. In *Ethics of Human Communication* (Johannesen, Valde, and Whedbee, 2008),

Rushworth Kidder discusses various levels of moral thinking. While these guidelines originate from ethical decisions regarding journalism, they can be useful when applied to decisions made within the public service sector.

According to Kidder (Johannesen, Valde, and Whedbee 2008), the four levels of moral thinking that occur are the following:

1. Ideal decision making, or what is absolutely right or wrong.
2. Practical decision making, or following common rules, such as: "Do not tell lies."
3. Reflective decision making, or the exceptions to given rules.
4. Political decision making, or making decisions for the good of the larger community.

In the end, ethical decision making and ethical judgment is ultimately a result of choices that should be freely made. Although the decision-making process may oftentimes result in there being more questions than there are answers, the recognition is there are various ethical perspectives, and varying levels of moral thinking. The utilization of the aforementioned decision-making strategies can often make the process much more manageable.

Existentialism

Existentialism is a relatively recent concept that has an emphasis on an individual's freedom to make decisions free of influence from others. This is often referred to as *free will*. If we are to discuss the concept of free will, it is necessary to discuss the supporting concepts of determinism and intentionalism.

Determinism

Determinism is a term that applies to the premise that all occurrences, thoughts, and actions are beyond the control of an individual. This concept can often cast doubt on the validity or usefulness of individual choice, and may reveal itself in a personal expression or attitude, typically appearing in such remarks as, "It wasn't in the cards," "I was destined to fail," or "It was fate that. ..." A more in-depth concept, known as **scientific determinism**, deals with an individual's actions, character, and decisions as results associated with genetics or one's surroundings. More specifically, this concept is grounded in the following:

- An individual's genetic make-up (specific genes and chromosomes) affects one's physiological make-up, which directly impacts one's decision making.

- An individual is a product of his environment. More specifically, climate and geography play a part and may directly influence personality and disposition, which will impact decision making.
- The society in which an individual lives and the cultures present within the society provide the individual with traditions, values, and foundational information that influence one's actions.
- An individual's education and experience provide for a personal knowledge base from which the decision process can be made.

Intentionalism

Intentionalism is a term given to the premise that individuals have free will and, thus, are accountable for their actions and the results of their decisions. More specifically:

1. External pressures on individuals are viewed as influences upon them rather than as preexisting determinants. When an individual assesses his or her surroundings and becomes aware of these external pressures, their impact on the decision-making process is considerably reduced.

RIPPED FROM THE HEADLINES

ETHICAL DECISION MAKING

CBS 4 of Miami, Florida, reported a story on how Miami police officers were given a lecture on ethical decision making. The officers spent several hours of in-service training studying the topic of ethics and being quizzed on what constituted ethical and unethical behavior. While the training was a necessary component to retain departmental accreditation, the timing was in large part due to recent occurrences at the agency.

Several months prior, the chief was found guilty of violating ethics laws by accepting a free sport utility vehicle, and then after lying about whether or not he had in fact accepted a gift, he was found guilty criminally for being untruthful. This administrative example of unethical gift acceptance and lying needed to be pointed to and have departmental personnel learn that such behavior is not only unacceptable, but illegal.

As a result, senior Miami police administrators issued a memo instructing all personnel to take part in the ethics lecture and tutorial which stated, "the department will maintain the highest professional ethics and integrity," a goal that had been compromised at the highest level and which the department was hoping to avoid in the future. www.ethics inpolicing.com/article.asp?id=5081 (accessed February 2, 2017).

2. Each individual possesses logic; therefore, it is possible to make use of logical reasoning to assist with ethical decision making.

Based on the above concepts, is persuasion then considered to be unethical? Determinism would state that "yes, persuasion is unethical because it can manipulate a person's decision" (Bowen, 2010). Whereas, intentionalism would state that "no, persuasion is not unethical because people are accountable for their decisions" (Bowen, 2010).

Logic of Ethics

Logic is a basic tool in the study of ethics and, as such, it is important to mention some techniques relating to logical evaluation with regards to ethical decision making. From a logical standpoint, a decision is a good ethical one when its "**premises**" (evidence/reasons) support it, and a decision is a bad ethical one when its premises lack support. Therefore, when one attempts to make an ethical decision and evaluate the decision options, he or she must attempt to answer three questions:

1. What is the argument attempting to prove? Or, more specifically, what is the "**conclusion**"? (Sentence that an argument claims to prove. This is sometimes referred to as a *decision*.)
2. What are the "**premises**"? (Any sentence that an argument offers as proof or evidence of the conclusion.)
3. Is the conclusion supported by the premises?
   a. If the premises are not all true, then the conclusion is not adequately supported.
   b. If the premises are not all relevant to the question at hand nor enough to prove the conclusion, then the conclusion is not adequately supported.

Good versus Bad Arguments

After one assesses the premises laid out before him and attempts to ascertain whether or not he supports the stated conclusions, he can begin to decide if he has a foundation for a **good** or a **bad argument**. An "**argument**" is made up of any of a number of sentences that claim to prove one another. Therefore, an argument is a good argument if "the premises are true, the premises are relevant to the conclusion, and no premise simply restates the conclusion" (Dreisbach, 2009). And an argument is bad when "a premise is false, a premise is irrelevant to the conclusion, or a premise simply restates the conclusion" (Dreisbach, 2009).

Deductive versus Inductive Arguments

Arguments can be further characterized as being either deductive or inductive arguments. Those arguments that claim certainty are referred to as being "deductive." These arguments claim that because the stated premises are true, then the conclusion is certainly true. Whereas, arguments claiming probability are referred to as being "inductive." These arguments claim that because the stated premises are true, then the conclusion is probably true. Most inductive arguments have their foundation in past observations or experiences. It is important to understand the distinction between deductive and inductive arguments when one is faced with evaluating moral decision making, as each of these has a different kind of evaluation that is attached to them. Deductive arguments have conclusions that are either certain or uncertain. Therefore, when the given premises do not prove a conclusion certain, even if highly probable, the argument fails. Whereas, inductive arguments are often more difficult to evaluate because concepts of probability vary between individuals. What one individual considers probable, another individual may consider improbable.

Truth versus Validity

It is also important to differentiate between true and false, and valid versus invalid where decision making is concerned. As has already been discussed, arguments are sets of sentences, and these sets of sentences can either make up a good or a bad argument. A good argument is considered to be "valid," or more specifically, an argument is valid "if the premises are true and, thus, the conclusion must certainly be true (in a deductive argument) or as probable as the argument claims (in an inductive argument)" (Dreisbach, 2009). A bad argument, on the other hand, is considered to be "**invalid**," or more specifically, "even if the premises were true, that would not demonstrate the truth or probability of the conclusion" (Dreisbach, 2009). Individual sentences, on the other hand, do not make up an entire argument, but instead are concerned with stating either a premise or a conclusion. These individual sentences can be found to be either true or false.

Sound versus Unsound Arguments

There is a final level of evaluation that bares mentioning and that pertains to the soundness of valid arguments. Valid arguments are classified as being either "**sound**" or "**unsound**." A **sound** argument is one where all stated premises are true. An **unsound** argument is one that contains at least one premise that is false.

Evaluating the Result of Decisions

Upon reaching a decision, it is logical for an individual to evaluate the results of the decision. While this would have been hypothesized earlier in the decision-making process, now that the decision has been made, the real-time effects and results can be evaluated. Based on the information provided at the time of the decision, was the right choice made? If presented with the

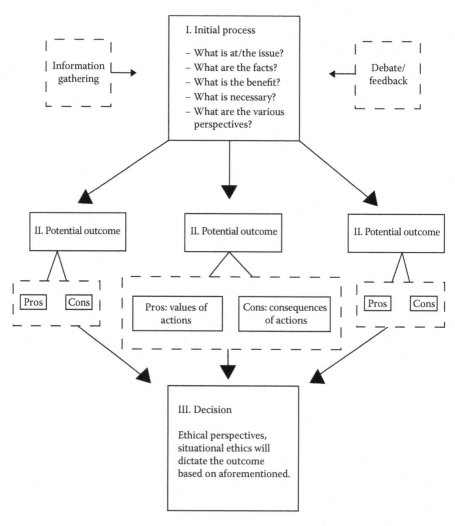

Figure 3.2 Ethical decision making. (Courtesy of Ellie Blazer.)

same options in the future, how would the decision change? It is here that the dilemmas of actions and consequences begin to show themselves. When actions occur, there are certain patterns that begin to emerge (**Figure 3.2**).

Due to variations in personal ethics, bias, and external influences, individuals do not always reach the same conclusions; however, this does not necessarily mean that the other individual is wrong. A particular situation may not have one "right" answer; however, it may have many "wrong" answers. Therefore, it is necessary that individuals use their best judgment (based on personal ethics) and common sense when attempting to reach the "best" conclusion.

Conclusion

It is important for one to understand the decision-making process if one is to evaluate whether or not a decision is an ethical or unethical one. This chapter has discussed the arguments and support that go into making a decision and coming to a successful conclusion. Chapter 4 will look at how organizational leadership can impact this decision-making process and impact the ethical outcome of decisions made due to professional obligations, which are dictated by agency, professional organizations, and accrediting bodies.

Questions for Review

1. Additional factors that may serve as an impetus for ethical decision making may include, but are not limited to _____, _____, _____, _____, _____, and _____.
2. True or false: When attempting to make a decision, analyzing the issue is the best place to begin.
3. What are the four levels of moral thinking that occur?
4. The term _____ applies to the premise that all occurrences, thoughts, and actions are beyond the control of an individual.
5. Scientific determinism deals with an individual's _____, _____, and _____ results associated with genetics or one's surroundings.
6. _____ is a term given to the premise that individuals have free will and, thus, are accountable for their actions and the results of their decisions.
7. True or false: A decision is a good moral one when its premises lack support.
8. True or false: An argument is bad when a premise is false, a premise is irrelevant to the conclusion, or a premise simply restates the conclusion.
9. Distinguish between being deductive and being inductive.
10. Valid arguments are classified as being either _____ or _____.

References

Bowen, R.T. 2010. *Ethics and the practice of forensic science*. Boca Raton, FL: Taylor & Francis Group.

Dreisbach, C. 2009. *Ethics in criminal justice*. New York: McGraw-Hill.

Johannesen, R., K. Valde, and K. Whedbee. 2008. *Ethics in human communication*, 6th ed. Long Grove, IL: Waveland Press, Inc.

Kem, J.D. 2006. *Ethical Decision Making: Using the "Ethical Triangle" in Military Ethical Decision Making*. Public Administration and Management. 11.1 (2006): 22.

Kidder, R.M. 1995. *How Good People Make Tough Choices*. New York: William Morrow and Company, Inc.

Roetzel, R. 2003. *Towards the Army's Ethical System*, U.S. Army Command and General Staff College Leadership Instruction Division, Leadership Course Materials.

Leadership Ethics

4

Ethical conduct is something that becomes inherent in an organization over a long period of time.

Lee R. Raymond

We should never be afraid of the truth, regardless of where it leads us.

Thomas Jefferson

Key Terms

Esprit de corps
Leadership
Morale

Learning Objectives

1. Identify ways in which individuals become leaders.
2. Identify characteristics of a successful leader.
3. Define qualities of leadership that are integral to engendering trust.
4. Define **morale** and its impact on leadership.

Introduction

History has shown that the vast majority of civilizations have been destroyed from internal forces, not from external ones. Corporations, agencies, and organizations are not immune from the same fate. Greed, power, competition, and materialism are just a few of the reasons behind internal destruction. The area of public service is not exempt from such tradition. The world that we live in very often can be morally disappointing. In many instances, this is often due to a lack of ethics with regards to the area of leadership.

Individuals become leaders as a result of a variety of possibilities and for a variety of reasons. Some are developed. Some possess qualities that lend themselves to being an effective leader. Some acquire leadership through force, wealth, social, or political connections. Yet, others become leaders as a result of circumstances or timing. However, regardless of the reason that an individual finds himself in a leadership role, he cannot be a leader without also having willing followers. "Leadership is not a person or a position. It is a complex moral relationship between people based on trust, obligation, commitment, emotion, and a shared vision of the goal" (Ciulla, 2004).

As discussed within *Ethics for Criminal Justice Professionals* (Roberson and Mire, 2010), "It is clear that leaders must consider a multiplicity of issues and concerns in making consistently ethical decisions and in developing a code of ethical behavior for their organizations. It is the leader's role to set a clear and uniform example of ethical behavior and to articulate specific expectations and goals so that ethical behavior becomes an integral theme of the organization."

Deciding How to Lead

Leadership is as complex a topic as that of ethics, so when one stops to combine the two, the result can be quite intimidating. To simplify the concept, in his book, *George Washington on Leadership*, Richard Brookhiser (2008) describes **leadership** as "knowing yourself, knowing where you want to go, and then taking others to that new place." There are countless leadership styles employed to accomplish this daunting task. One way is to focus analysis upon the ends/means/consequences equation that is suggested by Brookhiser. This leads to three primary questions:

1. What is the goal?
2. What means will we use to get there?
3. What types of tradeoffs and compromises must be made along the way?

Establishing Trust through Leadership

"Ethics lie at the heart of all human relationships and, hence, at the heart of the relationship between leaders and followers" (Ciulla, 2004). Throughout history, successful leaders have been those who have gained the trust of those who they have been responsible for leading. There can be much debate over how "trust" is defined; however, regardless of this lack of agreement, most individuals are well aware when trust is in place and when it is not. Trust is a result of proper communication and clarity of purpose within an organization. Trust is confidence and reliance upon an individual, organization, or object. It includes possessing confidence in strength and integrity of the same. Through the establishment of trust within an organization and, if able to maintain the trust, leaders will be able to provide effective guidance and work on the proper development of the organization. As with personal relationships, a proper foundation of trust serves to support an organization through difficult times and enable leadership the time and ability to find and implement solutions that will assist the organization in overcoming challenges and obstacles when they are presented.

In their book, *Learning to Lead* (1997), Warren Bennis and Joan Goldsmith mention qualities of leadership that are integral to engendering trust. The qualities mentioned by the authors are vision, empathy, consistency, and integrity.

Vision

Successful leaders are those who inspire and create vision. Leadership vision serves to provide a foundation for organizational purpose and engender trust, which can enable followers to develop personal identity and feel vested in the vision and its creation. The leader involves us in the visions, empowers us to create it, and communicates the shared vision so that we integrate it into our lives.

Empathy

Leaders who possess unconditional empathy for those working within the organization will emerge as the most successful. Although their opinions may vary considerably from those who work for them, trust is established when employees believe that a leader understands their view and can relate to where they are coming from.

Consistency

A leader who maintains a level of consistency with regard to his stance on topics, his vision, his leadership style, and organizational placement will be trusted and emerge as successful. Although consistent, the successful leader also will be willing to consider new evidence and new events when making organizational decisions.

Integrity

A leader who maintains integrity that is above question will have the trust of his employees and co-workers. When a leader takes a stance on topics, based on his moral standard, and these actions are observable to those who work with and for the leader, he will gain their trust. This same leader must be ready, as well, to hold others accountable for their actions and decisions based on the standard of ethics laid out and adhered to by the leader.

Ethical Behavior as an Organizational Theme

As typically witnessed within sports, motivation originates with leadership. The leadership values and motivation of an organization must start at the top if it is to find its way to those farther down the line. If the ethical behavior of an organization is in question, or there is a need for change, then the establishment, or modification, of an organizational ethical code may be necessary. Chapter 5 discusses more extensively ethical codes and standards; however, with reference to organizational leadership, it is important to recognize that any change must be made at, and lived at, the top before those outside of leadership positions can be expected to adhere to it.

Why Morale Is Important in Organizational Ethics

The definition of **morale** as it applies to the workplace has changed over time, but a recent definition would be "the mental and emotional condition (as of enthusiasm, confidence, or loyalty) of an individual or group with regard to the function or tasks at hand" (Merriam-Webster.com). This includes a sense of common purpose with respect to the group, sometimes referred to as **esprit de corps**. When morale is high, typically ethical violations are low. When morale is low, ethical violations increase. Therefore, the benefits of increasing and maintaining organizational morale are obvious.

Although many organizations suffer from poor morale, leaders often overlook it. This indifference can be devastating to organizational cohesion. Failure of leadership to recognize or respond to poor morale can be due to a number of reasons including the following:

1. *Ignoring it*: Ignoring poor morale will not change it. In fact, it typically results in matters deteriorating even further.
2. *Lack of understanding*: Even with a desire to do something, without knowing what to do or how to do it, leaders are (or appear to be) just as helpless or indifferent to the issues. Proper leadership training will minimize the instances of this occurring.

3. *Negative attention on self*: Many leaders will fail to address morale issues or concerns for fear of bringing negative attention on themselves. Leaders fail to recognize that poor morale is often a result of failure of the leader to be a role model and to provide proper motivation, while exuding positive morale. This self-centeredness approach to leadership will almost certainly lead to the demise of the organization.

Assessment of Ethics in the Workplace

Oftentimes employers are perplexed with where to go to acquire in-depth, appropriate-to-the-job, and effective ethics-based training. Many turn to local universities or private consultants to assist with such matters. One past example of this was the National Institute of Ethics. Before it was disbanded, the National Institute of Ethics was the nation's largest provider of law enforcement and corrections ethics training. Established in 1991, the Institute was a Congressional award winning, nonprofit 501(c)(3) organization dedicated to furthering ethics and integrity throughout America.

Specific to law enforcement and criminal justice, the institute has developed a series of training tools and manuals to assist agencies with determining "what policies, procedures, or practices within an organization need to be added or revised to ensure integrity and ethics in the workplace" (Roberson and Mire, 2010). The training provided by The National Institute of Ethics incorporated initial research in the form of two different surveys: (1) distributed to staff and (2) distributed to management. These surveys were used to determine the status of organizational ethics. All surveys were anonymous and sealed on completion. Each employee, management, and staff were asked to be specific with regards to any criticisms relating to organizational ethics. They were asked to take into account each level of the organization with regards to their responses, and to also suggest ways to improve, related to their concerns. The premise was to have the surveys serve as a starting point for the training discussions that will follow, and that are related to organizational ethics. After the surveys were conducted, the organization gained insight into shortcomings or discrepancies with regard to the status of organizational ethics. If it appeared there was a chasm, then training might be deemed necessary. Even if training did not take place, simply distributing the surveys and gaining the feedback was often enough to instill trust and motivation within the members of the agency, as it assured each individual that ethics was seen as being an important component of organizational behavior.

The aforementioned model is an example that can be mirrored by academic institutions and local consultants if an organization makes the decision to reach out and ask for assistance with assessment of organizational ethics. The authors of this text are always another option to aid organizations, should they deem it necessary.

LEADERSHIP ETHICS: LOOKING TO WEST POINT

For all of the criticisms about today's military, the U.S. Military Academy at West Point seems to be doing the most effective job of developing leaders and citizens of character. To be fair, the majority of military criticisms come from how the military is used, not for how it operates, or the ethical decisions employed within.

Of important note is that West Point (as with all military academies) places a serious emphasis on the candidate selection process, selecting applicants not only based on academic qualifications, but also based on their leadership qualities and potential, and their moral character.

The motto at West Point is: Duty, Honor, Country. The honor code, which all cadets must adhere to, will not tolerate lying, cheating, or stealing. These are not simply words, but rather a way of life. It is just as wrong for someone to commit one of these acts as it is for a cadet to know about it and not report it. Cadets live and work together, thus having an inherent hierarchy that facilitates enforcement.

So, what does the model of West Point have to offer those within public service? The entire four-year West Point experience was carefully developed to provide the military with officers who would demonstrate both competence and character throughout their lifetime. Simultaneous pursuit of character and competence is a life-long pursuit. Without continuous attention, an individual risks losing both. Character without competence is unacceptable. No one wants an ethical manager who cannot make a decision. However, if one has competence, but has no character, it can be even more dangerous. At every level, within every organization, and within every government, there are examples of competent people behaving detrimentally. Pick up any newspaper or watch any newscast and you are certain to find account after account of individuals whose actions are threatening the well-being and lives of those around them.

Ethics are an essential component of enduring relationships at every level. Organizations, governments, friendships, and families prosper on the basis of trust. Everyone wants the people who surround them to be trustworthy and people of character. All want leaders who have character, just as all leaders want subordinates who are trustworthy and of good character as well. Character, just as competence, is developed, not given or won. And yet, organizations often neglect the development of character, taking it instead for granted. Even in instances where character is explicitly addressed, the focus is typically not on development, but rather on motivation.

It is from this aspect that organizations can look toward West Point for assistance. This model was carefully designed to incorporate simultaneous pursuit of both character and competence development. This developmental process requires four essential elements:

1. **Knowledge** of the academy's standards and values.
2. **Adherence** to the academy's standards of conduct.
3. **Belief** in the process, the standards, and values.
4. **Leadership**, which includes role modeling, mentoring, and developmental leadership of character in others (www.usma.edu).

Through the incorporation of these aspects and the simultaneous development of both character and competence, an organization can improve both its leadership and its overall ability. Such attention is not simply for those who serve within the military, but are valuable components that should be ingrained into any leadership development model, and within each organization that seeks to have the greatest impact, while doing so in the most competent and ethical manner.

Conclusion

It is illogical to believe, or to expect, that agencies are capable of eliminating all corruption. However, what is of paramount concern if ethical violations are to be reduced, is that the leadership of an organization establishes an environment that fosters trust and integrity and that, if unethical behavior is discovered, makes it clear that such violations will not be tolerated. Leadership is not simply day-to-day administrative tasks. Leaders must be aware and have a pulse of their people. When mistakes are made, from an organizational leadership standpoint, they must be owned and acknowledged. Perfection is an impossibility. Mistakes will happen. What is important is that mistakes not be repeated and that they be learned from. Failure to learn from them, and repeating them, is tantamount to incompetence. At each step of the way, leadership must continue to question whether the decisions that are made are consistent with the organization's values that have been identified, as well as being in line with the individual's ethical beliefs, the one who is tasked with making them and serving in a leadership capacity.

Questions for Review

1. Trust is a result of proper _____ and _____ of purpose within an organization.
2. The four qualities of leadership that are integral to engendering trust include _____, _____, _____, and _____.
3. True or false: Motivation originates with leadership.
4. The mental and emotional condition of an individual or group with regard to the function or tasks at hand is known as _____.
5. True or false: Although many organizations suffer from poor morale, leaders often do not overlook it.
6. The National Institute of Ethics incorporates initial research in the form of two surveys: one distributed to _____ and one distributed to _____.
7. _____ are an essential component of enduring relationships at every level.
8. The four essential elements required for the developmental process established at the U.S. Military Academy at West Point include _____, _____, _____, and _____.

References

Bennis, W. and J. Goldsmith. 1997. *Learning to lead.* Boston: Addison Wesley.

Brookhiser, R. 2008. *George Washington on leadership.* New York: Basic Books.

Ciulla, J. B. 2004. *Ethics, the heart of leadership,* 2nd ed. Westport, CT: Praeger Publishers.

Roberson, C. and S. Mire. 2010. *Ethics for criminal justice professionals.* Boca Raton, FL: CRC Press.

The National Institute of Ethics. www.ethicsinstitute.com/ (accessed September 24, 2016).

U.S. Military Academy. 2016. *Building the Capacity to Lead,* West Point, NY.

www.merriam-webster.com (accessed May 10, 2016).

Ethical Codes and Standards

5

A long habit of not thinking a thing wrong gives it a superficial appearance of being right.

Thomas Paine

Key Terms

Code of ethics   Specific codes
General codes   Personal codes

Learning Objectives

1. Define and understand the purpose of a code of ethics.
2. Define and differentiate between the types of codes of ethics.
3. Identify the components of a successful code of ethics.
4. Define and understand transparency.

Introduction

A **code of ethics** (sometimes called an ethical code) is an assembly of institutional guidelines used to reduce ethical vagueness within an organization and serve as a means of reinforcing ethical conduct. As was discussed in Chapter 4, the formation of organizational ethics begins at the top. Organizational leadership establishes these codes based on moral values. A typical code of ethics contains general, nonspecific expectations and target guidelines that attempt to reduce vagueness and, thus, lessen the burden of ethical decision making with regards to gray areas. The codes are developed based not only on past organizational or individual experience, but also based on actions that the organization wishes to prevent from ever occurring.

According to Robin Bowen (2010), in *Ethics and the Practice of Forensic Science*, codes of ethics have two primary purposes. "First, they provide moral guidelines and professional standards of conduct. The professional codes hold people accountable for proper performance and devotion to honesty and obligation. The second purpose of codes is to define professional behavior to

promote a sense of pride, tolerance, and responsibility among professionals."
The codes typically serve as the foundation for disciplinary action relating
to ethical violations. Sometimes a code of ethics may incorporate personal
expectations that are significantly beyond what is legally expected of employees. These may include such matters as morality, honesty, and truthfulness. A
well-written code of ethics should properly dissuade people from committing
unethical acts, and should incorporate procedures for discipline as well as the
consequences for unethical actions.

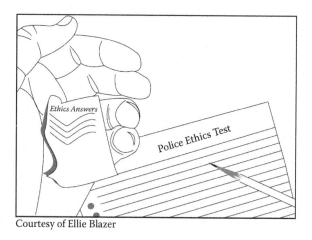

Courtesy of Ellie Blazer

Through the establishment of a code of ethics, an organization displays
its willingness to take responsibility for organizational ethics. However, this
being said, not having a code of ethics does not in any way imply that an
organization is uncaring about or oblivious to organizational ethics. Some
agencies make use of codes of conduct for individuals rather than a code of
ethics for the organization. In this case the code of conduct typically incorporates provisions that would otherwise be contained in a code of ethics, so it
is unnecessary to have both. The code also serves as a decision-making guide
and waiver of liability in some instances. If adhering to the stated code, a
person will receive organization support for a course of action if he or she
properly applied the code of ethics to the decision process associated with it.
This reliance upon guidelines to provide support for decisions, which would
otherwise be difficult to explain, helps to reduce cognitive dissonance and
stress associated with some decision-making processes. However, although
many organizations find ethical codes to be necessary for professional practice, simply developing and having ethical codes is not enough to eliminate
corruption or ensure that individuals will make the "right" decision. In fact,
often codes are revised and re-written based on new or innovative ways individuals have behaved that wasn't specifically covered under the previous
version.

CODE OF CONDUCTS PROHIBIT CERTAIN TYPES OF BEHAVIOR SUCH AS THE FOLLOWING:

Disruptive profanity, excessive loitering, firearms possession, horseplay, disorderly conduct, violations of the law, being disrespectful, cell phone or social media usage while at work, and being late for work.

A code of conduct covers specific behavior. Examples might include lending coworkers money, being late for work, unexcused absences, gambling while at work, taking long lunch breaks, or leaving work early. A code of ethics provides a broad and general rule for guidance. Examples include core values such as service expectations, treatment of individuals, integrity, and competence.

Establishing Organizational Support

Organizational support for a code of ethics is important. Support is established when an organization has implemented procedures that will properly maintain the organizational effectiveness of the code. These procedures may include the following:

- *Guidelines for the filing of complaints*: The established procedures must be easily understood and non-intimidating, so as not to dissuade the filing of proper complaints, but should not be so easy as to allow individuals to use the process as a method of workplace harassment.
- *Guidelines for receiving complaints*: Procedures must be in place to ensure that each complaint is received properly and recorded.
- *Guidelines for the investigation of complaints*: An organization must have guidelines established relating to how to incorporate hearsay information and personal morals while investigating the veracity of the complaint.
- *Guidelines for reviewing complaints*: Proper documentation of investigative efforts is of paramount concern in reaching, and supporting, a proper conclusion.
- *Guidelines for discipline associated with founded complaints*: Discipline serves to dissuade others from committing the same violation while also serving to punish those responsible for the violation. Discipline should be harsh enough to serve both purposes, but not so harsh as to be counterproductive in future decision-making efforts.

- *Guidelines for time and fairness*: Procedures must provide for complaints to be investigated in a timely manner and define a level of discipline impartially and uniformly applied to all organizational members.
- *Guidelines for transparency*: In today's public climate, transparency is very important. Integrity is constantly in question and solid rules for transparency can lessen disparagement and improve accountability.

Developing Codes of Ethics

We have discussed what a code of ethics is, but how does an organization go about creating this code? First, leadership must attempt to reach a mutual agreement regarding the moral principles of the organization. This can be an extremely challenging step because reaching a consensus is often a seemingly insurmountable task. Ideally, a code must represent the moral principles of the organization as a whole, not simply be a compilation of principles of the majority who impose views upon the minority. During the development process, the organization should be cognizant not to avoid or exclude controversial matters because it is typically these issues that are the chief causes of concern with regard to ethical violations. Codes should not be overly specific or they risk excluding potentially important issues, but not so broad as to fail to serve as an effective tool for decision making.

The development of a code of ethics requires an organization to identify a dedicated group of leaders who are aware of what the result of such development hopes to achieve, and are able to identify a type of code specific to these related outcomes. There are four criteria that may assist those tasked with the development process, if taken into consideration.

1. *The code must be desirable*: The code that is developed must meet with the expectations and desires of the organization and fit the organizational theme.

CONSIDER THIS

In early 2000, a married public servant employee went out of state for training. While he was at this training, he had sexual relations with a woman other than his wife. His employer discovered the behavior and fired him on the grounds he violated the organizational code of ethics. The specific code he violated was, "…shall not bring discredit to the agency." Was this a justifiable termination? Why or why not? Would your answer change if this happened a decade earlier or later?

2. *The code must be feasible*: Goals are great, if attainable. This holds true for the development of a code of ethics as well. There are no perfect employees. The code must not be so impossible as to prohibit the ability to adhere to it.

3. *The code must be enforceable*: Just as laws without punishment make for useless laws, so too is a code of ethics that is unenforceable and fails in its purpose.

4. *The code must be enforced*: There are many laws that go unenforced and, as a result, individuals lose respect for the law (speeding, for example). This is true of ethical codes as well. Failure to enforce the codes results in a lack of respect for the codes and the underlying intent is lost. This often diminishes the integrity of the process and causes diminished support for the ethos.

When individuals tasked with the development of a code of ethics begin the writing process, they would be wise to keep in mind that the code should:

- Be written to a general audience
- Be attainable
- Be written in clear, yet specific language
- Follow a logical order

A well-written code is one that remains applicable decades after it was drafted. While the code should be written to be more general than specific, the code should find a way to focus on unique organizational features. "If written correctly, the code should encourage discussion and reflection, should provide ethical guidance for the whole profession, and should make basic ethical values of the group clear" (Bowen, 2010).

Code of Ethics Types

An organization may choose to make use of three general types of codes.

1. **General Codes:** Provide minimal guidance in specific circumstances. This type may serve to supplement a code of conduct, if present.

2. **Specific Codes:** Help to establish guidelines and define a profession or organization for the first time.

3. **Personal Codes:** If the organization has not specified a code, individuals must default to their personal ethics for decision-making guidance. These codes assist in the development and implementation of more formalized organizational codes of ethics.

Purpose of Establishing a Code of Ethics

It is generally held that codes of ethics serve three main purposes:

1. Codes assure people outside of the profession or organization that they can expect a degree of uniformity as relates to expectation of performance and moral conduct from employees of the profession or organization.
2. Codes assure individuals within the organization or profession that they can rely upon colleagues within the organization and profession to maintain a level of standards in exchange for that individual conducting himself in adherence to the same principles upon which the others are held.
3. Codes serve as a notice that people outside of the organization or profession are not bound by the code and, perhaps, may be seen as adhering to lower standards or no standards pertaining to ethics.

Arguments against Ethical Codes

The purpose of a code of ethics is to establish formal guidelines for ethical behavior. However, a code of ethics cannot provide guidance for every individual in every situation. This is the reason that some positions, such as police officers, allow for the use of discretion in decision-making situations. In this case, a code of ethics cannot account for every instance where a decision would be made. With the ability to make discretionary decisions, having a code of ethics does not ensure ethical behavior.

Often an ethical code policy will provide guidelines that help ensure public trust but cannot be enforced through criminal or civil code. While it may be the intent of the organization to moderate individual morality on the job, it serves little purpose to establish codes of ethics that cannot be defended in court. Therefore, an organization should not implement policies that are not enforceable by law.

The argument is made that codes of ethics are "limited to the imagination of the individual" (Watson, 2010, p. 44). Having a code of ethics is an unnecessary reminder of integrity and professionalism that is expected from those within public service. Behavior cannot be governed by a set of rules; it must come from within the individuals and the organization. Simply providing a set of ethical rules and guidelines does not make an organization ethical. An organization that does not follow or enforce a partial set of guidelines can cause more damage than an organization that has no guidelines at all.

REFLECTION

When should codes be rewritten?

CONSIDER THIS

In the late 1990s a supervisor, while involved in jocularity with a subordinate, stated, "bite me." The humorous engagement ended with both parties appreciating the friendly exchange. Several months later the head administrator of the organization learned of the exchange, initiated an investigation, and turned the case over to human resources as sexual harassment. During the investigation, it was determined by a linguist that for a short period, during the 1980s, the phrase "bite me" had a sexual connotation attached to it. The ruling by human resources determined the recipient of whom the phrase was directed had no inference to sex. It was further determined that this form of horseplay was not a violation of the organization's code of ethics or code of conduct.

Another argument has been made that a code of ethics that governs public service ethics cannot be learned through a set of rules; the characteristics that are associated with these rules must become a part of an individual's life as early as their teenage years. Oftentimes, public service is a profession that must be governed by an inherent set of rules that do not come from reading a specific code. The public service sector is made up of dynamic professionals that must be poised to change as quickly as the society they are charged with serving.

Code of Ethics Examples

Throughout the text, as each segment of public service is discussed, there is an incorporation of or reference to a code of ethics example pertinent to that sector. The reader is reminded that these are examples only and may vary by agency or organization. It is important to keep in mind that these codes are guidelines and should be revisited regularly for update consideration so as to stay abreast of the dynamic environment in which we live and work. Real human resource and internal affairs cases are presented to give the reader application on how and why a solid code of ethics or code of conduct is important.

The IACP adopted the Law Enforcement Code of Ethics at the 64th Annual IACP Conference and Exposition in October 1957. The Code of Ethics stands as a preface to the mission and commitment law enforcement agencies make to the public they serve.

LAW ENFORCEMENT CODE OF ETHICS

As a law enforcement officer, my fundamental duty is to serve the community; to safeguard lives and property; to protect the innocent against deception, the weak against oppression or intimidation and the peaceful against violence or disorder; and to respect the constitutional rights of all to liberty, equality and justice.

I will keep my private life unsullied as an example to all and will behave in a manner that does not bring discredit to me or to my agency. I will maintain courageous calm in the face of danger, scorn or ridicule; develop self-restraint; and be constantly mindful of the welfare of others. Honest in thought and deed both in my personal and official life, I will be exemplary in obeying the law and the regulations of my department. Whatever I see or hear of a confidential nature or that is confided to me in my official capacity will be kept ever secret unless revelation is necessary in the performance of my duty.

I will never act officiously or permit personal feelings, prejudices, political beliefs, aspirations, animosities or friendships to influence my decisions. With no compromise for crime and with relentless prosecution of criminals, I will enforce the law courteously and appropriately without fear or favor, malice or ill will, never employing unnecessary force or violence and never accepting gratuities.

I recognize the badge of my office as a symbol of public faith, and I accept it as a public trust to be held so long as I am true to the ethics of police service. I will never engage in acts of corruption or bribery, nor will I condone such acts by other police officers. I will cooperate with all legally authorized agencies and their representatives in the pursuit of justice.

I know that I alone am responsible for my own standard of professional performance and will take every reasonable opportunity to enhance and improve my level of knowledge and competence.

I will constantly strive to achieve these objectives and ideals, dedicating myself before God to my chosen profession... law enforcement.

http://www.iacp.org/codeofethics

Conclusion

Recognizing that there is no utopia and laws are a necessary component of a free society, it is important that individuals realize the same is true with regards to organizational ethics. It is equally as necessary for organizations to develop codes of ethics for employees to serve as guidelines and to regulate behavior and decision making. However, as with laws, codes are effective only if they are explained to and understood by those whom they apply. Also, they will only maintain this level of effectiveness if they are enforced by those tasked with enforcing them. An increase in ethical violations is oftentimes an indicator that policies are out of date.

Questions for Review

1. A _____ is an assembly of institutional guidelines that are used to reduce ethical vagueness within an organization and serve as a means of reinforcing ethical conduct.
2. Developing and having ethical codes (is, is not) enough to eliminate corruption and ensure that individuals will make the "right" decision.
3. Codes should not be overly _____ or else they risk excluding potentially important issues, but not so _____ as to fail to serve as an effective tool for decision making.
4. The three types of codes of ethics include _____, _____, and _____.
5. What is the purpose for establishing a code of ethics?
6. True or false: A code of ethics can provide guidance for every individual in every situation.

References

Bowen, R. T. 2010. *Ethics and the practice of forensic science.* Boca Raton, FL: Taylor & Francis Group.

Watson, A. 2010. Clean as a hound's tooth: The origin of the military police creed. *Military Police* 43–44. (Retrieved from International Security & Counter Terrorism Reference Center database.)

Ethics in Law Enforcement

6

There is something a good patrolman puts into his work that is not found in the books of rules nor taught by police instructors.

August Vollmer (1933)

Key Terms

Absolutists
Authority
Blue wall
Code of silence
Conflict of interest
Discretionary authority
Economic corruption
Exceptionists

Idealism
Noble cause corruption
Relativism
Scope of authority
Situationists
Subjectivist
Whistle-blower fiduciary
  relationship

Learning Objectives

1. Define and differentiate between economic and noble cause corruption.
2. Define what is meant by a "**code of silence**" and its relationship to law enforcement ethics.
3. Define and differentiate between career stages and their impact on ethics and job performance.
4. Understand what is meant by "**scope of authority**" and how it applies to law enforcement ethics.
5. Define what is meant by "**discretionary authority**" and how it applies to law enforcement ethics.
6. Define and differentiate between common causes of corruption.
7. Define what is meant by "conflicts of interest" and how it applies to law enforcement ethics.

Introduction

Ethical behavior is the foundation of any professional organization. In law enforcement, many courses addressing ethics may be good, but they lack the knowledge of the ethical ideologies of the police officers that are being taught. Various divisions within a department may require different ethical framework because of the unit to which the officers are assigned. Patrol officers have different needs than narcotics officers, school resource officers, traffic officers, or special weapons and tactics (SWAT) officers. This makes the "one-stop shop" for ethics training not practical or efficient (Bayley, 2009).

Different Types of Corruption

Crank and Caldero (2000), as described by Cortrite (2007), state that unethical behavior of police can be broken down into two major types: economic corruption and noble cause corruption. **Economic corruption** refers to the practice of officers gaining some economic benefit from not enforcing a law. It is described as a steep downhill slope that gets steeper and more slippery the farther one goes. An officer's first step onto the slope may be as simple as a small gratuity and sliding to the bottom of the slope might represent extortion, drug sales, or even murder. Between the two extremes are incremental crimes such as burglary or theft. In most cases of serious corruption, an officer starts out by accepting small gratuities and moves on to bigger offenses. The correlation is believed to exist that officers who never take small gratuities, such as free meals, will not be involved in crimes of major corruption.

Noble cause corruption is the act of officers getting criminals off the street as a "noble cause." As a result, any means, including breaking the law, can be justified. If an officer knows that someone has committed a crime, then any means necessary to put them in jail is justified. Examples include planting evidence or using physical force to coerce a confession (Cortrite, 2007, p. 13). Unethical behavior of law enforcement officers occurs throughout the United States. Heinzmann (2009) reported misconduct complaints against the Chicago police force are up 19 percent. The complaints jumped from about 2,300 complaints every three months to almost 2,800, which is almost 1,000 a month. This problem is not new to law enforcement.

The Drug Reform Coordination Network (2000) reported widespread chaos in police corruption regarding drug investigations. In Cleveland, 51 law enforcement and corrections officers were charged with protecting the sale of cocaine. In Denver, Colorado, two officers were charged with destroying evidence in over 80 drug-related cases. Over 70 officers were investigated in Los Angeles, California for a veritable reign of terror including attempted murder. In Miami, Florida, three officers were investigated, tried, and convicted for protecting drug deliveries.

In July 2010, controversy resulted when the Detroit chief of police was fired for several issues with the city's mayor. One main issue was the chief dating a lieutenant in his department. The University of Michigan ethicist, John Chamberlin, believes when an administrator dates a subordinate, everyone between them in the chain of command is implicated. This is contrary to Jack Rinchich, president of the National Association of Chiefs of Police, who believes an officer shouldn't be faulted for a personal matter that isn't covered by policy (Goodman, 2010).

Justnews.com (2010) reported a veteran Florida trooper was arrested and pled guilty to writing fake traffic tickets. Prosecutors found 85 cases where the state trooper wrote traffic tickets to drivers for offenses they did not commit. Many of the falsely ticketed drivers had their driver's licenses suspended for not paying tickets they didn't know existed.

An officer from Stoughton, Massachusetts recently resigned after fellow officers reported the officer had attended a strip club while on duty and in uniform. That same officer had recently saved someone from a burning car and was honored for his involvement in catching an accused killer (Wedge and Johnson, 2010). However, the officers reporting the strip club incident to the administration were recognized for their work in attempting to change the reputation of the department.

Wlwt.com (2010) reported that a Milford, Ohio police officer audiotaped himself having sex with the town's mayor while he was on duty. The investigation that followed the report of his unethical behavior revealed this was somewhat of a common occurrence.

Recent events may have a longer-term impact than those in previous decades. A series of incidents that occur in a compressed time period and gain massive traction in the media can tarnish the image not only of the police in the cities where the incidents took place but can also damage the reputation of police nationwide. This contamination-by-association is occurring today in a cumulative manner. Each incident pollinates ensuing occurrences, in part, because activists and the media are drawing connections between them. This perfect storm gained added momentum in December 2014 with the creation of the President's Task Force on 21st Century Policing (Weitzer, 2015).

REFLECTIONS

The formation of a presidential committee signals police behaviors are in need of change or at minimum, police reforms are necessary. Is this a fair assessment? Is this a reality of police actions or is it the product of unfair media coverage? The number of police complaints is currently 7 complaints for every 10,000 contacts (Ariel, Farrar, and Sutherland, 2015).

Ethical Frameworks Related to Ethical Training

Four ideologies are derived from two dominant ethical frameworks in the teaching of law enforcement ethics. The first framework is the concept of **idealism**. This principle is anchored in the belief that a desirable outcome is always obtained by using the right or correct action. The second framework is the concept of **relativism**. It is grounded on the belief that everything is relative to a given circumstance and, therefore, undesirable outcomes will be a fact of life as well. The four ideologies derived from these ethical frameworks are as follows:

1. **Situationists:** Individuals who are closely aligned to this orientation believe that everything is relative and tend to reject any type of universal moral rule or code. Actions are often based on an individual assessment of the situation.
2. **Subjectivists:** As with the situationist, the subjectivist supports the relative nature of events and as such, also rejects the concept of universal moral rules or codes. Unlike the situationist, however, subjectivists subject each event to a personal assessment based solely upon his or her own moral principles.
3. **Absolutists:** A strong supporter of idealism, the absolutist is grounded in the belief that the best outcome to any situation can be obtained by following absolute universal moral principles.
4. **Exceptionists:** Like the absolutist, the exceptionist is also grounded in the belief that the best possible outcome to a situation can be obtained by following absolute universal moral principles. The distinction, however, is that the exceptionist also acknowledges that certain situations may require a deviation or exception to those ideals (Bayley, 2009, p. 2).

Codes of Ethics in Law Enforcement

Most law enforcement agencies operate with a code of ethics or a code of conduct. These codes, however, are generally written addressing one of these ideologies. What complicates the issue further is that the codes are written to address all divisions. A code of conduct that addresses all divisions through a single code may state that it is unacceptable for an officer to lie. Yet, an officer working in an undercover narcotics capacity is expected to immerse himself into the criminal element to be able to buy drugs. If someone trying to sell an undercover officer drugs, questions if the buyer is a police officer, he will not be successful if he answers that question truthfully. Codes that address lying as an officer are easier to keep for a street officer than for a narcotics

Figure 6.1 Ethics is everyone's responsibility. (Courtesy of Ellie Blazer.)

officer when, to be successful, a narcotics officer must immerse himself into the criminal environment (**Figure 6.1**).

Police Culture

Paoline (2001, p. 7) defines culture as a culmination of various definitions that include "attitudes and values that are shared and socially transmitted among groups of people in an attempt to cope with common problems and/or situations." The culture of a police agency is complex and can be defined and controlled by any number of influences.

Murphy (2008, p. 174), in an autoethnographic study, identified police culture as everything he encountered during his experience. His experience was the trust of officers, trust of administration, core values of an organization, the mission and vision of the organization, the true north, and the ability of living up to your word and deed. Police culture is the developed trust of leaders, both administrative and below, that must stand a test of time.

Organizations with stronger cultures have better motivated personnel. In environments with strong organizational ideology, shared participation, charismatic leadership, and intimacy, personnel experience higher job satisfaction and increased productivity (Dimitrov, 2006). Culture has a direct correlation to the attitude of personnel. However, Friedman (2005) states that law enforcement lacks a clear and consistent definition of culture. Law enforcement culture is used synonymously with a variety of concepts including climate, ethos, and saga.

Brooker (2003), as described by Wright (2008), stated that the study of police culture has traditionally been from one of two perspectives: the sociological or the psychological.

The sociological concepts are represented by the following:

1. **Cynicism.** This is a hardened, institutionalized kind of outlook. There are four stages: over idealism, frustration, disenchantment, and full-blown cynicism. This is experienced during the middle portion of a police career.
2. **Isolation.** This is associated with the "bluewall" or the brotherhood of police officers where the feeling of an attack on one officer is an attack on all.
3. **Stress.** The organization produces the kind of personalities it needs, causing a unique type of stress.

The psychological concepts are represented by the following:

1. **Authoritarianism.** This is represented by nine basic components: conventionalism, submissiveness, aggressiveness, being unreflective, superstition, toughness, destructiveness, projection, and sexual exaggeration.
2. **Anchor.** This is the approach of suspicion as healthy, cynicism as unhealthy, and authoritarianism as a personality trait.
3. **Stress.** Self-selection or predispositional; the organization attracts people with the personalities it needs.

Recently, there is the emergence of a third perspective: the anthropological. The concepts of the anthropological police culture include the following:

1. **Worldview.** This is a mentality of cognitive orientation involving how people see themselves and see others. Police are said to have a "we–they" or "us–them" worldview. This in-group, we (police) versus they (civilians) solidarity is associated with the idea of police subculture, but, in practice, the more general term **culture** is commonly used to describe everything police share in common.
2. **Ethos.** This is the idea of a spirit or force in the organization that reflects an unwritten and largely unspoken value system. It's what

makes daily life worth living. Police culture is said to have the following elements in its ethos: bravery, autonomy, and secrecy.

3. **Theme.** This is the idea of a belief system that regulates or guides the kinds of relationships or social interactions that people have inside and outside of their culture. In the case of policing, for example, the belief that police officers are never off duty would be a theme constraining a full interactive life with the general public.

4. **Postulate.** These are the beliefs that integrate the people of a culture. This occurs through proverbs that simplify a vast amount of complex information. These are the concepts closest to norms that are threatened by police deviance (Wright, 2008).

RIPPED FROM THE HEADLINES

CODE OF SILENCE

A *Los Angeles Times* story in May of 2009 quoted the Orange County district attorney as saying, "There is evidence of deputies' code of silence." The story revolved around an incident of police response involving a Taser® deployment, where the DA said that veteran police officers "softened" their accounts of the incident, and "were not truthful." The DA further said that "inconsistencies" relating to the testimonies of the deputies involved prevented the case from being successfully litigated, and suggested that this was in part due to a "code of silence" among the deputies.

The case involved a deputy as the defendant accused of excessive force through the deployment of a Taser on an arrestee who was handcuffed and seated in the rear seat of a patrol car. Initially, none of the deputies at the scene reported the Taser deployment during their primary reports of the incident. However, a grand jury was convened, based on events transpiring after the incident, and several deputies were found to have changed their stories with regards to when the Taser was deployed, where each individual was at prior to and during the deployment of the Taser, and whether or not they felt the Taser deployment was justified. Several deputies told one version of a story before the grand jury, but when testifying in court, told another. One of the deputies with the most inconsistencies was a patrol trainee who stated, "I was just trying to pass training," when asked about the inconsistencies. The DA believed that the individual feared having to return to a jail assignment if he were to fail patrol training, which may have led the individual to be less than forthcoming, and that he "must have felt some sort of pressure."

Although inconsistencies in testimony were pointed out and there appeared to have been some collaboration amongst the deputies after the initial incident, there was not enough evidence to charge any of the deputies with perjury (www.articles.latimes.com/2009/may/13/local /me-da-sheriff13 (accessed February 2, 2010)).

Career Stages and Ethics

Brooker (2003) provides the stages that police officers usually go through in their career. The stages are broken down according to years in service. Between one and two years, a police officer is considered a "rookie." This stage is marked with learning how to "be 911 instead of calling 911" (personal communication with Sergeant Wendy Michaux, autumn, 1999). During this stage, an officer begins to develop his "police personality" that will help him survive the trauma he witnesses, the hatred, and the worst that humanity has to offer. During these years, he learns that people will hate him for no reason and he will be used by them if he is not aware of their manipulative behaviors.

After three to four years of service, an officer begins to identify with television police officers. He feels good about the excitement of the job and is anxious to get to his next case so he can solve it for the good of humanity. He believes he is making a difference and constantly is looking for that happy ending that occurs on television.

Five to ten years on the job and officers become filled with cynicism. They develop bitter feelings toward the system because the bad guys are let out of jail for no apparent reason. They tend to feel the courts and other support agencies are not doing their job. There is no such thing as rehabilitation; bad people will always remain bad.

Between 11 and 15 years, an officer comes to terms with realism. They realize behavior can be changed and they can make a difference if all the right elements are in place. They no longer expect every criminal to go to jail or every crime to be solved. They work at a steady pace, no longer living and dying for their job.

Retirement mindset is developed in officers from 16 years and more as a police officer. Officers here begin to look forward to their retirement. They become more in tune with their mortality and work so they can retire. All these stages are the components of the cultures prevalent in law enforcement.

In a study conducted by Marche (2009, p. 178), it was revealed that police culture fosters corruption and that corruption is not necessarily the result of a "bad apple" making poor choices. The study further indicated that the more stringent police agencies identify, investigate, and discipline corrupt behavior, the clearer police cultures define themselves. Further, it was discussed that to provide a higher level of certainty for addressing police corruption the higher the cost to an agency, a cost that did not necessarily provide a benefit that matched the scope of expense. In this same study, incentive structures within the culture of a police agency caused an increase in corruption as the scale of police agency operation increased.

In a study of major metropolitan area police agencies, 20 area police chiefs were interviewed in regard to their perceptions of police sexual misconduct (PSM). The police chiefs reported that they believed major sexual misconduct activities regarding rape, sexual assault, and sex with a juvenile were rare, and that less sexual misconduct activities, which included flirting on duty, consensual sex on duty, and pulling over a driver to get a closer look, were more common. The police chiefs cited police culture, police departments' complaint systems, opportunity for sexual misconduct, and lack of knowledge about PSM as the primary cause for this type of behavior (Maher, 2008).

Barker (1996, p. 77) believes that police culture is a major contributor to police misconduct. He states that a three-pronged approach is needed to control police corruption and misconduct. They include: decreasing the opportunity, undermining peer group support for unethical behavior, and increasing the risk of engaging in these types of behaviors. He further states, "Police corruption exists only where it is tolerated by the police officers themselves. Only the police peer group can permit unethical behavior and only the police peer group can eliminate it."

RIPPED FROM THE HEADLINES

ETHICS AND RACE

In a 2009 poll (released April 7 by the Pew Hispanic Center and reported April 22 in Chicago, Illinois), less than half of Hispanics present in the United States believe that they would be treated equitably by law enforcement or the justice system. This distrust was found to be almost twice as much as whites, but significantly less than African Americans. The report stated that, of those polled, approximately 46 percent of Hispanics believed that law enforcement would treat them with fairness when compared to other race or ethnicities (compared to 74 percent of whites and 37 percent of African Americans).

This poll was conducted during a time when Hispanics were a "targeted" group within the eyes of the justice system, with regard to illegal immigration. The associated director of the center, Mark Hugo Lopez, believed that the distrust stemmed primarily from Hispanic's apprehensions associated with immigration prosecutions and police ineffectiveness in aiding victims of crimes (www.ethicsinpolicing.com/article .asp?id=5360 (accessed February 3, 2010)).

Police Misbehavior

Klockars et al. (2000) conducted a study of police officers' understanding of agency rules concerning police misconduct and the extent of their support for their agency's rules. The study also evaluated officers' opinions regarding appropriate punishment for misconduct, expected disciplinary threat, disciplinary fairness, and their willingness to report misconduct. Based on the officers' responses to 11 hypothetical case scenarios involving police officers engaged in a range of corrupt behavior, the following information was presented:

- In assessing the 11 cases of police misconduct, officers considered some types to be significantly less serious than others.
- The more serious the officers perceived a behavior to be, the more likely they were to think that more severe discipline was appropriate, and the more willing they were to report a colleague who had engaged in such behavior.
- Police officers' evaluations of the appropriate and expected discipline for various types of misconduct were very similar; the majority of police officers regarded the expected discipline as fair.
- A majority of police officers said that they would not report a fellow officer who had engaged in what they regarded as less serious misconduct (for example, operating an off-duty security business; accepting gifts, meals, and discounts; or having a minor accident while driving under the influence of alcohol).
- Most police officers indicated that they would report a colleague who stole from a found wallet or a burglary scene, accepted a bribe or kickback, or used excessive force on a car thief after a foot pursuit.
- The survey found substantial differences in the environment of integrity among the 30 agencies in the sample (Klockars et al., 2000, p. 2).

Newburn (1999), as noted by Cortrite (2007, p. 13), describes key categories in the range of police corruption: a police officer taking bribes in the form of money or other favors in exchange for not enforcing the law, brutalizing or using excessive force against arrestees, fabricating evidence to help convict a person accused of a crime and destroying evidence that might be helpful to a person accused of a crime, and using race or other criteria to give favorable or unfavorable treatment to a person or group.

Police officers deal with life-changing decisions constantly. Any code of ethics cannot cover every situation for every officer. Officers are given the discretion to choose whether or not to write a ticket or to make an arrest because they work without direct supervision.

Police officers also work in an environment where they are constantly being tempted by opportunities to take something they didn't earn: a fountain drink, a meal, unclaimed beer from a traffic stop, or even drugs from an undercover operation. These temptations are further enhanced by what is considered an officer's code of silence. A code of silence is developed through a culture that poises one group against another (Rothwell and Baldwin, 2007).

The Christopher Commission (Christopher, 1991) that investigated the Los Angeles Police Department reported that officers are governed by an unauthorized and unwritten rule often referred to as the "Code of Silence" (sometimes also called "The Blue Wall"). The "code" requires that an officer not give negative information about any other officer to anyone. This allows corrupt officers to work in the presence of honest officers.

Law enforcement officers constantly see the worse that society has to offer. After saving a spouse from serious injury, that spouse will often turn on the officer that has saved him or her and try to injure the officer. Videos are common place where officers have recorded their own deaths from "routine" traffic stops. Officers at the scene of large civil disputes have to rely on each other for survival and when they need backup for any reason, fellow officers must be relied upon to come to their aid.

Schafer and Martinelli (2008), in a study they conducted examining police supervisor's perceptions of police integrity, found that supervisors viewed themselves as more willing to report unethical and illegal conduct than other officers in their agency. They believed they would take officer transgressions more seriously than other officers. These results were taken from a study that asked respondents to respond to 11 vignettes regarding officer misconduct and criminal activity. In doing so, they were asked to evaluate themselves compared to "most officers in your agency." This study shows that the Code of Silence is not as entrenched among supervisors as it is with their subordinates.

Current Practices for the Prevention of Unethical Behavior

The Office of Community-Oriented Policing Services (COPS) is a division of the United States Department of Justice. The organization provides policing and ethics training to law enforcement agencies and community members through its national network of Regional Community Policing Institutes (RCPI). Ethics and integrity training curricula have been developed through many of these RCPIs. In an effort to standardize ethics-based training throughout the country, COPS has designed a course titled "Police Officer Ethics: A Self-Assessment" (Rubio, 2010).

It has become the national trend to include ethics and integrity training as a subtitle for perishable skills equal to firearms training, emergency vehicle operation, and other skills that demand annual demonstrated proficiency. Subcategories for ethics and integrity in this training include racial profiling, use of force issues, early warning systems, and citizen complaint processes (Rubio, 2010).

Berger and Peed (2010, p. 1) introduced an ethics toolkit entitled "Enhancing Law Enforcement Ethics in a Community Policing Environment." The toolkit was introduced through the International Association of Chiefs of Police and the United States Department of Justice Office of Community-Oriented Policing Services in 2010. The toolkit was the product of three years of research in which the research committee determined that "ethics remains our greatest training and leadership need today."

After leaders identify an organization's ethical system, the next step to developing ethics training is ascertaining the ethical ideologies and/or moral judgments of those who will be required to attend. The final step to improving organizational ethics training is a move toward a proactive mindset. Ethics training is a vital component of any organization's annual instruction. On a superficial level, it helps provide a potential buffer to any disciplinary and/or legal ramifications that may arise from members of an organization making poor decisions when faced with challenging issues (Bailey, 2012).

A topic that has recently challenged the ethical framework of police organizations is the use of body cameras. Proponents for their use believe they provide an extra level of accountability, transparency, legal reforms and improved police-community relations (*Harvard Law Review*, 2015). Opponents to their use cite eavesdropping and privacy laws. Also of consideration is the enormous expense and time commitment to labeling and storing the videos (Kambic, 2015).

Authority

The term **authority** means the power to determine or otherwise settle issues or disputes, the right to control, command, or determine something or someone. In law enforcement, it is necessary for police officers to exercise authority on a regular basis throughout an infinite number of actions and in an infinite number of scenarios. Due to the paramilitary structure of policing agencies, police officers also exercise authority over one another. With so much emphasis on authority, it is wise to discuss how to exercise authority wisely, and the ways in which one can abuse his or her authority. Therefore, it is important to discuss the concept of authority. This can be a rather complex concept. First of all, it must be understood that a "fiduciary relationship" exists with regard to police authority.

A fiduciary relationship involves a relation between two or more persons—the person who has or is in authority and the person or persons to whom the authority is directed. Some view authority as power. And, if power is defined as the ability to impart change or have an impact on the desired outcome, then authority may be viewed as a form of power, since often times a person in a position of authority may be able to influence a person to do what he wants him/her to do. The difference between authority and other types of power, such as coercion, is that with authority a person to whom an order is issued responds in accordance with that order because he accepts that the issuer of the order is entrusted with the authority to tell him how to act, and that the order should be carried out simply because the person in position of authority says so.

Regardless of the type of authority, all authority is limited in its scope. **Scope of authority** means that anyone who has authority has that authority over only a certain group of persons or matters, and this authority does not translate to other persons or matters. For instance, the office manager in the records division of the police department has authority over the persons that work for him as to how reports should be written regarding format and department policy issues. However, this same individual does not have the authority over officers working in a patrol division as to how they document the information within their reports.

How does this discussion of authority relate to the concept of police authority? First of all, police authority is remarkably wide in scope. That is to say, it is wide both in terms of its application, with reference to the number of persons it applies to, and also in terms of the area of action to which it applies. In their role as police officers, police have the authority to direct people with regards to any matter involving enforcement of the law or in the maintaining of public order.

Although wide in scope, police authority has boundaries. It is here that it is necessary to differentiate between compliance with laws and obedience to directives. In their roles as police officers, authority is exercised both within the confines of the law and within the confines of the paramilitary, hierarchical organization in which they work. This means they must both obey the law and obey their superiors. Most times this is not an issue because the majority of the time the orders given by superiors will be lawful orders and consistent with the law. However, in rare occasions, orders may not be lawful and, thus, the two points of authority are in conflict. Police officers are held to be responsible both for the law and to their superiors; however, their primary obligation is to the law. In other words, they should disobey an unlawful command if obeying it would be illegal.

Another aspect of police authority is that of its relationship to coercive force. However, coercive force is exclusive of effective authority. The need for one to resort to coercive force shows a sign of a breakdown in effective authority, implying that the person coerced would not have otherwise done as ordered, if not coerced. However, sometimes as police, it is necessary to make use of coercion in the act of one's duty. For instance, the majority of criminals understand what the law is and accept the law as generally in order; however, many will still attempt to evade or resist arrest. It is then necessary

ABUSE OF AUTHORITY

On July 17, 2009, CNN reported the story of a California police officer who admitted to sexually assaulting a woman while on a traffic stop. While on trial in District Court, the officer admitted to pulling over a female for a traffic violation and then subsequently forcing her to perform oral sex on him. The officer pulled the woman over for speeding and weaving in traffic, and had suspected her of being under the influence of alcohol while operating a motor vehicle. In the course of the traffic stop, he ascertained that the female did not have a valid driver's license and was driving while impaired. He offered to drive her to her job, but instead drove to a parking lot where he placed his hand on his gun and forced the woman to perform oral sex on him while in his patrol car. U.S. Attorney Thomas O'Brien was quoted as saying the officer "brutalized a person he had sworn to serve. ... His conduct eroded public confidence in law enforcement and cast a pall over his former colleagues who obey the law, proudly working to preserve public safety" (www.cnn.com/2009 /CRIME/07/17/officer.sex.assault/index.html (accessed August 23, 2010)).

for officers to coerce those evading arrest into custody by a manner of methods or else risk damaging police effectiveness and perceived authority.

While the previous example explains why coercion by police may be justified, it's impractical to think that effective policing could rely solely or mainly on the use of coercive force. At a certain point, the coercive force is more likely to undermine police authority as the police are looked at by the community that they police as an organization that will have their way regardless of the opinions and desires of the community that they are hired to serve and protect.

Authority brings with it responsibility. Having seen that the scope of police authority is wide, it is important to recognize that the responsibility associated with police authority is quite demanding and quite literally may involve matters of life and death.

Discretion

Police authority, including legal powers, are often times discretionary, that is, it is up to individual officers to decide whether or not they choose to exercise their authority in a given situation. For example, in many cases, an officer's decision to arrest, to issue the individual a summons, or to issue a verbal warning is a matter of discretion by law. Although discretionary, the law requires that such discretion be based on considerations that may include the severity of the offense, the likelihood that the suspect will appear in court, the individual's criminal history, the location of residence, and others.

Police discretion is present in many stages of police work. It is typically involved in the decision-making process of whether or not to investigate a possible crime, as well as being involved in the decision of whether or not to affect an arrest. Police work often involves never-before-seen situations that require an immediate resolution. In these instances, it is quite necessary that police have discretionary powers to aid them in providing solutions.

It is impossible to identify every situation and all conditions that influence an incident a police officer can experience. In science, this type of phenomenon is described as the Chaos Theory. This is the concept that holds a seemingly insignificant action, like a butterfly flapping its wings can have a dramatic effect on the weather thousands of miles away (Ambika, 2015). This is a good comparison to the influence officers often experience when dealing with what otherwise appear to be routine calls. An officer's decision to use physical force can be influenced by something as simple as a lack of eye contact. Subsequently, officer discretion is a necessary element of the position.

The topic of discretion is of special concern with regard to ethics when one stops to think about the reasons for the use of a discretionary decision. While police are given discretionary authority, this authority must be used in an unbiased, moral, ethical, and legal manner. It would be unethical and prejudicial for a police officer to issue a verbal warning to all female drivers who have broken the speed limit, but to issue citations to all male drivers who have broken the speed limit. The same would be true if this discretionary authority was used to make decisions based on race, ethnicity, or religious background.

There are some who argue that, if police abuse of power is to be reduced, their discretionary authority should be curtailed. A viewing of the evening news or a perusal of a recent newspaper will document abuse of power in relation to suspect rights based on police discretion. However, there are also those who hold an opposing point of view, that a corralling of police discretionary authority is a dangerous mistake. Perhaps, rather than a reduction in power, what is needed is an increase in accountability for the use of such discretionary power.

Corruption

The book, *Police Ethics*, by Miller, Blackler, and Alexandra (2006, p. 135) suggests that there are three defining features of a good police officer. These include the following:

1. The possession of specialized expertise.
2. The use of this expertise in the morally correct way.
3. For the morally correct ends.

As with any profession, not all police officers are good police officers. However, there is a difference between failing to be a good police officer and being a corrupt police officer. For instance, incompetence may be viewed as a type of corruption. It is typically not thought that incompetence could be morally blameworthy, even in instances leading to a bad outcome, since an individual cannot be blamed for failing to bring about something that they did not have the capacity to cause to occur. However, if this failure was a result of failing to equip themselves or train and be in possession of necessary skills or knowledge when given the opportunity, then this incompetence is morally blameworthy.

Blame is also possible in instances where individuals continue in a job when they no longer possess the aptitude or the ability to perform the requirements of the job. One example is what is referred to as someone being "retired on duty." This is an officer who continues to work, but, as a result of laziness, burnout, and perhaps myriad physical and mental reasons, is no longer capable or does not desire to perform his duty properly, but continues to work anyway. While not seen as being overtly corrupt, continuing in the job for reasons of self-interest, such as a paycheck and insurance, has a negative institutional impact and could even be seen as unsafe and an improper use of police authority and community property, which is a degree of corruption.

The police officers who are competent may be considered corrupt if they use their knowledge and skills in illegal or immoral ways. For example, an officer engaged in illegal activity may use his knowledge of interview and interrogation tactics as a way to intimidate or discover individuals who threaten to expose the officer's illegal activity.

QUESTION OF ETHICS

A TANGLED WEB

During my 25+ years working in law enforcement, I have unfortunately seen first-hand many careers end by poor ethical decisions. Many times these situations were so cut and dry they don't really lend themselves to interesting reading, such as the officer who took a purse he found in a recovered stolen vehicle and tried to sell it to nurses at the local emergency room. I thought a more interesting example might be that of the "slippery slope," where the initial poor ethical decision was not in and of itself a career ender, but the beginning of the end.

Even something as mundane as a traffic stop requires that officers maintain impeccable integrity and avoid even a hint of unethical behavior. In a police department in the Midwest, an officer made a traffic stop for an equipment violation. Like possibly hundreds of stops prior, the officer conducted a "routine" traffic stop. Another officer recognized, through radio communication that a passenger in the vehicle might have used a false name and had an outstanding warrant for his arrest. After hearing this, the on-duty supervisor drove by to check on the safety of the officer. When he arrived at the location where the stop was supposed to be occurring, no one was there. The supervisor called the officer on the radio and was informed the stop moved to a different location. The stop was now about one-half mile from where the original stop was reported.

Later, it was learned the violator felt he didn't need to remain at the stop and drove to an auto parts store to purchase a necessary part to repair an equipment violation. The officer never notified dispatch or fellow officers the location of the stop had moved and initially did not realize the violator had driven away from the stop.

When the Sergeant arrived at the auto parts store, the driver was standing by the driver's side of the patrol vehicle and the passenger was missing. It was determined the passenger had provided a false name and indeed had an outstanding warrant for his arrest. Other officers and deputies from the sheriff's office responded to the area and a short time later, the suspect was taken into custody. Once arrested, the suspect was placed in the initiating officer's car. That officer was handed a bag containing items taken from the suspect upon his arrest. Without looking in the bag the officer placed it on the front passenger's floorboard of the patrol vehicle.

A few days later, it was determined not all of the contents of the bag were turned into police evidence. During the investigation, information was obtained that the officer placed food items and beer from the bag in his refrigerator at his residence. He also kept possession of narcotic pills the suspect had on his person. However, during the officer's next shift, he turned in the suspect's wallet and a few personal affects, without turning in these other items. In addition, during the investigation, the officer attempted to cover up his mistakes with mistruths. What started as a "routine" traffic stop, followed by apathetic police procedure, ended the career of this veteran officer. Had the officer accepted responsibility for his poor police work and steered away from the slippery slope, he would have received discipline but maintained his job.

Chief Chuck Wynn

Chino Valley, Arizona Police Department

Lastly, police can be considered corrupt if they make use of proper skills and knowledge to achieve improper results. For instance, enforcing the law against only one social or cultural group, even if by the book, is prejudicial and biased. While the enforcement of the law may be legal, the overall situation is corrupt.

What Are the Causes of Corruption?

There is significant documentation of instances involving police corruption within the mainstream media and an even larger number of unreported instances. If one were to look at the various incidents, there are a number of causes of police corruption that can be identified. Having been given such powers as police discretion and coercive power, police have many opportunities every shift to abuse these powers. These can include harassment of the innocent, threats with trivial charges, turning a blind eye to more serious crimes, and many more. Police also are faced with myriad temptations throughout the course of their obligations. These can include the offer of money or favors in return for police protection, getting out of a charge, looking the other way, or using evidence for personal gain. In the majority of jurisdictions, public service is not a well-paid area of employment and, thus, the temptation to take shortcuts or to seek benefits that offset this lack of compensation is often quite considerable.

Another significant contributing factor in police corruption is the regular usage of what would normally be regarded as morally unacceptable activity within the capacity of their job. For instance, deception, threats of force, deprivation of personal liberty, etc. are all activities that would be considered morally wrong under normal circumstances. However, in the performance of one's duties as a police officer, detective, undercover operative, etc., these are all acceptable behaviors and are not seen as being morally or ethically wrong. These normally immoral activities are morally justified in police work in terms of the ends that they serve. Nevertheless, the use of these methods by police officers in circumstances, which are morally justified, can begin to have a corrupting influence upon the individuals who make use of them. For instance, a police officer may begin engaging in the morally justified telling of lies and in the development of elaborate deception in a role as an undercover officer, and proceed to tell morally unjustified lies and engage in deceptive behavior with innocent individuals, co-workers, and family members.

As has been discussed, and sometimes referred to as the **blue wall**, police display a high degree of group identification and solidarity. The solidarity can be a good thing without which effective policing may not be possible. However, it is also a contributor to police corruption. For instance, individuals who fail to act against corrupt colleagues out of a sense of loyalty are often morally and ethically compromised and become more likely to engage in corrupt activities in the future.

There are some general conditions that are viewed as being contributory to police corruption. These (adapted from Miller et al., 2006) may include the following:

- Necessity for and use of discretionary authority by police officers.
- Street-level interaction between law enforcement and corrupt individuals who often have a motivation or interest in manipulating or corrupting police.
- Ability for police officers to use methods, such as deception and coercion, which are typically viewed as immoral, but which are legal within the course of their employment.
- Employment of and operation of law enforcement in an environment that includes large amounts of money, drugs, weapons, and other items of value, or which are of temptation to abuse or misappropriate based on external pressures.
- Presence of corrupt administration or leadership, sometimes combined with a corrupt or seemingly futile political and court system.
- Compensation not commensurate with obligations and responsibilities.

Within the profession of policing, the tendency toward corruption should be considered as a basic occupational hazard and should be trained on and treated accordingly (Miller et al., 2006). Just as police officers are trained and tested with regards to the usage of firearms and the application of deadly force, understanding that the threat to their life is an occupational hazard, so too should police officers be trained and tested against moral vulnerability. It is necessary to enact measures to protect those engaged in the policing profession from the possibility of corruption.

How Is Corruption Overcome?

If measures are to be enacted to attempt to reduce police corruption, there are four basic areas that must be considered. These (adapted from Miller et al., 2006) areas include the following:

1. Personnel hiring and recruitment
2. Reduction of corruption opportunities
3. Detection of corruption
4. Reinforcing effort to motivate individuals to do what is right

It would seem self-evident that, if within policing there is a tendency toward corruption, it would be of paramount concern for those selected to possess the highest of moral character. It is important to reduce the opportunities for corruption; however, the nature of police work is such that it does not allow for complete reduction in such opportunities.

With regards to the detection and even the deterrence of corruption, these are in large part achieved through institutional accountability. These methods of accountability may be either internal or external and can include such things as complaints investigation, report and incident audits, surveillance, and personnel examinations. Methods of accountability should include a partnership involving both police and community. This ensures that the community is able to make the police aware of potential problems and to hold police accountable for these problems. It is further suggested that any such review boards composed of police and community might be wise to include retired police officers who no longer have a vested interest in the goings-on, but who have knowledge and experience possibly associated with the event in question. Sometimes it is a practice for agencies to offer an officer immunity in order that he testify and implicate others. Informants may not only consist of police officers, but also may consist of the public or even criminals who have been granted immunity; all of the latter should be carefully considered because often times the information provided turns out to be false.

Lastly, in an effort to reduce corruption, it is important that an agency support and make known its motivation to do what is morally right. It is obvious to all concerned that reducing corruption opportunities is important. It is equally apparent that there will always be those who will engage in illegal or immoral behavior and, thus, there will always be a need for techniques of corruption detection. However, a reduction in opportunities or the development of a sophisticated system of detection typically comes with a large price tag. Therefore, it is suggested that an agency spend considerable effort and time motivating its personnel to do what is morally right and to recognize those who do the right thing and make smart decisions. There is no system of detection, no matter how sophisticated, that could possibly hope to control corruption. This is why it is wise to institute a system of rewards and penalties within a police agency for decisions and actions that will help to motivate personnel in doing the right thing and discouraging personnel from making poor ethical, even corrupt, decisions. Even things such as clearly defined promotion procedures and disciplinary procedures vary greatly in this area. This helps to reduce or limit a feeling of resentment or injustice relating to these thoughts, which lead to corruptive behavior or, at the very least, a hostile work environment. The chain of command also should be further reinforced in doing what is right. With great power comes great responsibility and, as relates to police work, great discretion. The proper use of this discretionary power within the chain of command can be proper reinforcement of moral decision making and aid in reducing corruption.

The nature of police solidarity can be reinforcing as well. Placing emphasis on the collective responsibility of the police to police their own reinforces the need for and acceptance of proper moral decision making. Policing is cooperative in nature and, thus, corruption undermines the effectiveness of policing. Rather than blind loyalty to one's co-workers, collective responsibility requires selective loyalty. That is, maintaining loyalty to those individuals who do what is right, but not to those individuals who do what is wrong. This deep-seated loyalty is only warranted to those and by those who uphold the ideals of policing and who embody those ideals within their decisions and actions. This collective responsibility also may include an individual engaging in what is commonly known as **whistle-blowing**, as well as proper support for, rather than hostile action toward, properly intentioned individuals involved in whistle-blowing. A whistle-blower is a "person who informs on another or makes public disclosure of corruption or wrongdoing" (www .dictionary.com).

Conflicts of Interest

While perhaps not overtly corrupt, an individual may be engaged in corrupt behavior if he or she has a conflict of interest regarding the incident or person in question. The **conflict of interest** exists when a person is (1) in a relationship with another individual that requires that person to make judgments based on the other's behalf, or (2) when that person has a special interest that tends to interfere with proper decision making within that relationship or incident. The important terms to pay attention to within this definition are those of relationship, judgment, and interest.

The term **relationship**, which is mentioned, must be fiduciary in nature, which means it must involve one individual entrusted to work while trusting another in order to make a judgment on his behalf. This **judgment** is the ability of the individual to make reliably correct decisions requiring knowledge or skill. The term **interest** refers to any concern, loyalty to, influence over, or other instance in which a person's judgment in that situation could be deemed less reliable based on one of the aforementioned reasons.

The fundamental concern relating to a conflict of interest is that an individual's judgment is fundamentally less reliable than it ought to be and, thus, results in a failure by this individual to properly execute a fiduciary responsibility.

Conflicts of interest may be conducive to institutional corruption. However, even when an individual, in fact, does not act corruptly (he or she may have good moral intentions in the performance of the obligation), a conflict of interest still may remain in the perception of this conflict of interest and may impact the apparent ability to properly discharge his/her role. It is best to avoid conflicts of interest when at all possible; however, often times a conflict of interest may be a minor one that could be avoided only through difficulty. In such a case, it may be acceptable for an individual to simply disclose the conflict of interest rather than avoiding it and ensure that there is a proper process of accountability in place to ensure proper decision making.

Recruitment

The hiring and recruitment process is one of the chief areas in which ethics issues is most effectively addressed. If an organization has a well-established recruiting and hiring process, it is possible to identify those individuals who may have a tendency toward making poor ethical decisions or who would be more easily influenced and likely to make poor or unethical decisions. A proper hiring process that will assist with reducing the likelihood of ethical violations in the future should consist of:

- Criminal history check
- Professional references check
- Personal references check
- Financial history check
- Educational references check
- Psychological examination
- Polygraph examination

An organization is wise to invest significant resources of time, money, and personnel in its recruiting and hiring efforts. Identifying those individuals most likely to be tempted or influenced, rather than adhering to a strong set of personal beliefs in line with organizational ethics, will result in a minimization of ethical violations in the future.

Conclusion

Police ethics is a subject that has been studied and evaluated due to the tremendous need based on public responses through reported corruption and police misconduct. With over 2,000 police agencies in the United States, the majority of officers, however, are not involved in scandals or police misconduct. When widespread complaints are headline news, the public's trust is often shaken because of the unknown. The culture of most police agencies are closed cultures. This closed culture environment breeds mistrust, due to an inability to have transparency at all levels. This mistrust is heightened further through the widespread belief that officers protect one another (Rothwell and Baldwin, 2007). A proper recruitment and training process can minimize the potential for corruption within law enforcement.

Questions for Review

1. _____ is the act of officers getting criminals off the street as a "noble cause."
2. The belief that a desirable outcome is always obtained by using the right or correct actions is the concept of _____.
3. The four ideologies derived from the framework of idealism and relativism are _____, _____, _____, and _____.
4. Organizations with stronger cultures (have, do not have) better motivated personnel.
5. True or false: Law enforcement lacks a clear and concise definition of culture.
6. The sociological concepts are represented by _____, _____, and _____.
7. Five to ten years on the job officers become filled with _____.
8. What is the "code of silence" as it relates to law enforcement officers and what does the code allow?
9. The concept that anyone who has authority has that authority over only a certain group of persons or matters, and this authority does not translate to other persons or matters is known as _____.
10. True or false: Coercive force is exclusive of effective authority.
11. The idea that it is up to the individual officer to decide whether or not he chooses to exercise his authority in a given situation is known as _____.
12. Why do police officers need to have discretionary powers?
13. A police officer who is competent may be considered _____ if he uses his knowledge and skills in illegal or immoral ways.
14. True or false: The chain of command also can be further reinforcement to do what is right.
15. When does conflict of interest exist?

References

Ambika, G. 2015. Ed Lorenz: Father of the 'Butterfly effect.' *Resonance*, 20 (3), 198–205. doi:10.1007/s12045-015-0170-y

Ariel, B., W. A. Farrar, and A. Sutherland. 2015. The effect of police body-worn cameras on use of force and citizens' complaints against the police: A randomized controlled trial. *Journal of Quantitative Criminology*, 31 (3), 509–535. doi:10.1007/s10940-014-9236-3

Barker, T. 1996. *Police ethics crisis in law enforcement*. Springfield, IL: Charles C Thomas.

Bayley, B. 2009. Improving ethics training for the 21st century. From www.police one.com (accessed February 12, 2010).

Berger, W., and C. Peed. 2010. Introduction to ethics toolkit. *International Association of Chiefs of Police global leadership in policing*. Advance online publication: www.theiacp.org (accessed July 28, 2010).

Brooker, P. 2003. *A glossary of cultural theory, second edition*. London: Arnold.

Christopher, W. 1991. *Report of the independent commission on the Los Angeles Police Department*. Los Angeles.

Considering Police Body Cameras. 2015. *Harvard Law Review*, 128 (6), 1794–1817.

Cortrite, M. D. 2007. Servant leadership for law enforcement. PhD diss., University of California, Los Angeles.

Crank, J. P., and M. A. Caldero. 2000. *Police ethics: The corruption of noble cause*. Cincinnati, Ohio: Anderson Publishing Co.

Dimitrov, D. 2006. Cultural differences in motivation for organizational learning and training. *International Journal of Diversity in Organisations, Communities & Nations*, 5 (4): 37–48.

Drug Reform Coordination Network. 2000. *A barrel full of bad apples: Police corruption and the war on drugs*. From http://stopthedrugwar.org (accessed July 25, 2010).

Friedman, C. A. 2005. *Spiritual survival for law enforcement*. Linden, NJ: Compass.

Goodman, D. 2010. Detroit mayor: Ousted chief 'blindsided' him. *Officer.com*. From http://www.officer.com (accessed July 23, 2010).

Heinzmann, D. 2009, October. Police misconduct allegations up almost 19%. *Chicago Tribune*. From http://articles.chicagotribune.com (accessed July 25, 2010).

Justnews.com. 2010. *Ex Fla. trooper pleads no contest in fake tickets case*. From http://www.officer.com (accessed July 23, 2010).

Kambic, R., and P. Press. (2015, February 19). Mundelein police eye body cameras. *Chicago Tribune*. Retrieved from https://search.proquest.com/docview/165597 1921?accountid=35812.

Klockars, C. B., S. K. Ivkovich, W. E. Harver, and M. R. Haberfeld. 2000. *The measurement of police integrity*. Washington, D.C.: National Institute of Justice.

Maher, T. 2008. Police chiefs' views on police sexual misconduct. *Police Practice & Research*, 9 (3): 239–250.

Marche, G. E. 2009. Integrity, culture, and scale: An empirical test of the big bad police agency. *Crime, Law and Social Change*, 51 (5): 463.

Miller, S., J. Blackler, and A. Alexandra. 2006. *Police ethics*. Crows Nest NSW, Australia: Allen & Unwin.

Murphy, M. 2008. The role of emotions and transformational leadership on police culture: An autoethnographic account. *International Journal of Police Science and Management*, (10) 2, 165–178.

Newburn, T. 1999. *Understanding and Preventing Police Corruption: Lessons from the Literature*. London: Research, Development and Statistics Directorate.

Paoline III, E. A., ed. 2001. *Rethinking police culture: Officers' occupational attitudes*. New York: LFB Scholarly Publishing LLC.

Police Corruption. 2004. *Issues & controversies on file*. From Issues & Controversies database: www.2facts.com/article/i0400270 (accessed February 16, 2010).

Rothwell, G., and J. Baldwin. 2007. Ethical climate theory, whistle-blowing, and the code of silence in police agencies in the State of Georgia. *Journal of Business Ethics*, 70 (4): 341–361.

Rubio, M. 2010. *COPS ethics and integrity training*. From International Association of Chiefs of Police Global Leadership in Policing: www.theiacrg (accessed February 10, 2010).

Schafer, J. A., and T. J. Martinelli. 2008. First-line supervisor's perceptions of police integrity: The measurement of police integrity revisited. *Policing*, 31 (2): 306–323.

Wedge, D., and O. Johnson. 2010. *Cop quits after on-duty viewing of midget stripper show*. From www.policeone.com (accessed July 23, 2010).

Weitzer, R. 2015. American policing under fire: Misconduct and reform. *Society*, 52 (5), 475–480. doi:http://dx.doi.org/10.1007/s12115-015-9931-1

Wlwt.com. 2010. *Ohio officer suspended for on-duty affair with mayor*. From www .officer.com (accessed May 15, 2010).

Wright, A. L. 2008. *Spirituality-centered leadership: Perceptions of law enforcement leaders*. Huntsville, TX: Sam Houston State University.

www.dictionary.com (accessed December 26, 2010).

Ethics in Forensic Science

7

I can discover facts, Watson, but I cannot change them.

Sir Arthur Conan Doyle (1859–1930)
(Sherlock Holmes, "The Problem of Thor Bridge")

Key Terms

American Society of Crime
Laboratory Directors
Laboratory Accreditation
Board (ASCLD-LAB)
American Academy of Forensic
Sciences (AAFS)
American Board of
Criminalistics (ABC)
Daubert test
Chain of custody
Criminalistics
CSI effect

Drylabbing
Forensic science
Forensic Science Educational
Program Accreditation
Commission (FEPAC)
Frye test/rule, Federal Rules of
Evidence, Rule 702
International Association of
Identification (IAI)
National Institute of Forensic
Science

Learning Objectives

1. Define what is meant by "**forensic science**."
2. Define what is meant by "**drylabbing**" and explain how it relates to forensic science ethics.
3. Explain what should be the ultimate obligation of a forensic practitioner.
4. Define and explain what is meant by the "**CSI effect**."
5. Define and differentiate between "accuracy" and "precision."
6. Understand the ways in which ethics can be involved within crime scene investigation efforts and laboratory analyses.

Introduction

Forensic science, the application of science to civil and criminal law, is a field that is grounded in applied ethics. The identification, collection, and preservation of any piece of forensic evidence will ultimately involve numerous individuals. At any step within the process, evidence can be deliberately or accidentally mishandled. This risk begins at the scene of the crime where there is the possibility of evidence planting, destruction, or mishandling. After the scene has been processed, evidence is then sent to a forensic laboratory for analysis. Here, it can be subjected to contamination through poor testing methods, excess consumption, mislabeling, and even loss or destruction. After the analysis has been performed, those analyzing the evidence must then report on their findings. With regards to the reporting of examination results, personnel must be accurate and honest with regard to their findings. There have been instances uncovered where individuals trusted with such reporting have misrepresented their findings and have even been involved in **drylabbing**, which is the reporting of results based on forensic analysis when no test or analysis was ever performed.

These errors, omissions, or completely fraudulent testimonies or reporting are of special concern due to the fact that forensic evidence, which is testified to or reported on by "experts," is routinely given more weight and consideration by jurors. As a result, false testimony, inflated statistics, and laboratory fraud have led to wrongful conviction in many states due to juror trust in the system, but with forensic fraud being the impetus.

Expert Witnesses

Emergency responders, crime scene personnel, and forensic scientists are often called upon to testify as expert witnesses. An **expert witness** is someone who is called to answer questions on the stand in a court of law in order to provide specialized information relevant to the case being tried. Oftentimes, scientific principles relating to physical evidence are often beyond the knowledge of lay people. As a result, courts permit persons with specialized training and skills to appear in court to explain and interpret scientific evidence to juries. When this occurs, he or she may be deemed an "expert."

A person can be considered an "expert" when they have sufficient skills, knowledge, or experience in their field to help the "**trier of fact**" to determine the truth. It therefore is the duty of the expert witness to educate the jury and provide testimony using terminology that is easily explainable and will not be misunderstood (Fish et al., 2014).

Unlike non-expert witnesses an expert witness can provide opinions based on the outcomes of the examinations and the significance of their findings. Non-experts who state opinions as part of their testimony will have such statements ruled as inadmissible due to them being classified as **hearsay**. Hearsay is unfounded information that is heard from other people. However, the court allows experts to state opinions due to their ability to assist the court in better comprehending the topic under consideration.

In the case of an expert rendering an opinion on their findings, the opinion has a foundation in the expert's training and experience, and is not an arbitrary opinion with no factual relevance. It should be mentioned that simply because there is this ability to state an opinion, it does not mean that it is always a legal possibility.

The facts or data in the particular case upon which an expert bases an opinion or inference may be those perceived by or made known to the expert at or before the hearing. If of a type reasonably relied upon by experts in the particular field in forming opinions or inferences upon the subject, the facts or data need not be admissible in evidence in order for the opinion or inference to be admitted. Facts or data that are otherwise inadmissible shall not be disclosed to the jury by the proponent of the opinion or inference unless the court determines that their probative value in assisting the jury to evaluate the expert's opinion substantially outweighs their prejudicial effect (Expert Pages, 2008).

Although it is not possible for an expert to render an opinion with absolute certainty, as an advocate of truth, the expert must base opinions on a reasonable scientific certainty. An expert must be confident in their statements made within a court of law. If they are found to be contradictory, or if it is pointed out that the witness intentionally lied or misrepresented the facts, they could be charged with **perjury**. Perjury is the telling of a lie within a court of law by somebody who has taken an oath to tell the truth.

Since experts are permitted to express their opinions, based upon his or her training, experience, and knowledge, it is important that he or she communicate in a manner which is clear, simple, and honest. Witnesses cannot deliberately omit relevant facts or encourage incorrect conclusions; these are distortions of the facts. Overstatements of the facts or a suggestion that an individual is guilty will cost an expert witness their integrity. Individuals must be

QUALIFYING AS AN EXPERT WITNESS

Usually when one talks about experience, the term **credentials** is used. Often this refers to a certificate, letter, experience, or anything that provides authentication for a claim or qualifies somebody to do something. However, as pertains to forensic and crime scene–related work, credentials as an expert will be established by the court through questioning pertaining to the witness's education, training, and experience. The ability and competence of the witness must be demonstrated through testimony relating to college degrees, continuing education, attendance at conferences, publications, ongoing research, and a variety of other possibilities that show rigor and knowledge within the area of expertise under consideration.

RIPPED FROM THE HEADLINES

In May of 2001, the FBI was called in to investigate an employee of the Oklahoma City crime lab. A 21-year veteran of the Oklahoma City Police Department, Joyce Gilchrist, was being investigated about credibility issues that had surfaced with regard to her forensic analysis in hundreds of cases. Gilchrist was a chemist for the police lab and her work was being questioned due to inconsistencies and inaccuracies. According to one report, "her expert testimony went beyond the acceptable limits of forensic science." Gilchrist was involved in 11 cases that resulted in executions due to the death penalty, and there were an additional 13 individuals on death row awaiting execution, where her testimony or work had been a key piece of trial testimony. Gilchrist was eventually relieved of her duties and terminated and a review of 583 of her cases was conducted, resulting in several exonerations. It was determined that there was "no indication that any innocent people had been executed" as a result of Gilchrist's errors, omissions, or inaccuracies.

http://archives.cnn.com/2001/LAW/05/01
/oklahoma.evidence/index.html

familiar with the scope of his or her actions and knowledge, and know where his or her level of expertise ends. Once credibility as an expert witness is compromised, it is nearly impossible to recover in court (Rogers, 2004).

Ethics and Forensic Testimony

As was stated earlier, juries and jurors give increased weight to the testimony of forensic experts. They are correct in doing so in some respects because **criminalistics** (the field of forensic analysis) "has as its primary objective a determination of physical facts, which may be significant in legal cases" (Barnett, 2001). Therefore, an ethical analyst has an obligation to the truth and, as such, they have an obligation not to mislead the jury, defense, or the state when testifying before the court or when preparing their reports relating to their analyses of forensic evidence.

Chapter 5 covered ethical codes and standards and, while there exists no single ethical code that applies to all disciplines of forensic science or to all practicing criminalists, there are two primary organizations that have developed ethical codes relating to forensic testimony and the presentation of forensic analyses within court. The **American Board of Criminalistics (ABC)**, and the **American Academy of Forensic Sciences (AAFS)** are the two primary certifying bodies for forensic scientists within the United States. The ABC code of ethics requires each certified member to ensure that any opinions rendered with regards to his/her analyses are done so "only to the extent justified" by the evidence in question, and also to ensure that the testimony given is presented "in a clear, straightforward manner," which in no way misrepresents or extends "themselves beyond their field of competence." Testimony should be given "in such a manner so that the results are not misinterpreted" (ABC, 2017). The AAFS code is equally as articulate in spelling out the expectation of its members, stating that it forbids a "material misrepresentation of data upon which an expert opinion or conclusion is based" (AAFS, 2017). An addition to the AAFS code is a section that lists "Guidelines" for members and analysts. Under this section, it says that analysts should "adopt good forensic practice guidelines and that, unlike attorneys, forensic scientists are not adversaries. They take an oath in court to tell the whole truth. They should make every effort to uphold that oath. Every reasonable effort should be made to ensure that others (including attorneys) do not distort the forensic scientist's opinions" (AAFS, 2017).

Forensic Science Gone Awry

The *Virginia Law Review* (www.virginialawreview.org) included an article entitled "Invalid Forensic Science Testimony and Wrongful Convictions." This study, conducted by Brandon L. Garrett and Peter J. Neufeld, was the first study undertaken to explore the relationship between forensic testimony and convictions ultimately leading to exonerations based on postconviction DNA analysis. The study sought out court transcripts and results for the 156 exonerees who had been identified at that time, with ultimately 137 being located for review. The testimony that was reviewed for the 137 exonerees primarily involved serological analysis testimony (100 cases) and testimony regarding microscopic hair comparison (65 cases), with the majority of the cases being cases of sexual assaults (**Figure 7.1**).

Of those reviewed for the study, 82 of the cases, or approximately 60 percent, included invalid forensic testimony by prosecution experts, or "testimony with conclusions misstating empirical data or wholly unsupported by empirical data." According to the article, two basic categories of invalid scientific testimony were recurring themes within the cases reviewed: "(1) The misuse of empirical population data; (2) conclusions regarding the probative value of evidence in the absence of empirical data."

The six types of invalid testimony that were identified pertained to the following:

1. Evidence that was nonprobative presented as probative.
2. Discounting exculpatory evidence.

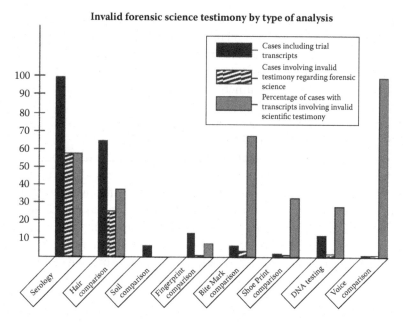

Figure 7.1 Invalid forensic testimony by type of analysis. (Courtesy of Ellie Blazer.)

3. Inaccurate presentation regarding statistics or frequency.
4. Providing statistics without supporting empirical data.
5. Nonstatistical statements made without supporting empirical data.
6. Conclusion of evidence originating from defendant without supporting empirical data.

In a statement made at a hearing before the Committee on the Judiciary, 107th Congress, Senator Orrin Hatch commented on the need to provide new resources for forensic science, while referring to the unethical work of an Oklahoma City forensic analyst (see Ripped from the Headlines).

This isolated situation should not be used unfairly to indict the thousands of forensic scientists who perform their work professionally and responsibly. It should, however, remind us that those who work in our criminal justice system have an obligation to be diligent, honest, and fair-minded.

*(http://frwebgate.access.gpo.gov/cgi-bin/getdoc
.cgi?dbname=107_senate_hearings&docid=f:78008.pdf)*

However, while not attempting to disagree with the senator's remarks, what this study found was that it was not necessarily a "few bad apples" who were making the bunch bad, and was not simply isolated incidents involving a handful of analysts. The trials reviewed included invalid testimony by 72 forensic experts, employed by 52 different agencies, in 25 different states. As shocking as these statistics may seem, more shocking is that in the majority of these instances, "defense counsel rarely cross-examined analysts concerning invalid testimony and rarely obtained experts of their own." In the rare case in which invalid forensic testimony was challenged or in dispute between the prosecution and defense, "judges seldom provided relief."

Legal Rulings Regarding Expert Testimony in U.S. Courts

What qualifies an individual to be deemed an expert within a court? When is such testimony admissible? There has been great debate and much litigation pertaining to what should be allowed as "expert testimony" and what should qualify an individual to be considered as an expert within courtrooms. To answer these questions, one must look back at a few historical rulings within U.S. courts.

Frye v. United States 54 App. D.C., at 47, 293 F., at 1014

The "**Frye test**" or "**Frye rule**" was produced by *Frye v. United States* in 1923. This test/rule directly affected the admissibility of scientific evidence for over 70 years. According to the National Criminal Justice Reference Service (NCJRS), "The Frye rule determined that to have scientific evidence admitted into court, the evidence must be generally accepted by the scientific community" (*NCJRS, Frye v. United States*). Thus, in order for scientific evidence to be admitted, it must be shown that the evidence itself and the examination of that evidence are generally accepted by the relevant scientific community.

Federal Rules of Evidence: Article VII. Rule 702

Federal Rules of Evidence (FRE) Rule 702 is fairly significant in regards to forensic science and the ability of expert witnesses to testify about scientific evidence. Rule 702 is essentially a legal "check" on experts who are expected to be rendering opinion in a trial. The rule is spelled out as follows:

> If scientific, technical, or other specialized knowledge will assist the trier of fact to understand the evidence or to determine a fact in issue, a witness qualified as an expert by knowledge, skill, experience, training, or education, may testify thereto in the form of an opinion or otherwise, if (1) the testimony is based upon sufficient facts or data, (2) the testimony is the product of reliable principles and methods, and (3) the witness has applied the principles and methods reliably to the facts of the case (Legal Information Institute, 2009).

DIFFERENCE BETWEEN FRYE AND FRE

The underlying difference between the Frye standard and FRE 702 was that there was no incorporation of a "general acceptance standard." Instead, three provisions of the FRE governed admission of expert testimony in court:

- Scientific knowledge. Nothing is known with absolute certainty; however, the "knowledge" had to be arrived at by use of the scientific method.
- Assist the trier of fact. The scientific knowledge offered must be an aid in assisting either a jury or a judge in understanding the evidence or determining a fact or issue in the case.
- The judge makes the threshold determination. Such an assessment is meant to focus on methodology and principles, not the ultimate conclusions generated. It is left up to the judge to determine if the reasoning or methodology upon which the testimony is based is properly applied to the facts at issue.

Federal Evidence Rule 702 was enacted in 1975, nearly 52 years after the Frye Rule was created.

Daubert v. Merrell Dow Pharmaceuticals Inc. 509 U.S. 579

The "**Daubert test**" was as a result of the case of *Daubert v. Merrell Dow Pharmaceuticals Inc.* that occurred in 1993. The Daubert test was intended to replace the Frye Rule/Test that was imposed in 1923, nearly 70 years earlier. Having scientific evidence admitted into trial due to its general acceptance within the relevant scientific community was considered insufficient. *Daubert v. Merrell Dow Pharmaceuticals Inc.* established that the scientific evidence must pass four tests before it can be admitted into trial. "The four tests determine whether the theory or technique has been tested, whether it has been peer reviewed, its known or potential error rate and the existence and maintenance of standards controlling its operation, and whether it has been accepted within a relevant scientific community" (NCJRS, *Daubert v. Merrell Dow Pharmaceuticals Inc.*). This new test serves more or less as a checklist for judges to follow when analyzing the admissibility of scientific evidence. It is, of course, the burden of the experts to show that the scientific evidence and the examination of such evidence satisfies each of these four criteria within the test. If the evidence passes the test, the defense or prosecution, based on which party submits the evidence, is then given the task to provide evidence that challenges the validity and reliability of the evidence and the methods used to examine it (depending on if such contradictory evidence exists).

Kumho Tire v. Carmichael 119 S. Ct. 1167

In *Kumho Tire Co. v. Carmichael* (1998), "the wording of the *Daubert v. Merrell Dow Pharmaceuticals* decision came into question" (NCJRS, *Kumho Tire Co. v. Carmichael*).

The Daubert test only addressed the scientific nature of expert testimony when assessing the admissibility. What if the expert testimony is not necessarily scientific? "*Kumho Tire v. Carmichael* brought to question that not all testimony given by experts is scientifically based; instead it can be nonscientific technical evidence. It was determined that the text of the Daubert rule when determining reliability and relevancy can be "flexible" based on the occupation of the expert witness" (NCJRS, *Kumho Tire Co. v. Carmichael*). Making the reliability and relevancy of the evidence and testimony "flexible" based on the occupation of the expert, the use of the Daubert test is not limited to evidence considered scientifically based. Thus, the courtroom is opened to all areas of forensics if it can pass the four criteria listed in the Daubert test.

National Academy of Sciences (NAS) Report

In 1989, in an article entitled "DNA Fingerprinting on Trial," Eric Lander stated, "At present, forensic science is virtually unregulated—with the paradoxical result that clinical laboratories must meet higher standards to be allowed to diagnose strep throat than forensic labs must meet to put a defendant on death row" (Lander, 1989). Now, over two decades later, little has changed. There continues to be no legislation or oversight mechanisms that regulate the quality of forensic science testimony or reporting. However, there are rumblings of change on the horizon.

In early 2009, the National Academy of Sciences produced a document titled *Strengthening Forensic Science in the United States: A Path Forward*. This was the first step in attempting to standardize forensic science throughout the United States, and to back such standardization with legislation. Of specific importance was the suggestion of a need for better "oversight of practices." Such oversight would pertain to accreditation, quality control, proficiency testing, certification, and codes of ethics. "A uniform code of

ethics should be in place across all forensic organizations to which forensic practitioners and laboratories should adhere" (p. 214). With regards to
such a code of ethics, the National Academy of Sciences recommended the
following:

> The **National Institute of Forensic Science (NIFS)**, in consultation with
> its advisory board, should establish a national code of ethics for all foren-
> sic science disciplines and encourage individual societies to incorporate this
> national code as part of the professional code of ethics. Additionally, NIFS
> should explore mechanisms of enforcement for those forensic scientists who
> commit serious ethical violations. Such a code should be enforced through
> certification process for forensic scientists (p. 26).

While there would be both positives and negatives to a nationalized code
of ethics, the implementation of such a code would undoubtedly reduce gray
areas that analysts often find themselves within, and it would also create a
uniform way in which to deal with associated misconduct.

The NAS report also recommended the establishment of an independent federal agency, a National Institute of Forensic Science, which would be
responsible for standardizing terminology, that would greatly impact report
writing and forensic testimony. If such an agency was created, and made up
of truly independent scientists (not those employed by state or federal crime
laboratories), they could be responsible for developing criteria and protocols
for the interpretation of data within forensic subdisciplines, which would
promote consistency.

The National Commission on Forensic Science

In 2013, the United States Department of Justice established the National
Commission on Forensic Science, in partnership with the National Institute
of Standards and Technology (NIST), to enhance the practice and improve
the reliability of forensic science. (The Commission was subsequently non-
renewed in 2017, as a result of the change in Executive Branch leadership.)
The Commission was composed of federal, state, and local forensic science service providers; research scientists and academics; law enforcement
professionals; prosecutors, and defense attorneys and judges. (justice.gov).
Among other areas, the committee was charged with exploring issues of
cognitive bias and ethics in forensic science. After much deliberation and
sub-committee work, the workgroup charged with assembling best-practices
issued guidance associated with expert testimony, in an effort to improve
consistency in forensic testimony, and to reduce the occurrence and possible
perception of impropriety associated with such testimony. The committee's
guidance is found below:

Expert Testimony Guidance by the National Commission on Forensic Science

1. Experts should be asked to identify and explain the theoretical and factual basis for any conclusion, and the reasoning on which the conclusion is based—and any limitations of their conclusions.
2. Experts should present testimony in a manner that accurately and fairly conveys the significance of their conclusions, avoiding unexplained or undefined technical terms or words of art.
3. Experts should remain neutral, and attorneys should respect this neutrality.
4. Experts should not testify beyond their expertise and should also appreciate the difference between testimony that the witness may give as an expert and testimony that the same witness may give as a lay/fact witness.
5. Experts should not testify on direct or redirect examination concerning case-specific conclusions not contained in the report(s)/documentation submitted in discovery—unless in fair response to issues raised on cross-examination. If an expert changes his or her opinion, a supplementary report should be submitted except where the change is occasioned by new information.
6. Experts should not testify concerning conclusions that are beyond the limits of a laboratory's testing protocols.
7. Experts should not use invalid or problematic terms in their reports or when testifying.
8. Experts should not use misleading terms that suggest that the methodology or the expert is infallible when testifying.
9. Experts should not use potentially misleading terms in their reports or when testifying without a clear explanation of the term's significance and limitations.
10. Experts should not use the term "scientific" when testifying unless the basis for their opinions has been scientifically validated.

Ethics at the Crime Scene

The variety of crime scene types and circumstances facing forensic investigators produces many ambiguous situations, which do not conform to a specific policy or procedure. This, coupled with the fact that their skills and knowledge in the forensic investigation may assist in establishing the innocence or guilt of a defendant mandate that professional ethics and integrity be essential to a forensic investigator's decisions and efforts. A forensic practitioner's ultimate obligation is to the truth. He or she must never be biased for or against a suspect in an investigation. Legal, scientific, and ethical values can become tangled in the courtroom; however, the most important aspect of the trial is that the guilty are convicted and the innocent are exonerated (Fish, Miller, and Braswell, 2014). The sole obligation must be to serve the aims of justice. Of ultimate importance is that the forensic practitioner conducted their efforts in a thorough, competent, unbiased manner.

To ensure ethical behavior, veracity of testimony, and professionalism amongst individuals engaged within the field of crime scene investigations, some departments and organizations have implemented a code of ethics that an employee must sign and agree to function by as terms of his/her employment or membership. For an example, for one of these codes, the reader is directed to the website of the **International Association of Identification (IAI)** to peruse their listed "code of ethics" for certified crime scene personnel. This can be located by going to: www.theiai.org/certifications/crime_scene/ethics.php. Other examples of codes of ethics can be located on the website, for various crime scene–related positions.

No forensic investigator wants to live with the possibility that a guilty person escapes prosecution or that an innocent person is punished based on his or her actions or inactions. Therefore, he or she should do everything possible to preserve the **chain of custody**, take all necessary precautions to prevent cross-contamination or deterioration of physical evidence, and leave the forensic analysis up to the criminalists and the courts. It is up to the judicial system, not the crime scene personnel, to weigh the evidence and come to a determination of guilt or innocence (Fish, Miller, and Braswell, 2014).

A search of recent cases involving mismanagement, improper documentation, unethical testimony, and improper analysis of physical evidence is bound to bring the searcher a plethora of cases associated with such matters. (The reader's attention is directed to Ripped from the Headlines at the end of this chapter.) Of course, these are only a sample of the ones that made headlines. For each that made the headlines, there are perhaps dozens that didn't. Ethics, or lack thereof, has been found to permeate all areas of the criminal investigative process. With very little research effort, the reader will find that there are ethical transgressions that occur at all steps in the evidentiary process, crime scene security, physical evidence collection and documentation, physical evidence processing and analysis, testimony regarding all aforementioned phases, and final evidence disposition. These issues are not isolated to particular geographic regions or to particular departments. They are instead a product of training (or lack thereof) and personal values (or lack thereof), that can be present in any setting.

An examination of unethical issues relating to crime scene work shows a variety of motivations for committing unethical acts. Sometimes the motivation is greed, other times it is power, status, or promotion. But more often it is a case of the individual forgetting that his or her obligation is to the truth and not to one side or the other. Many times individuals feel as though they are members of a particular team (prosecution) and, thus, may fail to present testimony or analysis that could prove damaging to the prosecutorial team and would be tantamount to letting the team down. As addressed previously, many times such instances can be avoided through a thorough background investigation, proper ethical training, and correct management practices.

Crime Laboratories

On September 12, 2016, the U.S. Department of Justice made a press release associated with forthcoming changes associated with the practice of forensic science within the United States. Among the changes to be implemented would be a new code of professional responsibility.

"The department believes the code will improve education and guidance on professional responsibility while establishing a process for identifying and addressing violations of professional conduct.

Department forensic laboratories will also review their policies and procedures to ensure that forensic examiners are not using the expressions "reasonable scientific certainty" or "reasonable (forensic discipline) certainty" in their reports or testimony. Department prosecutors will also abstain from using these expressions when presenting forensic reports or questioning forensic experts in court unless required by a judge or applicable law. This decision complements the department's efforts, announced earlier this year, to provide better guidance to forensic examiners and federal prosecutors on how to properly characterize the strength of forensic evidence in the courtroom.

The department also announced policies to implement greater transparency and access to forensic laboratory quality assurance documents and a plan to explore a grant funding of multiyear post-doctoral fellowships at federal, state, and local forensic science service providers and forensic medicine service providers (USDOJ, 2016). The suggested professional code of conduct can be found in Appendix B.

These new policies are derived from recommendations that were made by the National Commission of Forensic Science, pertaining to the establishment of greater reliability and scientific validity associated with forensic evidence. Among the concerns that were raised was that of unprofessional conduct.

Unprofessional conduct includes any actions that may tarnish the reputation of an agency or enable the public to lose trust. An example is a case where management publicly denies that one of its scientists was drylabbing, even though, in fact, he or she was drylabbing, demonstrates unprofessional conduct leading to unethical conduct. Drylabbing is creating scientific data without performing a test used in part to describe forensic laboratory actions

ETHICAL MISCONDUCT SPECIFIC TO FORENSIC SCIENCE

Barry Fisher's, (2000) *Techniques of Crime Scene Investigation* includes a list of ethical misconduct specific to forensic science:

- Planting evidence at a crime scene to point to a defendant.
- Collecting evidence without a warrant by claiming exigent circumstances.
- Falsifying laboratory examinations to enhance the prosecutor's case.
- Ignoring evidence at a crime scene that might exonerate a suspect or be a mitigating factor.
- Reporting on forensic tests not actually done out of a misguided belief that the tests are unnecessary.
- Fabricating scientific opinions based on invalid interpretations of tests or evidence to assist the prosecution.
- Examining physical evidence when not qualified to do so.
- Extending expertise beyond one's knowledge.
- Using unproved methodologies.
- Overstating an expert opinion by using "terms of art" unfamiliar to juries.
- Failing to report a colleague, superior, or subordinate who engages in any of the previously listed activities to the proper authorities.

or creating a report without performing tests on crime scene evidence (www .statemaster.com/encyclopedia/drylabbing). Some of the professional duties presenting ethical issues specifically for forensic scientists include the following:

1. The duty to *remain competent* in a wide range of scientific fields, while often limited resources for library and professional meetings are available. If appropriate resources are not provided and the forensic scientist cannot meet his or her responsibilities, is it ethical to continue to present oneself as such?
2. The duty to be as *objective* as reasonably possible in the selection of samples, examinations, and the interpretation of results. Is it ethical to ignore relevant samples known to exist simply because they were not submitted or marked? Can one refrain from certain significant tests on request and still be considered ethical?
3. The duty to act *thoroughly and to produce results* and conclusions within the capabilities and limitations of science and within the

expertise of the individual scientist. Forensic science often involves examinations of one-of-a-kind situations. In these cases, is it ethical to not fully reveal the procedures used, the supporting data, or the result of blind trials? Is it ethical to use a procedure in the absence of such data? How far is it necessary to go exploring things that are critical scientifically, but that may have little or no legal relevance? Should the reasons for inconclusive results not be explained?

4. The duty to be *openly communicative*. When open to communication among scientists is restricted by the demands of others, the scientist is faced with an ethical dilemma. Is it ethical for the scientist not to publish results of his or her research for the benefit of all? Should one refuse to talk to other scientists because they may have a different interpretation? Should scientists use a technique that has not received peer review?

Another area of scientific difficulty is having precision without accuracy. Accuracy is the degree of exactness possessed by an approximation or measurement, while precision is the degree of exactness with which a quantity is expressed. Although it is possible to have precision without accuracy and to have accuracy without being precise, the latter is actually the better situation. Accuracy is extremely important to forensic science; however, it has been argued that some forensic methods are more accurate than others. DNA is said to be the most accurate forensic evidence, while fingerprints are considered less accurate due to conclusions based on an examiner. A precisionist is a person who courts exact numbers instead of giving approximations (99 ft. 10.78 in. as opposed to 100 ft.). Although this person seems as though she is a wonderful scientist, juries may be wrongly seduced by her. In addition, such precision is an excessive and ineffective action. The aforementioned dimensions are useful for crime scene sketches requiring accurate measurements of bullet holes or angles. However, such an example is unnecessary for parking lots because the nearest inch is usually sufficient (although it depends on what is measured). As with any ethical situation, best practices and personal judgment are reliable guiding factors (Garrison, 2004).

The problem of practicing science in an adversary system is yet another reason why ethical dilemmas occur in forensic science. Some issues include the amount of detail tests or reports require and the amount of disclosure that the forensic scientist necessitates. An additional issue is how to decide what information needs to be presented. How does the information get presented? Should the expert offer extra information in which neither lawyer showed interest? What if additional information is pertinent to explain results? Unfortunately, these problems are nearly impossible to solve due to conflicting goals of science and law. Knowledge of the differences may help each side overcome some common obstacles.

RIPPED FROM THE HEADLINES

According to its website, the Innocence Project "is a national litigation and public policy organization dedicated to exonerating wrongfully convicted people through DNA testing and reforming the criminal justice system to prevent future injustice" (www.innocenceproject.org). As a result of its efforts, there have been numerous incidents where individuals and/or processes have been determined to be in error. More egregious issues, such as forensic misconduct by scientists, experts, and prosecutors, have been uncovered as well. Those that have led to wrongful convictions and are among the most notorious are as follows:

- Fred Zain, former director of the West Virginia state crime lab, whose testimony in 12 states showed that he had "fabricated results, lied on the stand about results, and willfully omitted evidence from his reports."
- Pamela Fish, a lab technician for the Chicago Police Department crime lab, was discovered to have testified "about false matches and suspicious results" in the trials of at a minimum of eight different defendants. DNA analysis proved her testimony incorrect and fraudulent.
- Houston Police Department crime lab, where a "two-year investigation, completed in 2007, showed that evidence in the lab was mishandled and results were misreported."

These are the more notorious examples; however, there have been numerous others since the Innocence Project began its work in 1992. As a result, the "Innocence Project calls for states to impose standards on the preservation and handling of evidence. When exonerations suggest that an analyst engaged in misconduct or that a facility lacked proper procedures or oversight, the Innocence Project advocates for independent audits of their work in other cases that may have also resulted in wrongful convictions" (www.innocenceproject.org/causes/misapplication-forensic-science/, accessed via the World Wide Web on October 11, 2018).

Ethics Education in Forensic Science

As Robin Bowen discusses within her text, "Ethics and the Practice of Forensic Science," "Forensic science has a few guiding principles for the profession. First, forensic scientists should have technical competence and employ reliable methods of analysis. Second, scientists should maintain honesty with respect to qualifications and should confine examinations to their areas of expertise. Next, scientists should partake in intellectual honesty concerning the scientific data on which their conclusions and opinions are based. Finally, objectivity in the review of evidence and the delivery of expert testimony is a principle of forensic science. The delivery of expert testimony refers to assuring the information is understandable to nonscientific fact-finders. These guiding principles are the basics of ethics in forensic science, but how do we provide all forensic scientists with this understanding of the profession? In a word, education" (Bowen, 2010).

The importance of educating those new to the field, and providing for continuing education for those within the field, cannot be overstated. It is imperative to the field of forensic science, and to the integrity of the legal system that those tasked with collecting, preserving, analyzing, and testifying about forensic evidence be given the education and training necessary to ensure that he or she is not testifying or performing beyond his or her knowledge or abilities.

It is further suggested (and is in fact a requirement of academic program certification) that programs which credential or award degrees specific to the fields of forensic science include ethics-related education within the curriculum.

Conclusion

Each time that a crime scene investigator responds to a crime scene or a criminalist performs an analysis, the potential exists that the actions taken and observations made will be presented within a courtroom. A forensic specialist's reputation is based on the veracity of their work and the integrity of their actions. Their actions, or lack thereof, are the voice of the victim. While justice may be blind, forensic scientists must present objective and unbiased testimony that clearly and accurately recreates the crime scene for the judge and jury. A forensic specialist's actions in no way should detract from the credibility of the physical evidence or tarnish its voice. As was said by Paul Kirk (1953):

Wherever he steps, whatever he touches, whatever he leaves, even unconsciously, will serve as silent evidence against him. Not only his fingerprints or his footprints, but also his hair, the fibers from his clothes, the glass he breaks, the tool marks he leaves, the paint he scratches, the blood or semen that he deposits or collects—all of these and more bear mute witness against him. This is evidence that does not forget. It is not confused by the excitement of the moment. It is not absent because human witnesses are. It is factual evidence. Physical evidence cannot be wrong; it cannot perjure itself; it cannot be wholly absent. Only its interpretation can err. Only human failure to find it, study and understand it can diminish its value.

Questions for Review

1. The application of science to civil and criminal law is known as _____.
2. What is drylabbing?
3. _____ is the field of forensic analysis.
4. An ethical analyst has an obligation to the _____ and not to mislead the jury, defense, or the state when testifying before the court, or when preparing his/her reports relating to his/her analyses of forensic evidence.
5. What are the two primary organizations that have developed ethical codes relating to forensic testimony and the presentation of forensic analyses within court?
6. Those who work in our criminal justice system have an obligation to be _____, _____, and _____.
7. The _____ determined that, to have scientific evidence admitted into court, the evidence must be generally accepted by the scientific community.
8. True or false: Federal Evidence Rule 702 is fairly significant in regards to forensic science and the ability of expert witnesses to testify about scientific evidence.
9. A forensic practitioner's ultimate obligation is to the _____.
10. It is up to the _____ system, not the crime scene personnel, to weigh the evidence and come to a determination of guilt or innocence.
11. True or false: It is mandatory for forensic laboratories to seek accreditation
12. Why do conflicts and frustrations occur among forensic scientists?
13. What is the "CSI effect"?
14. Differentiate between accuracy and precision.
15. _____ is said to be the most accurate forensic evidence.
16. The three core values in teaching ethics are _____, _____, and _____.
17. True or false: The technical standards guide experts in methodology, professional criteria, and assuring that adequate data are available.

References

American Board of Criminalists. 2017. Code of Ethics, www.abc.org (accessed January 23, 2017).

Barnett, P. D. 2001. *Ethics in forensic science: Professional standards for the practice of criminalistics.* Boca Raton, FL: CRC Press.

Bowen, R. T. 2010. *Ethics and the practice of forensic science.* Boca Raton, FL: Taylor & Francis Group.

Daubert v. Merrell Dow Pharmaceuticals, 509 U.S. 579 (1993).

Dutelle, A. W. 2017. *An Introduction to Crime Scene Investigation*, 2nd ed. Sudbury, MA: Jones and Bartlett Learning.

Fish, J. T., Miller, L. S., and Braswell, M. C. 2014. *Crime Scene Investigation*, 3rd ed. Newark, NJ: LexisNexis Group.

Fisher, B. A. J. 2000. *Techniques of Crime Scene Investigation*, 6th ed. Boca Raton, FL: CRC Press.

Frye v. U.S., 293 F. 1013 (D.C. Cir. 1923).

Garrett, B. L., Neufeld, P. J. 2009. Invalid forensic science testimony and wrongful convictions. *Virginia Law Review* 95(1). www.virginialawreview.org (accessed June 5, 2017).

Garrison, D. 2004. Precision without accuracy in the cruel world of crime scene work. *Midwestern Association of Forensic Sciences Newsletter*. April.

Kirk, P. L. 1953. *Crime investigation: Physical evidence and the police laboratory*. New York: Interscience.

Lander, E. S. 1989. DNA fingerprinting on trial. *Nature* 339 (501): 505.

Legal Information Institute. 2009. *Federal Rules of Evidence*. Ithaca, NY: Cornell Law School. From: www.law.cornell.edu/rules/fre/rules.htm (accessed June 6, 2017).

National Academy of Science. (2009). *Strengthening forensic sciences in the United States: A path forward*. From:www.ncjrs.gov/pdffiles1/nij/grants/228091.pdf (accessed June 6, 2017).

National Criminal Justice Reference Service. *Frye v. United States* 54 App. D.C., at 47, 293F., at 1014; *Daubert v. Merrell Dow Pharmaceuticals Inc.* 509 U.S 579; *Kumho Tire Co. v. Carmichael*, 119 S. Ct. 1167. http://www.ncjrs.gov/spotlight /forensic/legislation.html (accessed June 9, 2017).

National Commission on Forensic Science http://www.justice.gov/ncfs (accessed February 15, 2017).

The American Academy of Forensic Sciences. www.aafs.org (accessed January 23, 2017).

United States Department of Justice (September 12, 2016). "Justice Department Announces New Steps to Advance and Strengthen Forensic Science." https:// www.justice.gov/opa/pr/justice-department-announces-new-steps-advance -and-strengthen-forensic-science (accessed May 3, 2017).

Ethics in Corrections Systems

8

As a society, our decision to heap shame and contempt upon those who struggle and fail in a system designed to keep them locked up and locked out says far more about ourselves than it does about them.

Michelle Alexander

Key Terms

Deterrence   Retribution
Just desserts   Social contract theory

Learning Objectives

1. Define and explain the purposes of punishment.
2. Define what is meant by **retribution** and explain how it relates to correctional ethics.
3. Define what is meant by **deterrence** and explain how it relates to correctional ethics.
4. Define *rehabilitation* and explain how it relates to correctional ethics.

Ethics in Corrections[1]

The basic ethical questions in corrections involve asking whether our society has a right to punish or correct individuals who commit crimes against society and, if so, from where does the right come? We often answer these questions with the general assumption that the state has the power to control the population for the greater good of society.

The social contract theory is often used to justify a state's right to punish an offender. Under the **social contract theory**, we give certain powers to the state in return for protection by the state. If we overstepped the bounds of the retained rights, then the state has a right to punish us. Accordingly, there is a social contract between the individual and the state. As described by Thomas Hobbes (1985) in 1691, it is a voluntary agreement among people defining the

[1] By Roberson and Mire (2010, pp. 221–227).

101

relationship of individuals with one another and with government and by this process of forming a distinct organized society.

Punishment power by the state is limited under the social contract theory. As noted by von Hirsch (1976), it is generally assumed to be limited by the following restrictive guidelines:

- Our liberties are to be protected as long as they are consistent with the liberties of others.
- The state is obligated to use the minimum punishment necessary to protect our liberties. Excessive punishment by the state is in itself a violation of the social contract.
- The state must be prepared to justify any intrusion into citizens' liberty.
- Requirements of justice should constrain the pursuit of crime prevention.

Cesare Beccaria (1774), considered the founder of the classical school of criminology, in his *On Crimes and Punishment*, contended that the true measure of crimes is the harm they do to society. He stated that it is an error to believe that the true measure of crimes is to be found in the intention of the people who commit them. Sometimes men with the best intentions do the greatest injury to society; at other times, intending the worst for it, they do the greatest good. At the time of his writing, (January, 1764), Beccaria was objecting to the existing practices in the Italian penal system. He especially disliked the capricious and purely personal justice the judges were dispensing. He also objected to the severe and barbaric punishments of the day. The judges exercised their power to add to any punishments prescribed by law and, thus, to promote their personal views as to the special circumstances involved (Roberson and Wallace, 1998).

In his writings about the concept of the contractual society and the need for punishment, Beccaria stated that laws are the conditions under which independent and isolated men unite to form a society, and that men weary of living in a continual state of war and enjoying liberty rendered useless by the uncertainty of preserving it, sacrifice some of their liberty so that they might enjoy the rest of it in peace and safety. Tangible motives in the form of punishments are needed to protect society and to prevent it from plunging into its original chaos. Those who infract the law must be punished to protect society (Roberson and Wallace, 1998).

Beccaria contended that only laws can decree punishments for crimes, and the authority for making those laws resides only with the legislator who represents the entire society united by a social contract. A magistrate should not be allowed, under any pretext of zeal or concern for the public good, to augment the prescribed punishments.

RIPPED FROM THE HEADLINES

CORRECTIONAL OFFICER AND TWO OTHERS PLEAD GUILTY TO RACKETEERING CONSPIRACY AT EASTERN CORRECTIONAL INSTITUTION

Justice Department - U.S. Attorneys Offices Press Releases

Baltimore, Maryland—Correctional Officer Rachelle Hankerson, age 26, of Salisbury, Maryland; Ramel Chase, age 34, of Glen Burnie, Maryland; and Miguel Matos, age 46, of Ft. Washington, Maryland, pleaded guilty this week to racketeering conspiracy operating at the Eastern Correctional Institution in Westover, Maryland. Hankerson also pleaded guilty to deprivation of rights under color of law for participating in the stabbing of an inmate.

The guilty pleas were announced by United States Attorney for the District of Maryland: Rod J. Rosenstein; Special Agent in Charge Gordon B. Johnson, of the Federal Bureau of Investigation, Baltimore Field Office; postal inspector in charge, Terrence P. McKeown of the U.S. Postal Inspection Service—Washington Division; Secretary Stephen T. Moyer of the Maryland Department of Public Safety and Correctional Services; and Colonel William M. Pallozzi, Superintendent of the Maryland State Police.

According to their plea agreements and court documents, the Eastern Correctional Institution (ECI) is the largest state prison in Maryland, operating since 1987 near Westover, in Somerset County, on Maryland's Eastern Shore. During the conspiracy, Hankerson was a Correctional Officer (CO) at ECI, Chase was an inmate, and Matos was the father of an inmate at ECI.

Hankerson admitted that she accepted payments from facilitators and inmates to smuggle contraband into ECI, including narcotics, cell phones and tobacco. Hankerson charged at least $500 per package of contraband she smuggled into ECI. Hankerson also admitted that she approached a co-defendant who was a member of the Bloods gang at ECI for whom she smuggled contraband, and asked the inmate to confront inmate D.S., with whom Hankerson had had a verbal dispute. Hankerson twice allowed her co-defendant onto the tier where D.S. was housed. The second time that the co-defendant entered D.S.'s cell she violently attacked D.S., stabbing him multiple times. Another inmate told Hankerson about the violent confrontation, but rather than notifying prison authorities, Hankerson left the area. She later told an inmate to provide a false story to prison authorities that Hankerson had not been on the tier when the attack occurred.

Chase admitted that he bribed and attempted to bribe COs to smuggle contraband, including narcotics, into ECI. Chase managed a contraband smuggling and distribution network involving co-defendants and others. Matos admitted that he facilitated his son's contraband smuggling in ECI by obtaining narcotics and other contraband and transferring it to co-conspirators who smuggled it into the facility. In addition, Matos performed financial transactions in furtherance of the smuggling.

Law enforcement intercepted multiple calls in which Hankerson, Chase, Matos, and others working with them discussed contraband, arranging meetings with correctional officers, and payment for contraband. In calls between Matos and his son, investigators overheard them discussing COs who smuggled contraband into ECI for them. Matos was also overheard discussing the packaging and delivery of contraband with a supplier.

The defendants each face a maximum sentence of 20 years in prison for the racketeering conspiracy. Hankerson also faces a maximum of 10 years in prison for deprivation of rights under color of law for her participation in the stabbing of an inmate. U.S. District Judge James K. Bredar has scheduled sentencing for Matos on February 24, 2017, at 10:00 a.m.; for Hankerson on March 7, 2017 at 2:00 p.m.; and for Chase on January 17, 2017 at 2:00 p.m.

The U.S. Attorney expressed appreciation to Secretary Moyer whose staff initiated the ECI investigation and who has made the full resources of the DPSCS available to assist the three-year investigation. U.S. Attorney Rosenstein also recognized the efforts of the Maryland Prison Task Force which has brought together federal, state, and local agencies in meetings to generate reforms in prison procedures and facilitate joint investigations of prison corruption and prison gangs. Mr. Rosenstein thanked the members of the Maryland Prison Task Force and the other agencies who assisted in this investigation and prosecution.

United States Attorney Rod J. Rosenstein commended the FBI, U.S. Postal Inspection Service, Department of Public Safety, Correctional Services, the Baltimore Police Department, and Maryland State Police for their work in the investigation. Mr. Rosenstein thanked Assistant U.S. Attorneys Leo J. Wise, Robert R. Harding, and Daniel C. Gardner, who are prosecuting this Organized Crime Drug Enforcement Task Force case.

Department of Justice (DOJ) Documents/
FIND; Lanham (Nov 18, 2016)

Subculture in Corrections

The American Correctional Association published a code of ethics for correctional personnel. The overriding theme of the code is that the correctional personnel will respect and protect the civil and legal rights of all individuals, including prisoners. In addition, members are cautioned against using their professional position to secure personal privileges or advantages. It is often said that, within the corrections system, a subculture exists in which the inmate is the enemy and the use of force and deception is acceptable. Even the occasional use of deceit to cover up wrongs is acceptable (Muraskin and Muraskin, 2001). In examining the ethical considerations of correctional personnel, Pollock (2006) divided them into two general groups: correctional officers and their supervisors, and treatment professionals. She concluded that treatment professionals in the corrections system face a number of ethical issues that are similar to those faced by treatment professionals, such as medical doctors, in the outside world. The majority of the discussions within this chapter will center on the issues facing correctional officers and the public issues involving punishment.

Kauffman (1988, pp. 85–92) concluded that the correctional officer subculture accepts the following norms:

- Always go to the aid of another officer.
- Don't lug drugs.
- Don't rat on fellow officers.
- Never make an officer look bad in front of inmates.
- Always support an officer in a dispute with an inmate.
- Don't be sympathetic toward inmates.
- Maintain officer solidarity against all outside groups.
- Be concerned about fellow officers.

RIPPED FROM THE HEADLINES

Use of Position of Authority to Extort

In July 2014, the Federal Bureau of Investigation (FBI) in Raleigh, North Carolina initiated an investigation into the smuggling of contraband into Polk Correctional Institution. Jason Dean, 30, of Henderson used his position to obtain property and money from at least three inmates at the Polk Institution.

On February 9, 2015, Dean seized a custom-made gold grill (a gold plate shaped in the form of teeth designed to fit over an individual's natural teeth) from an inmate as contraband. Dean failed to turn the contraband over to his superiors or file the appropriate forms documenting the seizure. Instead, Dean secreted the gold grill from the institution. On February 18, 2015, Dean pawned the grill for $35.

Further investigation revealed that Dean also provided several inmates with pieces of paper containing his name, address, and phone number in order to facilitate monetary wire transfers. Specifically, Dean promised to supply the inmates with contraband cigarettes if the inmates wired him money through Western Union. One inmate wired Dean $175 in February, 2015; however, Dean failed to provide the cigarettes as promised. Dean was sentenced to 51 months imprisonment, followed by 3 years of supervised release (2016).

Sentencing

Judge Jack B. Weinstein, senior U.S. District Judge for the Eastern District of New York, noted in the 58th annual Benjamin Cardozo lecture at the Association of the Bar of the City of New York, November 28, 2007:

> A judge must remember whose government this is: it is the people's. This view controls the court's attitude toward those who come before it. The judges are the representatives of the litigants' government, there to serve and help them as well as the public at large. The attitude required of the people's servants plays out in a range of matters from sentencing of individuals by avoiding unnecessary harshness to devising effective techniques for satisfying valid claims of large masses of people injured in toxic tort or pharmaceutical cases.

Paradigm Shifts

A guiding principal for sentencing has long been that the punishment must fit the crime. Most recently, however, the concept of the Risk Principle is gaining popularity. The theory behind this principle is guided by the fact that the seriousness of a crime does not necessarily correlate to probability of a violator reoffending. By properly identifying the risk of a violator reoffending, resources are better appropriated to rehabilitating those who are most affected by the designated treatment. When an individual commits a serious crime, their treatment is not better determined by the severity of the crime, but rather by the proper assessment of their risk for recidivism (Lowenkamp, Latessa, and Holsinger, 2006).

Another paradigm shift in sentencing and incarceration is with the treatment of juveniles. Detention facilities across the nation are closing as a push to keep low risk youth from incarceration. Previously, an emphasis was placed on exposing troubled youth to an environment that resembled adult prisons and jails rather than the types of community and family-based interventions that were proven to be most effective (Holeman and Ziedenberg, n.d.).

One program gaining popularity in decreasing recidivism is restorative justice. The theory behind this principle is guided by holding a violator accountable through meeting with the person or persons they victimized. The meeting is in a controlled environment with a mediator trained in the process and philosophy of restorative justice. Restorative justice is a system of criminal justice that focuses on the rehabilitation of offenders through reconciliation with victims and the community at large.

Currently, legislatures across the country are considering bills promoting restorative justice in criminal, civil, and educational contexts. **Figure 8.1** provides an example model of the stakeholders involved in a restorative justice program.

Howard Zehr has written many books on restorative justice and is well known among restorative justice practitioners. In his book, *Changing Lenses*, he identified three questions which compare retributive justice to restorative

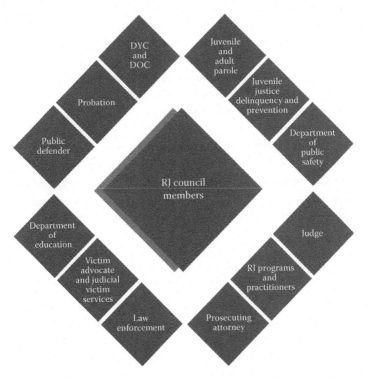

Figure 8.1 Example model of the stakeholders involved in a restorative justice program. (Adapted from Silva S. and Brown G. 2017. "Repairing the harm with 'VOD' high-risk victim offender dialogue." Figure prepared by Laura Rider Dutelle.)

justice. Retributive Justice looks to the state and asks: What law was broken, who did it, and how shall we punish the offender? Restorative Justice looks at the violations against individuals and asks: What harm was done, who is responsible for the repair, and what will repair the harm? This program has experienced much success in the reduction of recidivism (Zehr, 2015).

Dr. Beverly Title identifies five Rs for the foundational values and principles in restorative justice. They are the following:

- Relationship: When a crime occurs, individuals and communities have been violated. The central focus in restorative justice is repairing the damage to these relationships.
- Respect: The key ingredient that holds the container for all restorative justice practices.
- Responsibility: To qualify for restorative justice the person who caused the harm must be willing to take responsibility for repairing it.
- Repair: To the fullest extent possible, the harm is repaired. It is this principle that sets aside revenge and punishment and repairs the damage through taking responsibility and regaining self-respect.
- Reintegration: The process is complete when anyone who has felt alienated is welcomed back into the community. The person showing him or herself to be an honorable person through acceptance of responsibility and repair of harm, has transformed the criminal act. At the reintegration point, all parties are back in right relationship with each other and with the community.

In evaluating the responsibility of society in the sentencing and incarceration of violators, much is to be considered. Nothing outweighs the responsibility of critically evaluating credible research and adjusting sentencing and treatment accordingly. Proper handling of law violators is not only cost effective overall, it is an ethical responsibility (Silva and Brown, 2017).

The Case against Socrates

In 399 BC, Socrates was charged with the offense of impiety (corrupting young minds and believing in new gods). He was tried before a jury of 500 members. The trial lasted only one day. He was found guilty by a margin of 30 jurors. The prosecution proposed the death penalty. Socrates had a right to propose an alternative penalty. He stated:

> Shall I propose imprisonment? And why should I spend my days in prison, and a slave of the magistrates? Or shall the penalty be of fine and imprisonment until the fine is paid? There is the same objection. I should have to lie

in prison, for money I have none, and cannot pay. And if I say exile, I must indeed be blinded by the love of life, if I am so irrational as to expect that when you, who are my own citizens, cannot endure my discourses and arguments, and have found them so grievous and odious that you will have no more of them, that others are likely to endure them.

The jury condemned him to death. He committed compulsory suicide by drinking poison, the Athenian method of execution (Roberson and Wallace, 1998, p. 284).

Purposes of Punishment

The problem of punishment causes constant anguished reassessment, not only because we keep speculating on what the effective consequences of crime should be, but also because there is a confusion of the ends and means. We are still far from answering the following ultimate questions: What is the right punishment? On what grounds do we punish others (Schafer, 1969)?

There is an old Chinese proverb that states, "It is better to hang the wrong fellow than no fellow." This proverb is based on the concept that when a crime is committed, there should be certainty that punishment will follow. Accordingly, if a crime has occurred, punish the person most likely to have committed it. While this practice would probably reduce crime, how does it conflict with our requirement of establishing criminal's guilt beyond a reasonable doubt?

California rules of court ruled that Rule 410 provides that the general objectives of sentencing include the following:

1. Protecting society.
2. Punishing the defendant.
3. Encouraging the defendant to lead a law-abiding life in the future and deterring him from future offenses.
4. Deterring others from criminal conduct by demonstrating its consequences.
5. Preventing the defendant from committing new crimes by isolating him for the period of incarceration.
6. Securing restitution for the victims of crime.
7. Achieving uniformity in sentencing.

In 2011, California passed a resolution realigning many crimes in the state. This resulted in over 500 statutes being amended. The purpose of the realignment was to reduce the seriousness and sentencing of a large majority of the felonies in the state. Key factors to the legislations included the following:

- Convictions of one of about 500 felony crimes in California are considered "non-serious, non-violent, and non-sex-related" will result in sentences to county jail and/or non-custodial mandatory supervision (similar to probation), whereas before you could have been sentenced in California to state prison.
- If you are currently serving a prison sentence for a "realignment" crime, when you are released you will be supervised by county probation officers under the new scheme called Postrelease Community Supervision (PRCS) instead of by state parole agents.
- Realignment is not the same thing as felony probation in California, although California Penal Code Section 1170(h) provides that "mandatory supervision" shall be conducted in accordance with the terms, conditions, and procedures generally applicable to persons placed on probation.

The purpose of this realignment was to punish low-level felony offenders with local jail or out-of-custody mandatory supervision instead of prison. The change was directed at changing the method of dealing with low-level and low-risk offenders. Since this change, California's violent and property crimes rates have steadily increased over the last several reporting years (ppic.org).

Retribution

Retribution generally means *getting even*. Retribution is based on the ideology that the criminal is an enemy of society and deserves severe punishment for willfully breaking its rules. Retribution is often mistaken for revenge. There are, however, important differences between the two. Both retribution and revenge are primarily concerned with punishing the offender, and neither is overly concerned with the impact of the punishment on the offender's future behavior or behavior of others. Unlike revenge, however, retribution attempts to match the severity of punishment to the seriousness of the crime. Revenge acts on passion, whereas retribution follows specific rules regarding the types and amounts of punishment that may be inflicted. The biblical response of an "eye for an eye" is a retributive response to punishment. While the eye-for-an-eye concept is often cited as an excuse to use harsh punishment, it is less harsh than revenge-based punishment, which does not rule out two-eyes-for-an-eye punishment. Sir James Stephen, an English judge, expressed the retributive view by stating, "The punishment of criminals was simply a desirable expression of the hatred and fear aroused in the community by criminal acts" (Packer, 1968, p. 37). This line of reasoning conveys the message that punishment is justifiable because it provides an orderly outlet for emotions that if denied may express themselves in socially less acceptable ways. Another justification under the retribution ideology is that only through suffering punishment can the criminal expiate his sin. In one manner, retribution treats all crimes as if they were financial transactions. If you got something or did something, then you must give equivalent value (suffering).

Retribution is also referred to as **just desserts**. The just desserts movement reflects the retribution viewpoint and provides a justifiable rationale for support of the death penalty. This viewpoint has its roots in a societal need for retribution. It can be traced back to the individual need for retaliation and vengeance. The transfer of vengeance motive from the individual to the state has been justified based on theories involving theological, aesthetic, and expiatory views. According to the theological view, retaliation fulfills the religious need to punish the sinner. Under the aesthetic view, punishment helps reestablish a sense of harmony through requital and, thus, solves the social discord created by the crime. The expiatory view is that guilt must be washed or cleansed away through suffering. There is even a utilitarian view that punishment is the means of achieving beneficial and social consequences for the application of a specific form and degree of punishment deemed most appropriate to the particular offender after careful individualized study of the offender (Johnson, 1974, p. 173).

Deterrence

Deterrence is a punishment viewpoint that focuses on future outcomes rather than past misconduct. It also is based on the theory that creating a fear of future punishments will deter crime. It is based on the belief that punishments have a deterrent effect. There is substantial debate as to the validity of this concept. Specific deterrence deters specifically the offender, whereas general deterrence works mostly on others who might consider similar acts. According to this viewpoint, the fear of future suffering motivates individuals to avoid involvement in criminal misconduct. This concept assumes that the criminal is a rational being who will weigh the consequences of his or her criminal actions before deciding to commit them.

One of the problems with deterrence is determining the appropriate magnitude and nature of punishment to be imposed to deter future criminal misconduct. For example, an individual commits a serious crime and then feels bad about the act may need only slight punishment to achieve deterrent effects, whereas a professional shoplifter may need severe fear-producing punishments to prevent future shoplifting.

Increases in crime rates and high rates of recidivism are often used to cast doubt on the effectiveness of the deterrence approach. Recidivism may cause some doubt about the efficacy of specific deterrence, but says nothing of the effect of general deterrence. In addition, unless we know what the crime rate or rates of recidivism would be if we did not attempt to deter criminal misconduct, the assertions are unfounded. Are we certain that the rate would not be higher had we not attempted to deter criminals?

Incapacitation

In the incapacitation model, the individual is confined as a prisoner and, thus, incapable of committing crimes in the general public. At least while the prisoner is in confinement, he or she is unlikely to commit crimes against innocent persons outside of prison. To this extent, confinement clearly helps reduce total behavior. Under this viewpoint, there is no hope for the individual as far as rehabilitation is concerned. Therefore, the only solution is to incapacitate the offender.

There are two variations in the incapacitation viewpoint. Collective incapacitation refers to sanctions imposed on offenders without regard to their personal characteristics, such as all violent offenders. Selective incapacitation refers to incapacitation of certain groups of individuals who have been identified as high-risk offenders, such as robbers with a history of drug use. Under selective incapacitation, offenders with certain characteristics or history would receive longer prison terms than others convicted of the same crime. The purpose of incapacitation is to prevent future crimes, and the moral concerns associated with retribution are not as important as the reduction of future victimization. As Packer (1968, p. 55) stated, "Incapacitation is a mode of punishment that uses the fact that a person has committed a crime as a basis for predicting that he will commit future crimes." Packer also stated that the logic of the incapacitation position is that until the offender stops being a danger, we will continue to restrain him. Accordingly, Packer contended that the logical conclusion is that offenses that are regarded as relatively trivial may be punished by imprisonment for life.

Rehabilitation

The rehabilitation approach is that punishment should be directed toward correcting the offender. This approach also is considered the treatment approach. This approach considers criminal misconduct as a manifestation of a pathology that can be handled by some form of therapeutic activity. While this viewpoint may consider the offender as "sick," it is not the same as the medical approach. Under the rehabilitation viewpoint, we need to teach offenders to recognize the undesirability of their criminal behavior and to make significant efforts to rid themselves of that behavior. The main difference between the rehabilitation approach and the retribution approach is that under the rehabilitation approach, the offenders are assigned to programs designed to propel them for readjustment or reintegration into the community, whereas the latter approach is more concerned with the punishment aspects of the sentence. Packer saw two major objections to making rehabilitation the primary justification for punishment. First, we do not know how to rehabilitate offenders; second, we know little about who is likely to commit crimes and less about what makes them apt to do so. As long as we are ignorant in these matters, Packer contended, punishment in the name of rehabilitation is gratuitous cruelty.

VIEW FROM AN EXPERT

In the area of criminal justice, the corrections system is somewhat unique in regards to its role in dealing with persons who have been convicted by the court and sentenced to either a period of probation or prison. The offenders can be confined or supervised for varying lengths of time and, in some instances, for the remainder of their lives. As a result, interaction with offenders is much different than interaction with law enforcement, which, for all practical purposes, is completed at the time of disposition.

People working in the field of corrections can have daily contact with inmates in a prison setting. In probation and parole, contact can be less frequent, but can reach into all aspect of an individual's life.

The interaction with offenders is much more intense and requires one to develop at least a surface relationship. In order to be effective in performing one's job, it is important to be able to establish an amenable interaction in order to coexist. This relationship is needed in order to hopefully attain a degree of compliance in both the institution and community settings.

Consequently, the lines sometimes get blurred in regards to the relationship between correctional personnel and offenders. Depending on the setting, correctional personnel hold a great deal of influence over how an offender will be treated and possibly impacting their individual freedom.

As a result of the relationship that forms between correctional personnel and those for which they are responsible, it is important to set clear parameters that they must adhere to when involved with offenders. Most, if not all, departments of correction require all employees to sign what is referred to most commonly as a "fraternization policy." This policy outlines what behaviors are not allowed, and the consequences of violating the policy can in some instances result in dismissal and possible criminal charges. The following list is not all-inclusive, but addresses some of the more obvious behaviors that would be forbidden. (The following excerpts from a fraternization policy are taken from the State of Wisconsin Department of Corrections Executive Directive 16 dated August 2004.)

a. Employees shall not engage in sexual conduct with offenders. Today this behavior is against the State of Wisconsin Statutes Section 940.225(2) (b). Having personal contact with, meaning a one-on-one, such as dating, forming a close relationship, corresponding, or communicating without the exemption being granted.
b. Living within the same household.
c. Working for an individual or employing an individual under one's supervision.
d. Granting special privileges or consideration when they do meet the requirements.
e. Providing or receiving goods or services to or from an individual under one's supervision.
f. Employees are required to report in writing any present relationship or relationship being considered with an individual under the control of the department.

In summary, the relationship between offenders and staff in a correctional setting is ongoing and does result in a degree of familiarity, which can at times impact a person's decision-making process. What is important is that the person employed by a correctional institution is in a position of power over another person, and needs to be constantly vigilant not to abuse such authority for his own personal benefit either monetarily or emotionally. It is also important to note that any co-worker who is aware of such violations of conduct is required to report such, or be subjected to similar consequences as the offending party.

Edward Ross
Wisconsin Department of Corrections (Retired)

Conclusion

As with all areas of public service, a proper ethical foundation and proper ethics-based decisions are of equal importance within the public service field of corrections. Activities that are ethically questionable may pose a clear and obvious threat to the maintenance of correctional order and security. This can prove to not simply undermine authority, but, in fact, can place inmates and correctional employees at risk of physical harm. Proper hiring and recruiting methods, as discussed in Chapter 6, and the establishment of, and adherence to, a code of ethics, as discussed in Chapter 5, can aid in reducing unethical behavior related to corrections.

Questions for Review

1. Under the _____, we give certain powers to the state in return for protection by the state.
2. True or false: Punishment power by the state is not limited under the social contact theory.
3. What is the theme of the code of ethics for correctional personnel?
4. _____ generally means "getting even."
5. The _____ movement reflects the retribution viewpoint and provides a justifiable rationale for support of the death penalty.
6. _____ is a punishment viewpoint that focuses on future outcomes rather than past misconduct.
7. What is one of the problems with deterrence?
8. The two variations in the incapacitation viewpoint include _____ and _____.
9. The idea that punishment should be directed toward correcting the offender is known as the _____ approach.
10. True or false: Almost all departments of correction require all employees to sign a "fraternization policy."

References

Alexander, Michelle. http://www.goodreads.com/quotes/tag/incarceration (accessed June 12, 2017).

Beccaria, C. 1774. *Essay on crimes and punishment.* Trans. by Henry Paolucci. New York: Bobbs–Merrill, 1963.

Former polk correctional officer sentenced for corruption. (2016). Lanham: Federal Information & News Dispatch, Inc. Retrieved from https://search.proquest.com/docview/1783946610?accountid=458

Correctional officer and two others plead guilty to racketeering conspiracy at eastern correctional institution. 2016. Lanham: Federal Information & News Dispatch, Inc.

Holeman, B., and Ziedenberg, J. n.d. *The Dangers of Detention: The Impact of Incarcerating Youth in Detention and Other Secure Facilities,* A Justice Policy Institute Report.

Hobbes, T. 1985. *Leviathan.* ed. C.B. Macpherson. London: Penguin Books. (Original work published in 1691.)

http://www.ppic.org/main/publication_show.asp?i=1036 (accessed April 12, 2017).

Johnson, V. 1974. *Crime correction, and society.* Homewood, IL: Dorsey Press.

Kauffman, K. 1988. *Prison officers and their world.* Cambridge, MA: Harvard University Press.

Lowenkamp, C. T., Latessa, E. J., and Holsinger, A. M. 2006. The risk principle in action: What have we learned from 13,676 offenders and 97 correctional programs? *Crime & Delinquency, 52*(1), 77–93. doi:10.1177/0011128705281747

Muraskin, R., and Muraskin, M. 2001. *Morality and the law.* Upper Saddle River, NJ: Prentice Hall.

Packer, H. L. 1968. *The limits of criminal sanction.* Stanford, CA: Stanford University Press.

Pollock, J. M. 2006. *Ethics in crime and justice: Ethical dilemmas and decisions in criminal justice,* 5th ed. Belmont, CA: Wadsworth.

Roberson, C., and Mire, S. 2010. *Ethics for criminal justice professionals.* Boca Raton, FL: Taylor & Francis Group.

Roberson, C., and Wallace, H. 1998. *Introduction to criminology.* Incline Village, NV: Copperhouse.

Schafer, S. 1969. *Theories in criminology.* New York: Random House.

Silva, S., and Brown, G. 2017. *Repairing the Harm with 'VOD' High-Risk Victim Offender Dialogue* PP presentation Denver, Colorado.

Von Hirsch, A. 1976. *Doing justice.* New York: Hill and Wang.

Zehr, H. 2015. Reflections on lenses. *Restorative Justice, 3*(3), 460–467. doi:10.1080 /20504721.2015.1109370

Ethics in the Legal System 9

In law, a man is guilty when he violates the rights of others. In ethics, he is guilty if he only thinks of doing so.

Immanuel Kant

Key Terms

Canons	Perjury
Credentials	Trier of fact
Expert witness	Conflict of interest
Fair	Fruits of the poisonous tree
Hearsay	doctrine
Impartial	Good faith doctrine

Learning Objectives

1. Define and differentiate between **fairness** and **impartiality**.
2. Define **expert witness** and explain his/her role in the legal system.
3. Explain **credentials** and how they relate to ethics.
4. Define fruits of the **poisonous tree doctrine** and how it applies to ethics.
5. Identify the components of the **good faith** exception and how ethics plays a role in this exception.
6. Understand the various ways in which ethics impact the legal system.

Introduction

The legal system of the United States is based on fairness and impartiality. This is true for the litigation aspect as well as for the interpretation and application of the laws within the courts. But, what is meant by the terms **fair** and **impartial**? Fair typically refers to being free from dishonesty or injustice and being consistent with regards to dispensing discipline or justice. Whereas impartial refers to being free from bias and having the ability to be fair. As stated by the American Bar Association, "Our legal system is based on the principle that an independent, fair, and competent judiciary will interpret and apply the laws that govern us. The role of the judiciary is central to

American concepts of justice and the rule of law" (www.abanet.org/cpr/mcjc
/pream_term.html). For this to occur there has to be fairness and impartiality, as well as competence and virtue, at multiple levels and by all individuals
involved in the legal process.

Judges and Magistrates

Judges' and magistrates' roles within the criminal justice system and in the
greater area of public service are very visible positions with the ability to
enact change and greatly impact individuals and society as a whole. It is for
this reason that a strong ethical foundation is of paramount concern. For a
judge or magistrate to be effective within his or her position, it is necessary
for them to be trusted and for their integrity to be without question. If their
integrity is questioned or tarnished in any manner, so, too, will their rulings
and interpretations of law be called into question.

Most judges or magistrates begin their professional careers as lawyers and
then practice significant amounts of law prior to being elected or appointed
to the judicial court, and many belong to the American Bar Association. As
with many professions, the profession of law has codes of ethics and codes of
conduct for professionals practicing within the field. This is true for judges
as well. On its website (www.abanet.org/cpr/mcjc/toc.html), the American
Bar Association (ABA) lists a "Model Code of Judicial Conduct." This code
of conduct is separated into five principles or rules, referred to as **canons**.
The five canons of judicial conduct include the following:

Canon 1: A judge shall uphold the integrity and independence of the
judiciary.
Canon 2: A judge shall avoid impropriety and the appearance of impropriety in all of the judge's activities.
Canon 3: A judge shall perform the duties of judicial office impartially
and diligently.
Canon 4: A judge shall so conduct the judge's extrajudicial activities as
to minimize the risk of conflict with judicial obligations.
Canon 5: A judge or judicial candidate shall refrain from inappropriate
political activity.

Attorneys

In a November 2009 Gallup Poll, only 13 percent of those polled believed
attorneys to be ethical (http://www.gallup.com/poll/1654/Honesty-Ethics
-Professions.aspx (accessed August 29, 2010). This is reflective of a global

phenomenon that has been the result of many decades of the erosion of a profession's integrity due to ethical misconduct. Unfortunately, for the profession of law, this is not something that can be quickly or very easily rectified. The ABA has attempted to hold its members to a higher standard through the incorporation and recently revised code of ethics, but, as with all professions, it is the actions of a few that impact the abilities of the many. The ABA has been proactive in its attempt to provide practitioners with a 24-hour phone number that they can use to inquire about ethics-related questions and attempt to locate the correct resources to resolve whatever the dilemma presented to them is. The number is staffed by lawyers with experience in legal ethics research, enabling them to "provide citations to relevant ABA rules and opinions, and other ethics resources" (http://www.abanet.org/cpr/professionalism/home.html).

In order for attorneys to maintain the integrity of their profession, they must:

- Not knowingly make statements that are false as to material fact.
- Must not make false or reckless statements concerning the integrity or qualifications of judges.
- Must inform the appropriate professional authority when he or she knows that another lawyer or judge has committed violations of professional conduct.
- Must not imply or attempt to influence judges or government officials in an attempt to achieve results.
- Must not engage in conduct, criminal or otherwise, that adversely reflects upon his or her honesty, integrity, and ability as a lawyer.

Adhering to the above guidelines will not sway public opinion as to the overall integrity of the profession; however, it will have an impact on individual credibility and, with no further erosion of the profession, could prove to slowly gain back some credibility that has eroded over many decades of unethical acts by attorneys.

RIPPED FROM THE HEADLINES

In March of 2017, a grand jury indicted the Philadelphia District Attorney on federal corruption charges of accepting bribes of tens of thousands of dollars. The indictment alleged the district attorney compromised his position of public trust in exchange for private financial gain. The indictment further accused the attorney of seeking and accepting bribes in the form of cash, Caribbean vacations, airline tickets, a Jaguar convertible, expensive furniture and other items (Calvert, 2017).

Reporting Professional Misconduct

As with other areas of public service, those within the field of law have an obligation to report conduct that is unethical or inappropriate. Failure to report professional misconduct can impact a number of areas:

- The individual involved in the misconduct is not given the opportunity to learn from his error, or if intentional, is not brought to task on the misconduct and, thus, feel that he has successfully gotten away with the misconduct, which could lead to further misconduct in the future.
- The individual who observes the misconduct is affected by the mere fact that he has made the observation and could possibly have lost trust in the individual committing the misconduct, as well as losing trust in the system, which allows it to occur.
- The profession of the individual committing the misconduct is affected through association, and risks losing credibility as a profession if the misconduct is not identified, disciplined, and rectified. Failing to properly identify misconduct by individuals within a profession risks an erosion of the entire profession.

Most states have procedures for reporting judicial or attorney misconduct, both by clients and individuals involved in the litigation process, outside of the profession as well as by those within the profession. The code of ethics presented by the ABA requires its members to report misconduct or else failing to report such misconduct is tantamount to misconduct in itself.

In 1963, a landmark case was decided by the Supreme Court. Brady v Marilyn (373 U.S. 83, 1963) was a case where the prosecution in a murder case against Brady did not provide the court with a written statement of a co-defendant. In the written statement, the co-defendant claimed he acted alone in committing the murder. In the United States Supreme Court ruling, it was established that the prosecutor must turn over all evidence that might exonerate a defendant. The defense must have access to all exculpatory evidence that is material to either guilt or punishment.

Following the Brady decision, prosecutors must disclose evidence or information that would prove the innocence of the defendant or would enable the defense to more effectively impeach the credibility of government witnesses. Evidence that would serve to reduce the defendant's sentence must also be disclosed by the prosecution. Prosecuting attorneys throughout the U.S. began establishing what was coined Brady Lists, known as a roster to identify police officers, witnesses for the prosecution, whose testimony in court could be brought into question because of something they've done in the past.

A QUESTION OF ETHICS

The Brady list consists of law enforcement who, by in large, are determined to be dishonest through the opinion of an attorney. However, no such list exists for attorneys. Consequently, an opportunity exists where an attorney of questionable character determines the reliability of an officer who has impeccable character and has been unjustly accused.

With no set guidelines from one jurisdiction to another for who qualifies to be on the list and who does not, an officer's behavior is evaluated, with no uniform guidelines, by the area where he works. In January 2013, the court ruling Olsen v. U.S. created a standard that requires prosecutors to be notified by police agencies of pending internal affair cases that involve dishonesty (http://cdn.ca9.uscourts.gov/datastore/opinions/2013/12/10/10-36063%20 web.pdf). In most jurisdictions, no vehicle or procedure exists to remove someone from the Brady List. Subsequently, when an officer is exonerated from an allegation of dishonesty their career may still be hindered by a false accusation.

Expert Witnesses

In public service, there are many examples of specially trained personnel who are called upon to testify as expert witnesses. An **expert witness** is someone who is called upon to answer questions within a court of law in order to provide specialized information relevant to the case being tried, and to assist the **trier-of-fact** (judge or jury) with understanding the information presented. Therefore, it is the duty of the expert witness to educate the jury and provide testimony using terminology that is easily explainable and not misunderstood (Fish, Miller, and Braswell, 2007). An effective expert witness is one who speaks clearly, honestly, and with simplicity. Expert witnesses must not deliberately omit relevant facts or encourage incorrect conclusions. Doing so is a distortion of the facts and is unethical. The opposite is also true. Overstatements of the facts could impact an expert witness's credibility.

So, what qualifies an individual as an "expert"? And when is such testimony admissible? Historically, there has been great debate and much litigation pertaining to what should be permitted as "expert testimony" and what should qualify an individual as an "expert" within the court. Chapter 7 covered the primary cases relating to such matters. The reader is encouraged to revisit the mention of the Frye ruling, Daubert ruling, and Federal Rules of Evidence (FRE) pertaining to expert testimony mentioned in that chapter.

Typically, when one talks about experience, the term **credentials** is used. This usually refers to a certificate, letter, the individual's experience, or anything that can be used to provide authentication for a claim or that qualifies somebody to do something. However, as pertains to expert testimony within a court of law, credentials as an expert will be established by the court through questioning pertaining to the witness's education, training, and experience. The competence of the witness must be demonstrated through testimony relating to education, specific training, publications, research, and a variety of other possibilities that are evidence of thorough knowledge within the area of expertise being considered.

Once credentialing as an expert has been established by the court, an expert witness can provide opinions based on the outcomes of his examinations and present the significance of his findings. This is different from those who have not been declared as experts by the court. Nonexperts who state opinions as part of their testimony will have such statements stricken from the record due to their being classified as **hearsay**. Hearsay is unfounded information or opinions oftentimes, which is heard from other people. The court allows experts to offer opinions as testimony in an effort to assist the court in better comprehending the topic under consideration. However, simply because there is the ability to state an opinion does not mean it is always a legal possibility. Federal Rules of Evidence Rule 703 provides for an explanation of the bases of opinion testimony relating to expert witnesses.

> The facts or data in the particular case upon which an expert bases an opinion or inference may be those perceived by or made known to the expert at or before the hearing. If of a type reasonably relied upon by experts in the particular field in forming opinions or inferences upon the subject, the facts or data need not be admissible in evidence in order for the opinion or inference to be admitted. Facts or data that are otherwise inadmissible shall not be disclosed to the jury by the proponent of the opinion or inference unless the court determines that their probative value in assisting the jury to evaluate the expert's opinion substantially outweighs their prejudicial effect. (Expert, 2010)

> *www.expertpages.com (accessed August 20, 2010)*

An expert must be confident in the statements that he makes within a court of law. If such statements are found to be contradictory or in error, or if it is pointed out that the witness intentionally lied or misrepresented the facts, there remains the possibility that he could be charged with perjury. **Perjury** is the telling of a lie within a court of law by somebody who has taken an oath to tell the truth.

An expert witness must remember that his integrity and professionalism are open for inspection. He must be familiar with the scope of his actions and knowledge, and know where his level of expertise ends. When subpoenaed to testify as an expert witness, the way others perceive the expert is more important than the way experts perceive themselves. Once credibility as an expert witness is compromised, it is nearly impossible to recover in court.

Significant Rulings

There have been several historical rulings that impacted court procedures associated with the admission of evidence, sometimes associated with an ethical event.

Exclusionary Rule

The exclusionary rule prohibits the use of evidence or testimony obtained in violation of the Fourth and Fifth Amendments of the U.S. Constitution. This Supreme Court Decision was decided for federal officers in 1914 by Weeks v. United States and established for state and local officers in 1961 by Mapp v. Ohio. The exclusionary rule was a judicially created remedy to deter police misconduct in obtaining evidence.

Until 1984, the foundation for a judge to exclude evidence was simply if grounds existed to determine the evidence was obtained in violation of the defendants' rights. The **Good Faith** exception created by the Supreme Court in United States v. Leon significantly limited the exclusionary rule. Under the good faith exception, evidence obtained in violation of a person's rights will not be excluded from trial if the law enforcement officer, though mistaken, acted reasonably (Legal-dictionary.threfreedictionary.com/The+Exclusionary +Rule+and+the+Poisonous+Tree=Doctrine).

Fruits of the Poisonous Tree

The **Fruit of the Poisonous Tree doctrine** is a companion to the exclusionary rule and was established by the Supreme Court in 1939 (Nardone v. United States, 308 U.S. 338, 60 S. Ct. 266, 84 L. Ed. 307). This term is a legal metaphor used to describe evidence that is obtained illegally. The logic of this terminology suggests that anything connected to illegal evidence is not admissible in court (Legal-dictionary.threfreedictionary.com/The+Exclusionary+Rule+and +the+Poisonous+Tree=Doctrine).

While, in theory, the judicial system follows a set of guidelines, those guidelines are often like trying to follow an ever-changing bouncing ball. Consider, for instance, a judge has ruled an informant who was once used by the police is no longer creditable. The judge rules the police may no longer use the informant. One day the informant sees a vehicle he knows is stolen and calls the police. An officer drives by the vehicle and confirms the vehicle is stolen. As the officers move to seize the vehicle, a chase ensues. Once the suspect and case are brought before the court, how should the judge respond? On one hand, a criminal is apprehended, on the other, the police disobeyed a direction given by the court. Does anything change if someone is killed in the pursuit?

POINT OF DISCUSSION

In a community in the Midwest, a group of police officers responded to a residence where illegal activity was occurring. Noting the large number of people in the house, additional officers were requested to respond. Two additional officers arrived as the original officers were securing the main floor. The responding officers asked how they could help. One of the original officers stated that they had not searched the upstairs, yet. This was all the information the responding officers had as they went to the upstairs. Several minutes had passed and the original officer went upstairs to check on the officers he had sent up the stairs. The backup officers had searched and found substantial evidence. Unfortunately, when the original officer directed the backup officers to search the upstairs, he meant to search and secure the upstairs of any additional suspects, not to search the property. At the time the search of property was conducted, probable cause had not yet been established to search for property. What are the ethical considerations? Should the officers leave illegal substances that were discovered? Should the suspects be charged, do the officers put the evidence back and retrieve it later with a search warrant? Should the suspects get off free because of the officer's miscommunication? What rules of procedure apply here?

RIPPED FROM THE HEADLINES

UP AND COMING PENNSYLVANIA ATTORNEY GENERAL DOES HARD TIME

In 2012, Kathleen G. Kane was elected attorney general of Pennsylvania. Ms. Kane's running platform was, in part, to shake to its foundation, the state's male-dominated, corruption-prone political establishment. She mocked the institution as, "The Harrisburg old boys." In her efforts, she was convicted of illegally leaking grand jury records in an attempt to discredit a critic. She then lied about her actions to a grand jury (https://www.nytimes.com/2016/10/25/us/kathleen-kane-former-pennsylvania-attorney-general-is-sentenced-to-prison.html?_r=0).

After a very colorful couple of years in office, Ms. Kane succeeded in ousting two State Supreme Court justices and successfully prosecuting other government officials. Her aggressive tactics eventually led to a feud with Frank G. Fina, a top state prosecutor who oversaw the sting operation of the Pennsylvania State, Sandusky case. In an effort to undercut Mr. Fina, Ms. Kane leaked information to the Philadelphia Daily News about a grand jury investigation in which Mr. Fina was involved. Her actions led to her conviction of two felony perjury charges and seven misdemeanor counts, forcing her to resign from office in 2016.

During the Sandusky investigation, Ms. Kane gave various state agencies around 1,500 emails that she believed presented violations of rules of judicial conduct and general state ethics codes (http://www.pennlive.com/midstate/index.ssf/2015/12/judicial_conduct_board_files_c.html).

In March of 2016, Pennsylvania Supreme Court Justice Michael Eakin retired amidst an impending ethics trial on charges related to the emails. Earlier, in 2014, Justice Seamus McCaffery abruptly retired after being suspended by the court for his role in the email investigation (http://www.foxnews.com/politics/2016/03/16/second-pennsylvania-supreme-court-justice-resigns-over-pornographic-email-scandal.html).

A state judicial conduct board hears matters involving these types of violations. Their decision is forwarded to the state's Court of Judicial Discipline for a hearing. This Court consists of judges, lawyers and non-lawyers and acts like a regular trial court. The charges, to be upheld, are held to the standard of "clear and convincing evidence" (http://www.pennlive.com/midstate/index.ssf/2015/12/judicial_conduct_board_files_c.html).

No Hiding from Ethic's Violations in New Hampshire

On July 9, 2010, the *Concord Monitor* printed a story written by Ann Marie Timmins, that explained how there was a new site that had been created to list disciplined lawyers within the state of New Hampshire. If one is to visit www.nhattyreg.org, they will be able to search a lawyer by name or the penalties imposed. The penalties listed range from warnings, to censure, to disbarment. As of July, 2010, approximately 30 attorneys had already been posted as being in violation at some level. New Hampshire also makes more information pertaining to accused judges available than any other state, through a Judicial Conduct Committee website, www.courts.state.nh.us. The website is not searchable and does not include many case details pertaining to the accusation; however, it does explain how and when to file a grievance against a judge. The stated purpose of making such files mostly available to the public is to show that allegations of misconduct are thoroughly investigated and taken quite seriously (http://www.concordmonitor.com/print/208122 (accessed July 14, 2010)).

Keeping a Watchful Eye on Ethics

The people of Colorado have some assistance with keeping a watchful eye on public service ethics. Colorado Ethics Watch was founded in 2006 and is a nonprofit, nonpartisan group that lists its mission as using "high impact legal actions to hold public officials and organizations accountable for unethical activities that undermine the integrity of state and local government." The organization accomplishes its mission through litigation, use of open records, filing of ethics complaints, and requests for government audits and investigations.

This is by no means a unique organization and found only in Colorado. Many states have similar watchdog groups, basing themselves on the organization Citizens for Responsibility and Ethics in Washington (CREW), an organization that "targets government officials who sacrifice the common good to special interests." CREW has chosen to fight corruption at the federal level through aggressive litigation and research.

Whether at the state or federal level, watchdog groups, such as Colorado Ethics Watch and CREW, encourage cleaner, more responsible government (http://www.coloradoforethics.org/about (accessed July 14, 2010)).

VIEW FROM AN EXPERT

As a U.S. pretrial services officer for the Northern District of Illinois, United States District Court, I am considered a judicial employee and must follow the same ethical code of conduct as set forth in this chapter. To provide a little background, my job consists of interviewing all individuals arrested for a federal crime and assisting the judge in determining whether or not the individual should be released on bond. If the individual is released on bond, my job is to ensure that the defendant complies with his or her Order-Setting Conditions of Release throughout the duration of his or her pending criminal matter. A U.S. pretrial services officer is seen as the eyes and ears of the court and interacts with all parties throughout criminal proceedings. Pretrial services officers have the unique experience of working with all aspects of the judiciary system and experience firsthand how crucial ethics are in court proceedings.

Impartiality is the cornerstone to ethics within the judiciary system. While judges and their respective judicial employees have slightly varying degrees of ethics, one's ability to avoid impropriety and the appearance of impropriety in court proceedings is first and foremost for judges and judicial employees. It is essential that each order a judge or judicial employee imposes is based solely on the defendant's circumstances and not reflective of personal bias or opinions of the defense attorney, assistant U.S. attorney, arresting agency, or other judicial employee. To assist judicial employees in avoiding improprieties, "rules" are often set in place to further enforce the code of conduct. For example, a fellow pretrial services officer is married to an assistant U.S. attorney and rules have been established prohibiting that officer from handling any case to which her husband or his subordinates are also working on. An additional example is that the 7th District has enforced an order that pretrial or probation employees who have pending applications with other federal law enforcement agencies must disclose their potential employment with the respective agency to all parties on a case to avoid any appearance of impropriety toward the government.

Impartiality with all judiciary employees is necessary to uphold the integrity of court proceedings to ensure that rulings are unbiased and based solely on the laws in place. Even attorneys must be cognizant of their relationship with judges so that it does not create a view of impartiality between the plaintiffs and defendants. Many assistant U.S. attorneys started their career as a law clerk for certain judges. As a result, judges often will not accept cases with those individuals as a means to maintain fairness and equality with the case and to avoid any potential biases among all parties involved. In one court proceeding, an assistant U.S. attorney had to request permission from the judge and defense attorneys to represent the government on the case because he was engaged to one of the judge's law clerks.

Judges are required to be fair, impartial, and diligent in their performance of judicial duties. Judges are often the deciding factor in preventing unethical circumstances in court proceedings. I have seen judges disqualify themselves from a case for reasons such as owning stock from a company involved in the case, being a resident of the same neighborhood as the defendant, having purchased a home from a mortgage company that a defendant worked for, or being a client of a store owned by the defendant.

All parties in a case are required to withdraw from cases that bear a conflict of interest because they assume the same ethical responsibilities as the presiding judge. Most recently, I saw a defense attorney, who was fluent in English and Mandarin, called upon to assist during a 16-defendant arrest where the majority of the defendants spoke Mandarin. While the judge on the matter allowed the attorney to represent the defendants during the initial appearance, due to a shortage of court-certified interpreters of that language, the judge prohibited the attorney from representing all of the defendants throughout the duration of the case. This defense attorney had already spoken and told all of the defendants that he personally wanted to represent them in all of the proceedings without informing the defendants that he would represent other defendants as well.

While most judges address ethical boundaries upfront in the courtroom, there are times when the ethical issue of representation and conflict of interests are not as obvious. I supervised a former police officer who was indicted for mail fraud in a corruption case. After paying his attorney several thousands of dollars, three months before his trial was to begin, it was revealed that the defendant's attorney was also representing two witnesses in the case, and the judge prohibited the attorney from representing the police officer in his criminal case. The defendant was not given his money back by the defense attorney, even though he had been representing both parties throughout the previous 18 months of the case and knew that the behavior was not going to be allowed unless he obtained approval from all parties in advance.

As you've just read in this chapter, judicial employees must refrain from partisan political involvement. More specifically, judicial employees are prohibited from publicly displaying a campaign picture, sign, sticker, badge, or button for a partisan political candidate or organization in their yard, on their person, or any personal property. During election time, reminders are sent out to employees prohibiting them from publicly endorsing or opposing a partisan political organization or candidate during election time. By closely associating oneself with a certain political party, impartiality within the judicial system can be compromised. This is important in the federal judiciary because we prosecute political figures who are criminally charged with corruption within their position of power. Illinois itself has a history of corrupt politicians and public figures in position of power within the Northern District of Illinois United States District Court, such as former Governor George Ryan, who was convicted of corruption in 2006 and former Governor Rod Blagojevich, who was convicted with lying to federal agents in 2010. As a U.S. pretrial services officer, I have interviewed and supervised several individuals who were voted into their position of power, including police chiefs, aldermen, city officials, fundraising advocates, city contractors, and city workers. By enforcing impartial political involvement, one cannot request an appeal because someone in the case was biased toward a certain political party or campaign. It goes without saying that if a judicial employee feels at any time that he or she cannot be impartial and uphold the laws and regulations of his or her duties, then he or she is obligated to remove himself or herself from the case.

Ethical dilemmas will continue to be present throughout the judicial process, and there is often no clear guidance on the resolutions besides a code of ethical conduct that is discussed within this chapter. It's often the various interpretations of these ethical codes that lead to so many ethical issues noted above. Subsequently, continuous and ongoing ethics training is important for judicial employees in order to continue to uphold the integrity of the court system in a unified manner. Annual training is provided to judicial employees within my district, but it's the ethical dilemmas that I see on a daily basis throughout different courtrooms in all types of proceedings that provide the most knowledge. At the end of the day, it is up to each judicial employee to be aware of the ethical code of conduct that applies to him or her and to remember the duty to report any unethical behavior he or she is aware of to his or her superior.

Carrie J. Holberg, MS
Senior U.S. Pretrial Services Officer
Northern District of Illinois

Conclusion

The laws of a nation are only effective if they are properly enforced and interpreted. The interpretation of the law is left up to judges or magistrates. The litigation of law is left up to attorneys. Assisting each of the aforementioned are expert witnesses who attempt to clarify the issues at question so as to enable the proper interpretation and assist with the decision-making process. At each level within the legal system, it is necessary for the individuals involved to have a proper ethical foundation and to make good decisions. Doing so will maintain the integrity of the individual, and also the integrity of the legal system as a whole. Chapter 10 will discuss the importance of maintaining the same level of integrity within public office because, before laws can be enforced and interpreted, they must be proposed and implemented.

Questions for Review

1. The legal system of the United States is based upon _____ and _____.

2. For a judge or magistrate to be effective within his or her position, it is necessary for him/her to be _____ and for his/her _____ to be without question.

3. True or false: Those within the field of law have an obligation to report conduct that is unethical or inappropriate.

4. An _____ is someone who is called upon to answer questions within a court of law in order to provide specialized information relevant to the case being tried.

5. Expert witnesses must not deliberately _____ relevant facts or encourage _____ conclusions.

6. How are credentials as an expert established as pertains to expert testimony within a court of law?

7. Telling a lie within a court of law by somebody who has taken an oath to tell the truth is known as _____.

8. Judges often times (are, are not) the deciding factor in preventing unethical circumstances in court proceedings.

References

Calvert, S. Philadelphia district attorney indicted on federal corruption charges; R. Seth Williams accused of doling out favors in exchange for bribes. *Wall Street Journal (Online)* https://search.proquest.com/docview/1879382429?accountid=35812 (accessed March 21, 2017).

Fish, J. T., Miller, L. S., and Braswell, M. C. 2007. *Crime scene investigation.* Newark, NJ: LexisNexis Group.

http://www.coloradoforethics.org/about (accessed July 14, 2010).

http://www.concordmonitor.com/print/208122 (accessed July 14, 2010).

http://www.gallup.com/poll/1654/Honesty-Ethics-Professions.aspx (accessed August 29, 2010).

Kathleen Kane – Former Pennsylvania Attorney General Sentenced to Prison (2016) https://www.nytimes.com/2016/10/25/us/kathleen-kane-former-pennsylvania-attorney-general-is-sentenced-to-prison.html?_r=0 (accessed June, 25, 2017).

Second Pennsylvania Supreme Court justice resigns over pornographic email scandal (2016, March 16) Associated Press. Retrieved from http://www.foxnews.com/politics/2016/03/16/second-pennsylvania-supreme-court-justice-resigns-over-pornographic-email-scandal.html

The Exclusionary Rule and the Fruit of the Poisonous Tree... (n.d.). Retrieved June 25, 2017, from Legal-dictionary.threfreedictionary.com/The+Exclusionary+Rule+and+the+Poisonous+Tree=Doctrine

Thompson, C. (2015, December 8) PA. Supreme Court justice charged in email
    scandal. Retrieved from http://www.pennlive.com/midstate/index.ssf/2015/12
    /judicial_conduct_board_files_c.html
United States v. Olsen (2013 December 10) Retrieved June 26, 2017 from http://cdn
    .ca9.uscourts.gov/datastore/opinions/2013/12/10/10-36063%20web.pdf
www.expertpages.com (accessed August 20, 2010).

Ethics in Public Office 10

A country should be defended not by arms, but by ethical behavior.

Vinoba Bhave
Indian advocate of nonviolence and human rights

Key Terms

Effectiveness model
Government Transparency
Legal institutional model

Personal responsibility model
U.S. Office of Government
Ethics

Learning Objectives

1. Explain what should be the primary obligation of the legislators.
2. Define the role of the **U.S. Office of Government Ethics**.
3. Become familiar with Executive Order 12674 and identify the two core concepts underlying the 14 principles listed within.
4. Understand the concepts behind the movement for **Government Transparency**.
5. Define and differentiate between the three models that have been offered as framework to resolve the conflicts between the exercise of public discretion and political life.

Introduction

Often, when ethics is discussed as it relates to the criminal justice system, the emphasis is typically placed on law enforcement, the judicial system, corrections, and parole. However, law is the starting point for each of these and as such, legislators are the ones responsible for the formation of the law. "The field of legislation includes legislators—senators and representatives—primarily; legislative staff secondarily, but not insignificantly; and lobbyists, political action committees, and journalists somewhat less directly" (Dreisbach, 2009, p. 221).

The 14th Amendment to the U.S. Constitution states: "No State shall make or enforce any law which shall abridge the privileges or immunities of citizens of the United States." U.S. federal law should trump individual state laws if ever there is a conflict between them. In terms of ethics, there is sufficient similarity among federal, state, and local legislatures, therefore, this chapter will concentrate on the ethical discussions that focus on the federal legislator.

RIPPED FROM THE HEADLINES

CAPITOL HILL: IRS SCANDAL UPDATE: 'SMOKING-GUN PROOF' OF HARASSMENT

Another installment of Lois Lerner's emails has been released. Judicial Watch, which is using the Freedom of Information Act to force the IRS to produce the emails, believes that it has on its hands documents that "show that Lois Lerner and other top officials in the exempt organizations unit of the Internal Revenue Service, including soon-to-be acting IRS Commissioner Steve Miller, closely monitored and approved the controversial handling of tax-exempt applications by Tea Party organizations."

After sifting through 906 pages of documents, Judicial Watch President Tom Fitton announced, "This material shows that the IRS' cover-up began years ago."

There is now "smoking-gun proof," he says, that top IRS officials "unlawfully harassed taxpayers just to keep them from complaining to Congress about IRS' targeting and abuse."

It's no wonder, says Fitton, that the IRS "has had such little interest in preserving or finding Lois Lerner's emails."

Judicial Watch has indicated that prying the documents from the nation's tax-collecting service has been an arduous exercise. Most recently, the IRS waited until July 15 to respond to a July 1 court order to begin producing—every week—the nearly 1,800 newly recovered Lerner emails that Judicial Watch had asked for through a Freedom of Information Act request.

If the roles were switched and Judicial Watch were being audited, it's a good bet that the IRS would make sure the organization turned over—on time—all documents that the IRS was demanding. If Judicial Watch were not to comply, it would be punished.

The IRS isn't likely to suffer much from its reluctance to cooperate.

Capitol Hill, 2015

Ethics in Governance

The primary obligation of the legislator is representation of the persons or community that collectively appointed the official. Legislative representation is a two-part task, where the individual is tasked with both representing and legislating. Each have relevant issues associated with ethics. Throughout each task, representation, and legislation, a legislator must communicate with his or her constituents so that legislators can represent the community's best interests. Proper communication with constituents includes informing them and educating them as to the constitutional scope and limits of legislative rights and responsibilities. Proper communication also means informing them and educating them with regard to pending legislation, for instance, how a pending law will be worded and what impact, if any, it may have on the community. Lastly, it is incumbent upon the legislator to provide constituents and community members access to the legislator's time so that they may express their concerns and access information they require to be properly informed.

United States Office of Government Ethics

Background and Mission

The **Office of Government Ethics (OGE) (Figure 10.1)**, a small agency within the executive branch, was established by the Ethics in Government Act of 1978. Originally part of the Office of Personnel Management, OGE became a separate agency on October 1, 1989, as part of the Office of Government Ethics Reauthorization Act of 1988. The Office of Government Ethics exercises leadership in the executive branch to prevent conflicts of interest on the part of government employees, and to resolve those conflicts of interest that occur. In partnership with executive branch agencies and departments, OGE fosters high ethical standards for employees and strengthens the public's confidence that the government's business is conducted with impartiality and integrity (http://www.usoge.gov/).

Agency Program Services

Office of Agency Programs

The Office of Agency Programs (OAP) has three divisions that monitor and provide services to federal agency ethics programs. These are the Program Services Division, Program Review Division, and the Education Division. The three divisions coordinate their services to assist agencies in carrying out their programs. They work closely with agencies to identify and resolve problem areas, provide educational materials and training, stay abreast of budgetary concerns, and identify emerging issues to be addressed by OGE. OAP also hosts the annual Government Ethics Conference and maintains the *Ethics News* and Information List E-mail Service.

Figure 10.1 Office of Government Ethics poster. (Courtesy of the United States Office of Government Ethics, www.usoge.gov.)

Ethics News and Information E-mail List Service

The *Ethics News* and Information E-mail List Service is OGE's primary medium for communicating with the ethics community. OGE uses the list to provide timely information to ethics officials concerning changes in ethics regulations, statutes, interpretations, guidance, etc., as well as upcoming events, such as conferences and ethics training.

Annual Government Ethics Conference

OGE hosts an annual Government Ethics Conference to update executive branch ethics officials on the most recent developments in the government ethics area and to provide opportunities to enhance their understanding of the ethics statutes, regulations, and policies. Officials attend and participate in a mix of general sessions and smaller concurrent sessions. These sessions provide ethics officials an opportunity to meet and discuss common issues and problems and to share resolutions and solutions.

Program Services Division

The Program Services Division (PSD) provides dedicated liaison and program support services to each executive branch department and agency ethics office through the Desk Officer Program. Each department and agency is assigned an OGE desk officer who is responsible for providing assistance in maintaining effective ethics programs and providing advice and guidance on the Standards of Conduct for Employees of the Executive Branch.

In addition, PSD manages the annual and termination public financial disclosure reporting system for approximately 1,000 presidential appointees confirmed by the Senate (PAS positions) and 125 designated agency ethics officials (DAEOs). PSD collects, tracks, and reviews these reports to ensure that they are complete and do not raise any unaddressed questions of potential conflicts of interest. These reports are made available upon request to the general public and the news media. The staff also reviews public financial disclosure reports filed by PAS at the time of their nomination and tracks and ensures compliance with ethics agreements made by these presidential appointees during their confirmation process.

Public Financial Disclosure Reporting System

Under Title I of the Ethics in Government Act of 1978, as amended, senior officials in all three branches of government are required to file public reports of their finances. Officials must report information on their income and assets, financial transactions, gifts and travel reimbursements, liabilities, employment agreements, positions held outside the U.S. government, and sources of compensation greater than $5,000. The agencies review and certify that the reports are complete and that any potential or actual financial conflicts under the statutes or regulations are identified and resolved.

OGE oversees the executive branch reporting system. The statute and OGE regulations, contained in 5 C.F.R. part 2634, specify which officials are required to file a Standard Form 278 (SF 278). The approximately 1,000 PAS and approximately 125 DAEOs are required to file reports each year with their agency on May 15, and also when they leave federal employment. After agency review of these reports, they are forwarded to OGE for final review and certification. An additional 19,000 other high-level officials are required to file an SF 278 with their agencies for certification at the agency only. Within OGE, PSD has primary responsibility for tracking, collecting, reviewing, and certifying these public reports.

Public Document Service for Public Financial Disclosure Reports

The SF 278s are available to the public under the Ethics in Government Act of 1978, as amended. Within 30 days after receiving a report, agencies, including OGE, must permit its inspection and furnish a copy to any individual who presents a proper written request. Agencies must make reports publicly available for six years after receipt. An individual's written request for inspection or copying must include the following:

- His/her name, occupation, and address.
- The name and address of any other person or organization on whose behalf the inspection or copy is requested.
- That he/she is aware of the prohibitions on obtaining or using the report, which basically preclude use for any unlawful or commercial purposes.

OGE has developed a standardized application form, OGE Form 201, for this purpose. Individuals requesting an SF 278 should specify each requested report by the filer's name and the filing year of the report.

PSD oversees the public inspection process and provides copies of the reports OGE collects and reviews, which are primarily the reports to the president, vice president, and PAS. Currently, OGE charges a nominal copying fee only if the total number of report pages copied exceeds 333. Individuals may phone OGE to request a copy of OGE Form 201 at 202-482-9300.

Ethics Agreement Compliance

PSD also tracks each presidential appointee's compliance with any ethics agreements the appointee made during the Senate confirmation process. These agreements concerning the financial interests of the appointees, their spouses, and their dependent children are made to bring filers into compliance with applicable ethics laws and regulations and to avoid conflicts of interest with their government positions. Appointees are to certify, with documentation to OGE, that such agreements have been satisfied within 90 days of their Senate confirmation.

Program Review Division

The Program Review Division (PRD) conducts onsite ethics program reviews of headquarters and regional offices to determine whether an agency has an effective ethics program tailored to its mission. The reviews are accomplished in accordance with detailed **review guidelines** and are scheduled in advance as part of an annual program plan. The guidelines provide a step-by-step approach to examining each of the ethics program elements at an agency. **Tips** on preparing for an annual ethics program review and for administering a well-run ethics program have been developed by the PRD. The annual program plan sets forth which agency reviews will be conducted during the year. The plan lists headquarters offices in Washington, D.C. and various offices and military facilities throughout the United States. After establishing the commencement date of an ethics program review with the agency's ethics official, a confirmation letter will be prepared and sent to the designated agency ethics official along with a checklist of ethics materials.

Program Reviews

Program reviews entail a thorough analysis of the agency's implementation of all basic requirements of an ethics program as well as more unique elements of a program that may arise because of the actual mission of the agency. Individual ethics program elements that the PRD examines include ethics program structure and staffing, public financial disclosure, confidential financial disclosure, ethics education and training, ethics counseling and advice outside employment and activities, and post employment.

Following the review, a report is sent to the DAEO. That report may contain recommendations to improve the ethics program if deficiencies are found. Agencies are required to respond to OGE within 60 days concerning the actions they are taking pursuant to OGE's recommendations. To confirm that the agency has acted on OGE's recommendations, the PRD conducts a follow-up review six months from the date of the report.

Education Division

The Education Division (ED) develops and provides ethics training courses and materials for executive branch departments and agencies. The ED delivers training to both new and experienced agency ethics officials through workshops and seminars designed to improve their skills in performing ethics-related duties and maintaining effective ethics programs. In addition, the ED develops and makes available ethics training courses and materials for agency ethics officials to use in conducting ethics training for their employees. These courses and materials are available in a variety of formats, such as instructor-led, web-based, and video, and cover a variety of ethics topics to enable agency ethics officials to best meet their training needs.

Ethics Training Workshops

OGE offers a variety of ethics training workshops for agency ethics officials that focus on applying the standards of ethical conduct, criminal conflict of interest statutes, and the financial disclosure regulations in their day-to-day work. These workshops offer attendees the opportunity to work through case studies and problems that enhance their knowledge of the ethics rules. Many ethics officials use the knowledge and materials obtained through these workshops to train employees. These workshops are conducted in Washington, D.C., and other federal regions around the country.

Ethics Training Materials

OGE develops a wide variety of ethics training materials for use by all executive branch departments and agencies in meeting the mandatory ethics training requirements. These materials include computer and web-based training, videotapes, pamphlets, booklets, and reference manuals. All of the printed materials are available either from the website (http://www.usoge.gov/) or can be purchased from vendors. See ordering information on the site for OGE publications, videos, and software.

Agency Ethics Program Administration

At its heart, the purpose of the "ethics in government" program is to ensure that executive branch decisions are neither tainted by, nor appear to be tainted by, any question of conflicts of interest on the part of the employees involved in the decisions. Because the integrity of decision making is fundamental to every government program, the head of each agency has primary responsibility for the day-to-day administration of the "ethics in government" program.

Each agency head selects an individual employee of that agency to serve as the agency's DAEO. It is these individuals and the additional staff of each agency tasked with supporting an agency's ethics program (collectively known as the executive branch "ethics community") with whom OGE primarily deals and to whom we communicate policy and regulatory changes. Further information about agency-specific ethics programs can be obtained through contact with the DAEOs of the agencies.

Frequently Asked Questions of the Office of Government Ethics

1. *Does OGE have jurisdiction over the ethics programs of the legislative and judicial branches?*

   No, OGE is the supervising ethics office for the executive branch. Each branch of the federal government is responsible for its own ethics program and in the case of the legislative branch, each house has its own committee.

   Legislative Branch
   > Senate Select Committee on Ethics
   > 202-224-2981
   > http://ethics.senate.gov/ethics2.html
   > House Committee on Standards of Official Conduct
   > 202-225-7103
   > www.house.gov/ethics

   Judicial Branch
   > Judicial Conference Committee on Codes of Conduct
   > Office of the General Counsel
   > Administrative Office of the U.S. Courts
   > 202-502-1100
   > www.uscourts.gov

2. *Where do I get information about the rules relating to federal employees' involvement in political activities?*

   The U.S. Office of Special Counsel has jurisdiction on all matters involving the Hatch Act, which prohibits federal employees from engaging in certain political activities.

   U.S. Office of Special Counsel
   800-854-2824
   www.osc.gov

3. *I work in my office's government procurement division. Are there special conduct or postemployment rules for officials involved in procurements that I should know about?*

   Yes. There are several additional prohibitions, restrictions, and requirements that apply to certain agency officials involved in procurements or in the administration of contracts or who had access to certain sensitive procurement information. In some cases, these prohibitions apply to officials who have left government service.

For more information about the procurement integrity rules, contact your agency's ethics official or your immediate supervisor.

4. *Who is responsible for prosecuting alleged violations of the criminal conflict of interest statutes?*

U.S. Department of Justice–Public Integrity Section, Criminal Division
202-514-1412
www.usdoj.gov

or the

Appropriate U.S. Attorney's Office (generally in the jurisdiction where the alleged misconduct took place)
United States Attorneys
www.justice.gov/usao/offices/

5. *Who is responsible for investigating the alleged misconduct of federal employees?*
    The Inspector General of the department or agency involved and, when necessary, the Federal Bureau of Investigation of the Department of Justice. The 64 Inspectors General (IG) in the executive branch of the U.S. government conduct the majority of investigations into government wrongdoing. In addition, they also coordinate investigations with their regular financial and management audits of federal agencies and programs. The coordinating body for the Inspectors General is the President's Council on Integrity and Efficiency (PCIE) of which the Office of Government Ethics is a member.

President's Council on Integrity and Efficiency
http://www.ignet.gov (contains the URLs for individual inspector general's offices)
Federal Bureau of Investigation
www.fbi.gov

6. *Where are lobbyists registered and how do I find out how much money they have spent "lobbying" the federal government?*
    Two sources of information are:

House Legislative Resource Center
202-225-1300
Senate Office of Public Records
202-224-0758

7. *I have a question about how much money a candidate for public office is allowed to spend in any calendar year. Who should I call?*

For all questions relating to federal campaign financing and reports, you should call the Federal Election Commission. If the candidate is not running for a federal office, but a state or local office, you might check to see if that state has an elections agency.

Federal Election Commission
Press Office
202-219-4155
www.fec.gov

8. *Do state and local governments also have codes of conduct for their employees?*

Most state and many local governments have codes of conduct, as well as other components to their ethics programs, that govern the conduct of their employees. One source of information about who to contact about ethics matters in your state or city is the Council on Governmental Ethics Law (COGEL).

Council on Governmental Ethics Law
310-470-6590
www.cogel.org

9. *Are there other government offices that have ethics-related duties?*

Yes. For more information on other U.S. government entities with ethics/conduct-related authority, see the List of U.S. Government Entities with Ethics/Conduct-Related Authority provided on the OGE website.

10. *If a federal employee feels he/she has been discriminated against in the workplace based on race, color, religion, sex, disability, age, or national origin, what should he/she do?*

The first step is to contact your agency's Equal Employment Opportunity (EEO) counselor. The agency responsible for enforcing laws that prohibit this type of workplace discrimination is the Equal Employment Opportunity Commission.

Equal Employment Opportunity Commission
202-663-4900
www.eeoc.gov

Complaint Forwarding: Where can I send complaints against ...

1(a). Department of Justice attorneys accused of engaging in miscon-
       duct in connection with their duties to investigate, litigate, or
       provide legal advice?
           The Office of Professional Responsibility has jurisdiction to
       investigate these allegations, as well as related allegations of
       misconduct by law enforcement personnel. (The Department of
       Justice Inspector General (IG) also has jurisdiction to investigate
       certain allegations of employee misconduct. The Department of
       Justice IG hotline is: 1-800-869-4499.)

       Office of Professional Responsibility
       www.usdoj.gov/opr

1(b). Assistant U.S. attorneys and U.S. attorneys accused of other
       offenses?

       Legal Counsel's Office
       Executive Office for U.S. Attorneys (EOUSA)
       Bicentennial Bldg., Room 2200
       600 E. Street, N.W.
       Washington, DC 20530
       www.usdoj.gov/usao/eousa/

2.   Court-appointed attorneys?
           The Bar Association for the state in which the attorney is
       licensed to practice. For more information, refer to the American
       Bar Association's Directory of Lawyer Disciplinary Agencies,
       organized by state:

       American Bar Association
       Directory of Lawyer Disciplinary Agencies
       www.abanet.org/cpr/regulation/directory.pdf

3(a). U.S. District judges?
           Complaints should be referred to the clerk of the United States
       Court of Appeals in the circuit in which that judge presides. For
       more information, contact:

       Administrative Office for U.S. Courts
       www.uscourts.gov

3(b). State judges?

  To a judicial conduct organization for the state in which the judge presides. For a list of judicial conduct organizations by state, refer to:

Judicial Conduct Organizations
www.ajs.org/ethics/eth_conduct-orgs.asp

4. Federal prison wardens or other Bureau of Prisons employees?

Office of Internal Affairs
Bureau of Prisons
320 First Street, NW, Room 600
Washington, DC 20534
www.bop.gov/

(The above information was retrieved from: http://www.usoge.gov/.)

Common Ethics Issues

General Principles

Executive branch employees hold their positions as a public trust and the American people have a right to expect that all employees will place loyalty to the Constitution, laws, regulations, and ethical principles above private gain. Employees fulfill that trust by adhering to general principles of ethical conduct, as well as specific ethical standards.

Executive Order 12674, issued by President George H. W. Bush in 1989 and modified in 1990 by Executive Order 12731, states 14 general principles that broadly define the obligations of public service. Underlying these 14 principles are two core concepts:

- Employees shall not use public office for private gain.
- Employees shall act impartially and not give preferential treatment to any private organization or individual.

In addition, employees must strive to avoid any action that would create the appearance that they are violating the law or ethical standards.

By observing these general principles, and specific ethics standards, employees help to ensure that citizens have confidence in the integrity of government operations and programs.

Please note that an officer or employee who is appointed to perform temporary duties for 130 or fewer days is a Special Government Employee (SGE). Many of the provisions summarized below apply differently to SGEs. For a summary of these differences, see OGE Informal Opinion 00x1 (Feb. 15, 2000). Reference: *Executive Order (E.O.) 11222*; *E.O. 12674, as modified by E.O. 12731*; 3 C.F.R. 306-311 (1990); *5 C.F.R. § 2635.101*; *18 U.S.C. § 202.*

Gifts from Outside Sources

Executive branch employees are subject to restrictions on the gifts that they may accept from sources outside the government. Generally they may not accept gifts that are given because of their official positions or that come from certain interested sources ("prohibited sources"). Prohibited sources include persons (or an organization made up of such persons) who:

- Are seeking official action by, are doing business or seeking to do business with, or are regulated by the employee's agency.
- Have interests that may be substantially affected by performance or nonperformance of the employee's official duties.

In addition, an employee can never solicit or coerce the offering of a gift, or accept a gift in return for being influenced in the performance of an official act. Nor can an employee accept gifts so frequently that a reasonable person might think that the employee was using public office for private gain.

There are a number of exceptions to the ban on gifts from outside sources. These allow an employee to accept the following:

- A gift valued at $20 or less, provided that the total value of gifts from the same person is not more than $50 in a calendar year.
- A gift motivated solely by a family relationship or personal friendship.
- A gift based on an employee's or his spouse's outside business or employment relationships, including a gift customarily provided by a prospective employer as part of bona fide employment discussions.
- A gift provided in connection with certain political activities.
- Gifts of free attendance at certain widely attended gatherings, provided that the agency has determined that attendance is in the interest of the agency.
- Modest refreshments (such as coffee and donuts), greeting cards, plaques, and other items of little intrinsic value.
- Discounts available to the public or to all government employees, rewards and prizes connected to competitions open to the general public.

There are other exceptions, including exceptions for awards and honorary degrees, certain discounts and other benefits, attendance at certain social events, and meals, refreshments, and entertainment in foreign countries.

These exceptions are subject to some limitations on their use. For example, an employee can never solicit or coerce the offering of a gift. Nor can an employee use exceptions to accept gifts on such a frequent basis that a reasonable person would believe that the employee was using public office for private gain.

If an employee has received a gift that cannot be accepted, the employee may return the gift or pay its market value. If the gift is perishable (e.g., a fruit basket or flowers) and it is not practical to return it, the gift may, with approval, be given to charity or shared in the office. Reference: *5 C.F.R. §§ 2635.201–205.*

Impartiality in Performing Official Duties

Executive branch employees are required to consider whether their impartiality may be questioned whenever their involvement in a particular matter involving specific parties might affect certain personal and business relationships. A pending case, contract, grant, permit, license, or loan are some examples of particular matters involving specific parties. A general rulemaking, on the other hand, is not.

If a particular matter involving specific parties would have an effect on the financial interest of a member of the employee's household, or if a person with whom the employee has a "covered relationship" is or represents a party to such a matter, then the employee must consider whether a reasonable person would question his impartiality in the matter. If the employee concludes that there would be an appearance problem, then the employee should not participate in the matter unless authorized by the agency.

An employee has a "covered relationship" with the following persons:

- A person with whom the employee has or seeks a business, contractual, or other financial relationship.
- A person who is a member of the employee's household or is a relative with whom the employee has a close personal relationship.
- A person for whom the employee's spouse, parent, or dependent child serves or seeks to serve as an officer, director, trustee, general partner, agent, attorney, consultant, contractor, or employee.
- Any person for whom the employee has within the last year served as officer, director, trustee, general partner, agent, attorney, consultant, contractor, or employee.
- Any organization (other than a political party) in which the employee is an active participant.

An employee may have a concern that circumstances other than those expressly described in the regulation may raise a question regarding the employee's impartiality. In such a situation, the employee should follow certain procedures to determine whether or not participation in the particular matter would be appropriate.

RIPPED FROM THE HEADLINES

VA SCANDAL

The Department of Veterans Affairs (VA) Office of Inspector General (OIG) is investigating medical facilities in at least 26 cities. The scandal started in Phoenix where a retired VA physician, Sam Foote alleged that up to 40 patients in Arizona died awaiting care for over a year. Foote claimed that Phoenix VA officials were misrepresenting wait times to collect bonus checks while maintaining "secret lists" of patients. Dennis Wagner in an article in the *Arizona Republic* listed many of the accusations made against various VA hospitals outside of Phoenix. These include:

- Chicago, Illinois: Germaine Clarno, president of a federal employee union, said secret lists and falsified wait times had been an "everyday practice" at the Hines VA Hospital, and complaints of data fraud were ignored. Clarno also said the inspector general conducted an inquiry, but targeted tangential issues. "The problem is the government covers up for the government—the OIG is a bed partner of VA administration."
- Walla Walla, Washington: VA auditors who visited the Walla Walla VA identified improper and inconsistent patient-scheduling practices, according to the Walla Walla Union-Bulletin. A psychiatric nurse, who won a whistle-blower settlement after being terminated, told NBC News that intimidation and retaliation were commonplace at the medical center.
- San Antonio, Texas: Dr. Joseph Spann, who retired in January after 17 years with the VA, told federal investigators that physicians were regularly asked to alter the "request date" for medical procedures to hide backlogs for tests.
- Cheyenne, Wyoming: Congressional investigators uncovered an e-mail written by a nurse to other VA employees describing techniques for "gaming the system" by falsifying appointment records to meet goals set by bosses.
- Fort Collins, Colorado: OIG investigators in December found that medical clinic staffers were trained to make it appear veterans were getting appointments within 14 days, per department guidelines, even though waits were longer.
- Albuquerque, New Mexico: U.S. Sen. Tom Udall, D-N.M., called for an investigation after allegations that wait-time records were falsified. Phoenix and Albuquerque are both supervised by the same person.

The connections among these locations is striking. Beginning several years ago, according to internal VA records, VA central office in Washington realized medical centers around the country were finding ways to manipulate the numbers. The VA had been the subject of congressional inquiry and criticism not just due to long waits for care, but because of mismanagement. No action was ever taken.

Robbins, 2014

If someone who is entering government service has received a special severance payment or other benefit in excess of $10,000, which his former employer does not make to other departing employees not entering into federal service, and if certain other factors are present, then the employee must be disqualified for two years from participating in any particular matter in which the former employer is a party or represents a party. The agency may waive or shorten the disqualification period. Reference: *5 C.F.R. §§ 2635.501–503.*

Conflicting Financial Interests
An executive branch employee is prohibited by a federal criminal statute from participating personally and substantially in a particular government matter that will affect his own financial interests as well as the financial interests of the following:

- His spouse or minor child.
- His general partner.
- An organization in which he serves as an officer, director, trustee, general partner, or employee.
- A person with whom he is negotiating for, or has an arrangement concerning prospective employment.

Several kinds of financial interests are exempt from this prohibition. These include direct or imputed financial interests in securities that are worth $15,000 or less and financial interests in diversified mutual funds and unit investment trusts, regardless of their value.

Agencies may, by supplemental regulation, prohibit or restrict the holding of certain financial interests by all or a group of agency employees. A few agencies extend such restrictions to the employee's spouse and minor children. Reference: *18 U.S.C. § 208; 5 C.F.R. §§ 2635.401–403; 5 C.F.R. Part 2640.*

Executive branch employees must not use their public office for their own or another's private gain. Employees are not to use their position, title, or any authority associated with their office to coerce or induce a benefit for themselves or others.

Employees also are not to use or allow the improper use of nonpublic information to further a private interest, either their own or another's.

Employees may use government property only for authorized purposes. Government property includes office supplies, telephones, computers, copiers, and any other property purchased with government funds.

Employees may not misuse official time. This includes the employee's own time as well as the time of a subordinate. Reference: *5 C.F.R. §§ 2635.701–705.*

Executive branch employees may be subject to some limitations on the outside activities in which they may be involved. An employee may not have outside employment or be involved in an outside activity that conflicts with the official duties of the employee's position. An activity conflicts with official duties:

- If it is prohibited by statute or by the regulations of the employee's agency.
- If the activity would require the employee to be disqualified from matters so central to the performance of the employee's official duties as to materially impair the employee's ability to carry out those duties.

Employees of some agencies may be required by their agency's own supplemental conduct regulations to obtain prior approval before engaging in certain outside employment or activities.

The Supreme Court has held that prohibitions on the acceptance of honoraria contained in the Ethics Reform Act of 1989 violated the First Amendment. Thus, an employee generally may accept honoraria, but he may not be paid for outside teaching, speaking, and writing if the activity relates to his official duties. However, an exception permits him to be paid for teaching a course at an accredited educational institution, even where the subject does relate to his official duties. Employees may not use their official title or position (except as part of a biography or for identification as the author of an article with an appropriate disclaimer) to promote a book, seminar, course, program, or similar undertaking.

Presidential appointees to full-time, noncareer positions generally are prohibited from receiving outside earned income. Also, certain other noncareer employees are subject to monetary limitations on the amount of outside income that they may earn.

Employees may engage in fundraising in a personal capacity subject to several restrictions. An employee cannot solicit funds from subordinates. And an employee cannot solicit funds from persons who have interests that may be affected by the employee's agency, such as those who are regulated by, seeking official action from, or doing business with the agency. Also an employee cannot use or permit the use of the employee's official title, position, or authority to promote the fundraising effort. Reference: *5 C.F.R. §§ 2635.801–809*; *United States v. National Treasury Employees Union*, 115 S. Ct. 1003 (1995); *OGE DAEOgram DO-95-011* (March 3, 1995).

RIPPED FROM THE HEADLINES

ETHICS IN PUBLIC OFFICE: CORRUPTION

CNN aired a news story that announced that a Louisiana ex-congressman had received a sentence of 13 years in federal prison for a corruption conviction. "A jury found the congressman guilty of four bribery counts, three counts of money laundering, three counts of wire fraud, and one count of racketeering." Former U.S. Representative William Jefferson was also ordered to forfeit over $470,000 after it was determined he had used his public office to solicit bribes. During the investigation, agents found and seized over $90,000 in cash from a freezer in his residence. Principal Deputy Assistant Attorney General Mythili Raman stated, "In a stunning betrayal of the public's trust, former Congressman Jefferson repeatedly used his public office for private gain. The lengthy prison sentence imposed on Mr. Jefferson today is a stark reminder to all public officials that the consequences of accepting bribes can and will be severe" (http://www.cnn.com/2009/POLITICS/11/13/jefferson.sentencing/index.html (accessed August 30, 2016)).

Government Transparency

A universal, rudimentary definition of **government transparency** is defined as "the release of information which is relevant for evaluating institutions" (Bauhr and Nasiritousi, 2012). The concept of government transparency has gained momentum over the last 15 years. Transparency has been advocated as a necessary component for better government quality, greater accountability, and a more limited scope for corruption and immunity. The concept, while a valid premise, suffers from analytical ambiguities and normative complexities. Transparency contains a host of contested issues: individual integrity, an organization's desire for non-disclosure, whether government offices must publish information proactively or simply provide requested information, who incurs the costs, who decides what information is meaningful, how are transparency violations addressed, and when does national security outweigh the need for transparency (Bauhr and Grimes, 2012).

As this concept continues to evolve, universal standards for reporting information must be established that addresses these and other contested issues. Transparency, without universal standards, will continue to be defined by conceptual ambiguity. Further, an openness to transparency does not, on its own, provide for honest governance. Accountability mechanisms, citizen participatory arrangements, grievance procedures, and societal pre-conditions are important factors for responsible, credible, and non-corrupt governance.

Private Life and Public Office

Watch the news literally any day of the week, or pick up a newspaper, and there is most likely a news story related to a political scandal involving a public official's private life. However, when a person takes a position in public office, do they maintain a private life? Some would argue that taking public office makes one's entire life public. "Private life" scandals have destroyed the careers of a great many public officials throughout history. "Attacks upon the private lives of public figures are as old as politics" (Dobel, 1999). Today, many public officials find themselves almost completely devoid of a private life, a characteristic likely to remain for the foreseeable future. When Vincent Foster, former President Bill Clinton's White House lawyer, committed suicide, he left behind a personal note that underscores this feeling. Foster stated that within American politics "ruining people is considered sport" (Apple, 1993). In recent years, what would typically be considered as private matters (financial records, friendships, romantic and sexual relationships, family issues, and religious beliefs) have increasingly found themselves as topics brought up within campaigns, nomination hearings, and public smear campaigns.

A strong private life, with a proper network of support and privacy, is a necessary component of a public official's life if he is to maintain his integrity while in office. An individual's private life should provide for the social and emotional support he needs to ensure his moral commitments as well as provide for a place where he is able to reflect upon the challenges faced within public life. Unfortunately for most, the line of demarcation that notes where one's public life ends and private life begins is often blurred. Many point to indiscretions within one's private life as proof of unethical behavior or tendencies within public life and, thus, justify the intrusions and prying into the private lives of public officials. Hillary Rodham Clinton was once quoted as saying, "I have really been pulled kicking and screaming to the conclusion that if you choose to run for public office you give up any zone of privacy at all." She could most definitely speak to the veracity of this statement based on historical events.

There has been a steady erosion of privacy within the public sector and those who are considering employment within public service must accept this as a foregone conclusion and component of a position within the public trust. One's private life may not be that ... private.

RIPPED FROM THE HEADLINES

ETHICS IN PUBLIC OFFICE:
PERSONAL VERSUS PRIVATE LIFE

Fox News ran a story stemming from the Associated Press, which involved a mayor in Oregon being recalled due to her posing for photos in her underwear on a town fire truck. The ousted mayor explained that the photos had been taken for a fitness contest and were not intended to be provocative nor made public. She said that a relative had posted them on a social networking site (MySpace) "in hopes it would improve the social life of the single mother." The photos were taken prior to her being elected as mayor, so she saw no reason to remove them from the website. Those voting for the recall believed "it wasn't fitting for the mayor to be so depicted" (http://foxnews.com/story/0,2933,332870,00 .html (accessed March, 2017)).

Integrity in Office

Every elected, appointed, and career individual in public office must use good judgment and discretion while carrying out the duties and obligations of his/ her office. Society is dependent upon public officials to make conscientious decisions and to use good skill in an effort to provide for the foundations of public order. A proper foundation in ethics can assist in guiding public officials in exercising proper judgment and discretion.

Patrick Dobel, in his book *Public Integrity*, discusses the topic of public discretion. He mentions that the concept of public discretion is "an iterative process in which public officials move within a triangle of judgment" (Dobel, 1999) (**Figure 10.2**). In this model, public officials move between the three domains, attempting to hold them in balance when making decisions.

"No matter how strictly written the mandates or how clearly prescribed the hierarchy, at some point commitments will come into conflict" (Dobel, 1999). As a public official, it is difficult to accomplish what is "right" when faced with limited power of checks and balances, limited information, and oppositional governance. Add to this conflicting loyalties and temptations associated with power and it is a recipe for unethical behavior. It is with this in mind that there are three models that have been offered as a framework to resolve the conflicts between the exercise of public discretion and political life.

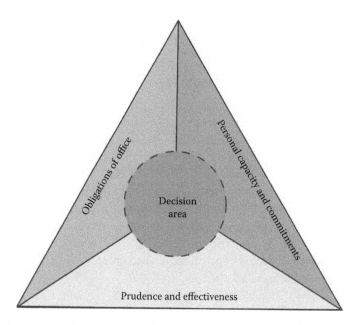

Figure 10.2 Decision triangle. (Courtesy of Ellie Blazer.)

Legal Institutional Model

The **legal institutional model** limits discretion in public office. All decisions that are made by public officials should be capable of being traced back to either clear lines of authority or clearly defined mandates. Government institutions utilizing this model would be designed in a manner that would minimize discretion and maximize oversight. Laws and regulations are to be clear and unambiguous. Such design limits abuse of discretion and ethical violations co-existing with them.

Personal Responsibility Model

The **personal responsibility model** is founded on the premise that an individual's commitments, abilities, and character, which he or she possesses prior to taking public office, are what form the heart of his/her integrity. These commitments and abilities are amplified when placed in a public service role. As a result, personal responsibility and discretion increases and personal judgment becomes paramount. This model has its core foundation in that if an individual maintains his personal integrity and responsibility when in public office, then that individual is unable to deny responsibility for any actions or decisions that were made in the course of his duties. All commitments and decisions are personal commitments, which then removes the possibility of blame from the institution or from others. In this model, officials are subject to praise and blame, shame and satisfaction alike.

Effectiveness Model

The **effectiveness model** incorporates the concept of prudence into its design. As seen within **Figure 10.2**, prudence and effectiveness balance out personal capacity and commitments and the obligations of office. Prudence is a necessary component as the world of politics is not without its share of friction and dynamic partnerships. Practicing prudent decisions is often deemed wise within the confines of political office. Any decision that is made to either initiate or oppose should incorporate evaluation of the decision's importance relating to the individual's obligations of office. However, the same individual also must question whether or not they have enough authority to enable a successful outcome based on the decision to be made. Further considerations include proper timing to make the decision so as to maximize success.

Conclusion

A foundation in ethical principles and ethical decision making in public office is as important as within other areas of public service. One of the primary differences, however, is that public official's decisions and actions are observed with more scrutiny. This exacerbates situations where poor decision making has occurred or where a lack of ethical foundation exists. Also, whereas a police officer, firefighter, or correctional officer may have their personal lives involved minimally with relation to the performance of their duties, public official's private lives are rarely seen as being entirely private, and the line separating their public and private lives is often indistinguishable. Possessing a healthy and supportive private life is of paramount importance with regards to holding public office. To ensure the integrity of public office, legislative and administrative actions are often undertaken. This can be seen through the establishment of the Office of Government Ethics and through the issuance of Executive Orders from the President of the United States, just to name a few. These measures are undertaken to ensure that the individuals charged with performing within an office of public trust do so with the best of intentions and while making "good" ethical decisions.

Questions for Review

1. What is the primary obligation of the legislature?
2. The Office of Agency Programs has three divisions. What are they and what do they do?
3. The _____ conducts onsite ethics program reviews of headquarters and regional offices to determine whether an agency has an effective ethics program tailored to its mission.

4. Which program develops and makes available ethics training courses and materials for agency ethics officials to use in conducting ethics training for their employees?
5. Executive branch employees fulfill trust by adhering to general principles of _____ as well as specific ethical standards.
6. What are the two core concepts underlying the 14 principles of Executive Order 12674?
7. True or false: Executive branch employees have no restrictions on the gifts that they may accept from sources outside of the government.
8. _____ employees must not use their public office for their own or another's private gain.
9. True or false: Employees may use government property only for authorized purposes.
10. Employees may not misuse _____ time.
11. True or false: There are no limitations on the outside activities Executive branch members may be involved in.
12. A strong _____ life, with a proper network of support and privacy, is a necessary component of a public official's life if he/she is to maintain his/her integrity while in office.
13. The _____ model limits discretion in public office.
14. Practicing prudent decisions (is, is not) often deemed wise within the confines of political office.

References

Apple, R.W. Jr. 1993. Note left by White House aide: Accusation, despair and anger. *New York Times*, August 11.

Bauhr, M., and Grimes, M. 2012. What is Government Transparency? New Measures and Relevance for Quality of Government, *2012:16 QOG The Quality of Government Institute. ISSN 1653-8919.*

Bauhr, M., and Nasiritousi, N., Linköpings universitet, Institutionen för tema, Tema vatten i natur och samhälle, Centrum för klimatpolitisk forskning, & Filosofiska fakulteten. 2012. Resisting transparency: Corruption, legitimacy, and the quality of global environmental policies. *Global Environmental Politics, 12*(4), 9-29. doi:10.1162/GLEP_a_00137

Capitol hill: IRS scandal update: 'Smoking-gun proof' of harassment. 2015. Chatham: Newstex. Retrieved from https://search.proquest.com/docview/1699708299?accountid=35812.

Dobel, J.P. 1999. *Public integrity.* Baltimore, MD: The Johns Hopkins University Press.

Dreisbach, C. 2009. *Ethics in criminal justice.* New York: McGraw Hill.

Robbins, R., and Phoenix Pulmonary and Critical Care Research and Education Foundation, Gilbert, AZ. 2014. VA scandal widens. *Southwest Journal of Pulmonary and Critical Care, 8*(5), 288–289. doi:10.13175/swjpcc070-14

Ethics in Other Areas of Public Service

11

It is the moral education of public servants, and the moral demands of their oaths of office, that cry out for more attention.

Terry Newell

Learning Objectives

1. Gain an understanding for ethical concerns as relates to military professions.
2. Be familiar with the primary obligation of the social work profession.
3. Recognize specific areas of ethical concern for emergency medical services personnel.
4. Explain how ethics is important within the realm of government contracts.

Introduction

Each chapter within this text could have its own textbook on the topic. It is virtually impossible to assemble a text that is all encompassing with regards to subject matter, position description, and application to each instance within the field of public service. While the most popular topics of criminal justice and law have been covered up to this point, it is equally as important to recognize that there are many other areas of public service that an individual may choose to be involved in, and which the topic of ethics is of equal importance to a strong foundation. This chapter attempts to assemble a number of those that are typically left out from other texts on the topic of ethics and, although not covered in as great of depth as those previous to this chapter, the reader will hopefully gain insight into other areas of public service to which the topic of ethics is of importance, and, thus, serve as an impetus to seek out other careers of applicability and apply the concepts discussed within the confines of this text to those fields.

A QUESTION OF ETHICS

Residents of Flint, Michigan were recently confronted with a life-threatening scenario. Due to a number of factors, the city's water supply was discovered to be nondrinkable, and thus, a state of emergency was declared and the state and federal governments were called upon to step in and provide assistance. Research this calamity and determine the following:

1. At what point were city officials aware of the issue?
2. At what point were residents made aware of the issue?
3. What (if any) ethical dilemmas or decisions were a part of this event?

City Management Ethics

There have been a multitude of events during the past several years which have brought further visibility to, and recognition of the necessity to have ethics within municipal management be of paramount importance. Terry Newell (Huffington Post) summed up the situation well, when he wrote about a recent crisis in Flint Michigan. "...laws and rules are never enough to prevent moral failure. By the same token, penalizing those responsible through judicial proceeding will address the need for retribution, but it will not prevent unethical, yet still legal, behavior in the future. Government workers owe their first loyalty

THE INTERNATIONAL CITY/COUNTY MANAGEMENT ASSOCIATION

According to the organization's website, "ICMA, the International City/County Management Association, advances professional local government worldwide. The organization's mission is to create excellence in local governance by developing and fostering professional management to build better communities." (http://icma.org/en/icma/about/organization_overview)

Fundamental within this organization, is the concept of ethics. "Since the development of the ICMA Code of Ethics in 1924, the organization has built an extensive collection of advice on ethics issues, case studies, and model local government documents." (http://icma.org/en/icma/ethics)

to the citizens they serve, not to their agencies or supervisors." (http://www.huff
ingtonpost.com/terry-newell/failure-in-flint-the-mora_b_9298824.html)

Military Ethics

A search of recent headlines will undoubtedly bring up examples of situations where members of the nation's military have been involved in unethical
decisions or confronted with ethical dilemmas. As with other areas of public
service, when one chooses to join the military, they give up a bit of his personal life in order to serve the greater good of society. This sacrifice is made
public when an individual commits an ethics violation or is involved in situations of questionable ethics. Few, if any, texts include military service as a
segment of public service ethics, but it is of paramount concern because the
members of our nation's military are ambassadors to foreign countries and
protectors of our way of life. In both, possessing a strong ethical foundation
is of great importance.

ETHICS IN THE MILITARY

The necessity for military personnel to make ethical decisions has far-
reaching consequences. Unethical decisions have consequences on the
battlefield and beyond. Two examples will illustrate these points. For
the baby boomer generation, the My Lai massacre during the Vietnam
War would be the poster child as an example of a military operation
that went wrong. Elements of the 23rd Infantry Division (the American
Division) were involved in an operation to seek out and destroy the 48th
Battalion of the National Front for the Liberation of South Vietnam
involved in recent attacks during the Tet Offensive, January of 1968.
A number of hamlets designated My Lai 1, 2, 3, and 4 were thought
to harbor elements of the Viet Cong (VC) 48th Battalion. Operations
started on March 16, 1968. At the end of the day, between 300 and 500
unarmed Vietnamese civilians, mostly women, children, and old men,
had been killed (Hersh, 1970). Initially reported that many Viet Cong
were killed in a fierce fire fight, it was not until later that the truth came
out. Attempts by senior army leaders to cover up the actions at My Lai
and claims of "just following orders" by those involved in the massacre
reveal a lack of integrity and leadership by the ones involved. As a result
of army investigations, 26 soldiers were charged with criminal offenses.
Only one, however, was convicted. Second Lieutenant William Calley,

a platoon leader, was given a life sentence for his actions on March 16. He would serve three years.

What went wrong? Why would a small number of American soldiers indiscriminately kill hundreds of noncombatants? Frustration by soldiers for not being able to engage in a visible enemy. The division had taken numerous casualties from mines and booby traps. There were no front lines in this war. There was no clearly visible enemy. Not like World War II or Korea where the enemy wore identifiable uniforms and engaged in conventional operations. This was a war of limited contacts with small groups of soldiers, with an enemy who would disappear after brief contacts, who for the most part dressed like local inhabitants. It was hard to tell combatants from noncombatants. Other explanations would include the limited one-year tour for U.S. military personnel. It was difficult to establish unit cohesion with new people constantly rotating in and experienced personnel rotating out. As the war continued on (major U.S. operations 1965–1973), the number of career and experienced soldiers decreased significantly. Increased reliance was put on draftees to fill out the ranks; individuals who did not necessarily want to be there. As the war continued, the popularity and support on the home front decreased. It became a very unpopular war.

What changed? The army became all voluntary. Whole units rotated in and out of operations. There was an increased emphasis on leadership, a refocus on values. The seven army values became the guiding moral compass for all soldiers. These values include: loyalty, duty, respect, selfless service, honor, integrity, and personal courage. Two of these values are directly related to ethics and ethical actions and decisions. First, respect: How we consider others, as in the Golden Rule—treat others as you would like to be treated. Second is integrity: That is, doing what is both legally and morally right, whether it is following the rules of engagement, the treatment of detainees or prisoners of war, or the treatment of noncombatants; actions on the part of American service personnel that are legally and morally right.

The second example of ethical issues relating to the military is the Abu Ghraib prison detainee abuse incident. In this case, the actions of a few soldiers in their mistreatment of detainees had an impact far beyond what happened at that prison. Actions by a few soldiers from the 800th Military Police Brigade and the 205th Military Intelligence (MI) Brigade and the photographs of their actions not only shocked the U.S. military, but condemnation by nations from around the world had a major impact on America's image. Between July, 2003 and February, 2004, the misconduct (ranging from inhumane to sadistic) by a small group of morally corrupt soldiers and civilians, a lack of discipline on the part of the leaders and soldiers, and a failure or lack of leadership by multiple echelons within the command structure accounted for this ethical breakdown.

The U.S. Army is an organization governed by rules and regulations. There are regulations or field manuals for every aspect of the army. For example Army Regulation (AR) 190-8 deals with enemy prisoners of war, retained personnel, civilian internees, and other detainees. Army regulations are similar to laws, violate one and you can be punished under the UCMJ (Uniform Code of Military Justice). A field manual describes how something should be done. FM 3-19 40, Military Police (MP) Internment/Resettlement Operations, explains how an MP unit establishes, operates, and manages an internment center or describes how to run a prison facility. For an MP, there are at least five different sources that explain appropriate behavior toward detainees. First is the Geneva Convention, which governs the treatment of prisoners of war, refugees, and the protection of civilians in time of war. Second are Department of Defense (DoD) directives that are from the Secretary of Defense. DoD Directive 5100 69 covers DoD program for prisoners of war and other detainees. Third is STANAGs NATO Standardization Agreements that establishes processes and procedures among member countries. STANAG 2033 covers the interrogation of PWs. Fourth are Army Regulations (ARs) AR 190-8, which cover enemy prisoners of war, retained personnel, civilian internees, and other detainees. Lastly, the fifth are field manuals (FMs). FM 3-18 40 covers military police internment/resettlement operations. It is the responsibility of the chain of command to ensure all soldiers are familiar with and have access to all relevant materials. For the MPs of the 800th MP Brigade, they should have had all relevant documents pertaining to the care and treatment of detainees. This was not the case. For the MI soldiers, their activities were governed by similar rules and regulations. Army regulations 190-13 (Army physical security programs), AR 380-67 (personnel security program), and AR 380-5 (Army Information Security) govern the action of military intelligence personnel. Field manual (FM 34-52) intelligence interrogations specifically lays out how interrogators are to conduct interrogations. Nothing in the ARs or FMs sanctioned the abuse of detainees by some of the military intelligence personnel of the 205th MI Brigade (Taguba, 2004).

Soldiers of the 800th Military Police Brigade were responsible for the security and operations of the Abu Ghraib prison facility. Members of the 205th Military Intelligence Brigade and civilian contractors were responsible for the interrogation of detainees thought to possess valuable intelligence; information that would have an impact on military operations (locations of weapons caches, IED (improvised explosive device) manufacturing, insurgent groups, and their plans of attack); information that is perishable. Information once obtained would be rapidly sent to affected units. The purpose is to save lives.

A main issue that developed during this time frame was the status of detainees. Were they considered prisoners of war, or enemy combatants, or civilian noncombatants, or common criminals? Which part of the Geneva Convention applied or did it? Did interrogation techniques approved for use in Afghanistan or Guantanamo also apply for detainees in Iraq?

The army's investigation of the actions of members of the 205th MI Brigade "found that from 25 July 2003 to 6 February 2004, 27 personnel from the 205th MI Brigade allegedly requested, encouraged, condoned, or solicited military police (MP) personnel to abuse detainees and/or participated in detainee abuse and/or violated established interrogation procedures and applicable laws and regulations during interrogation operations at Abu Ghraib" (Jones and Fay, 2004, p. 109).

Within the 800th MP Brigade, numerous officers and enlisted soldiers were reprimanded or disciplined for misconduct. Some were relieved of command and given letters of reprimand, and seven enlisted MP personnel were charged with brutalizing detainees (Higham and Stephens, 2004). Actions by Private Lynndie England and Sergeant Charles Graner were at the center of court martial proceedings against military police personnel. Photographs of the abuse surfaced. "In one photo, England is depicted with a cigarette dangling from her mouth giving the thumbs up sign, presumably to the photographer, and grinning at a naked Iraqi man as he masturbates" (Tucker and Triantafyllos, 2008, p. 84). Just as shocking in another photograph, "England stands looking at a naked Iraqi man while holding a leash attached to his neck." In the course of its investigation, the army investigators "discovered serious misconduct and a loss of moral values" (Kern, Jones, and Fay, 2004).

Another example of a small group of soldiers whose behaviors were outside the parameters of acceptable; behaviors that "were not the result of any doctrine, training, or policy failures, but violations of the law and misconduct" (Kern, Jones, and Fay, 2004).

Just like the soldiers at My Lai 4, soldiers at Abu Ghraib knew their actions were wrong and their supervisor/leader also knew these actions were wrong. They failed to take action to stop it. This brings us back to the two army values mentioned at the beginning of this piece: respect and integrity—treat others the way you want to be treated and do what is morally and legally right.

It is the responsibility of every supervisor and the responsibility of every soldier to do what is morally, legally, and ethically right. It is the responsibility of every soldier regardless of rank to prevent, to stop, and to report behavior that is wrong.

Tom Caywood, Ph.D.
U.S. Army Reserve (CW2, retired)
Professor of Criminal Justice (retired)
University of Wisconsin–Platteville

Ethics in Social Services

According to the National Association of Social Workers, the primary obligation of the social work profession is to "enhance human well-being and help meet the basic human needs of all people, with particular attention to the needs and empowerment of people who are vulnerable, oppressed, and living in poverty" (www.naswdc.org). Those involved with social work attempt to promote social change and justice through change on behalf of "clients." This term is an inclusive term, used to refer to individuals, groups, families, organizations, and communities.

As with many of the professions dedicated to public service, social work has a mission that is rooted in a set of core values. These include, among others, a specific listing of "integrity." The reader is directed to the website for the National Association of Social Workers (www.naswdc.org) to review a code of ethics specific to the profession, and ethical principles and standards that are expected of those who are certified within the field of social work.

Many professions have adopted journals as a forum to educate and train those within the respective field with regards to ethics pertinent to the job. Social work is no different. The *Journal of Social Work Values and Ethics* "examines the ethical and values issues that impact and are interwoven with social work practice, research, and theory development" (http://www.jswvearchives.com/). The reader is directed to this website to peruse how historical perspectives associated with social work ethics have changed and to expose themselves to the full range of social problems and issues that social workers typically encounter within the confines of their employment.

RIPPED FROM THE HEADLINES

PUBLIC PERCEPTION OF PUBLIC SERVICE ETHICS

A November 2009 Gallup News Poll reported that, in spite of many news stories reporting to the contrary, honesty and integrity of police officers is still high. While, for the eighth year in a row, nurses were the ones to top the Gallup's annual "Honesty and Ethics of Professions" survey, police officers finished fourth out of the 21 categories, with 89 percent of those polled believing officers to have above average or high ethical standards. Other than nurses, only pharmacists and medical doctors finished ahead of police officers.

Unfortunately, not all areas of public service were seen as being as ethical. Members of Congress finished 18th, seen as ethical by only 9 percent of those polled. State governors also were low on the list, most likely due to recent media events, posting a 15 percent above average ethical score. Finishing slightly behind the governors was the category of lawyers, with a 13 percent average. Car salespeople brought up the rear, with a 6 percent ethical average (http://www.gallup.com/poll/1654 /Honesty-Ethics-Professions.aspx (accessed August 29, 2010).

Ethics in Emergency Medical Services

While many of our nation's emergency medical services are made up of private industry, some are employed as components of our nation's public fire services or emergency management services, and, therefore, it is important to discuss services within the confines of this text. So, why discuss ethics in emergency medical services (EMS)? Imagine you are a paramedic who arrives at the scene of a multiple motor vehicle accident. The driver is assessed as being of emergent concern and requires medical transport. Although in urgent need of medical attention, she is unconcerned about herself and continuously inquires as to the status of her passenger, who is dead. How do you respond to her? The response may hinge on your actual job position. If you are a physician then the answer must be with complete honesty, based on the American Medical Association's Principles of Medical Ethics. "A physician shall be honest in all professional interactions" (www .ama-assn.org/ama/pub/physician-resources/medical-ethics/code-medical -ethics.shtml). However, if you are a paramedic or emergency medical technician (EMT), then there is no code that dictates that honesty must be the response. Therefore, if you were to tell the driver that her passenger was being attended to and was receiving the best medical care possible, but that your emphasis had to be placed on her for the moment, telling the truth would be avoided through deflection and information short of complete divulgence. These are the instances that one may be presented with within the confines of emergency medical services response, which would necessitate that an individual have a foundation in ethics and could make sound ethical decisions.

Specific areas of ethical concern for those in emergency medical services include the following:

- Confidentiality
- Consent
- Disclosure
- Limits to medical treatment
- Off-duty response

For a sample code of ethics associated with emergency medical services, the reader is directed to the code of ethics for the National Association of Emergency Medical Technicians: www.publicsafety.net/emtcode.htm

Ethics in Firefighting

Ethics with regards to firefighting is a sadly underexplored and undocumented field. Some believe that ethics associated with firefighting is comparable to medical ethics and, thus, does not necessitate unique identification or attention. However, firefighting is significantly less professional in some regions, sometimes made up almost entirely of volunteers and subsidized fire equipment. Also, a firefighter's role does not primarily involve care-giving, and instead is central on other aspects than life and limb. Firefighters also face much greater risks than most medical personnel and must make decisions and operate in conditions that are much more hazardous and sometimes more stressful. All of the aforementioned speak to reasons why the area of firefighting should be another area of public service which should have its own identified concern for and answer to ethical issues. The International Association of Fire Fighters' *Manual of Common Procedure and Related Subjects* contains a code of ethics that is assembled to assist firefighters with remembering their career and mission goals (www.affi-iaff.org).

FIREFIGHTER CODE OF ETHICS

The Firefighter Code of Ethics is a recommended Code of Ethics intended to mitigate and negate situations that may result in embarrassment and waning of public support for what has historically been a highly respected profession.

I understand that I have the responsibility to conduct myself in a manner that reflects proper ethical behavior and integrity. In so doing, I will help foster a continuing positive public perception of the fire service. Therefore, I pledge the following...

- Always conduct myself, on and off duty, in a manner that reflects positively on myself, my department, and the fire service in general.
- Accept responsibility for my actions and for the consequences of my actions.
- Support the concept of fairness and the value of diverse thoughts and opinions.
- Avoid situations that would adversely affect the credibility or public perception of the fire service profession.
- Be truthful and honest at all times and report instances of cheating or other dishonest acts that compromise the integrity of the fire service.
- Conduct my personal affairs in a manner that does not improperly influence the performance of my duties, or bring discredit to my organization.
- Be respectful and conscious of each member's safety and welfare.
- Recognize that I serve in a position of public trust that requires stewardship in the honest and efficient use of publicly owned resources, including uniforms, facilities, vehicles, and equipment and that these are protected from misuse and theft.
- Exercise professionalism, competence, respect and loyalty in the performance of my duties and use information, confidential or otherwise, gained by virtue of my position, only to benefit those I am entrusted to serve.
- Avoid financial investments, outside employment, outside business interests or activities that conflict with or are enhanced by my official position or have the potential to create the perception of impropriety.

- Never propose or accept personal rewards, special privileges, benefits, advancement, honors, or gifts that may create a conflict of interest, or the appearance thereof.
- Never engage in activities involving alcohol or other substance use or abuse that can impair my mental state or the performance of my duties and compromise safety.
- Never discriminate on the basis of race, religion, color, creed, age, marital status, national origin, ancestry, gender, sexual preference, medical condition, or handicap.
- Never harass, intimidate, or threaten fellow members of the service or the public and stop or report the actions of other firefighters who engage in such behaviors.
- Responsibly use social networking, electronic communications, or other media technology opportunities in a manner that does not discredit, dishonor, or embarrass my organization, the fire service, and the public. I also understand that failure to resolve or report inappropriate use of this media equates to condoning this behavior.

Developed by the National Society of Executive Fire Officer
https://www.usfa.fema.gov/downloads/pdf/code_of_ethics.pdf

Ethics in Government Contracts

"The Government relies on many contractors to provide products to the government and perform services for or on behalf of the government. Contractor personnel generally are not subject to the same general principles of ethical conduct and specific ethical standards as are executive branch employees. However, federal contractors and their employees are subject to other restrictions, many of which involve standards of conduct and ethical concerns, which are imposed by law or regulation, by contract, and often by the contractors themselves" (http://www.usoge.gov/).

In December 2007, Federal Acquisition Regulations (FAR) were enacted that now require a written code of business ethics be a component of many government contracts. Because government utilizes public funding, it is necessary that there be strict ethical standards in place. However, many contractors are not aware of the complexities and areas where ethical concerns may lurk. It is important that contracting officials properly inform contractors as to the basics of such things as gift giving/acceptance, and soliciting for and awarding of contracts. The end result of proper adherence to ethics with

RIPPED FROM THE HEADLINES

MILITARY MENTORS CASHING IN
(*USA Today*, NOVEMBER 18, 2009)

An increasing number of retired senior military personnel are finding "retirement" to be a lucrative venture. There are at least 158 retired generals and admirals that the Pentagon has hired to act as senior mentors. These mentors are paid hundreds of dollars an hour to offer advice to former colleagues, to help run war games, and to offer advice on tactical, technological, and strategic plans. This arrangement is in addition to their military pensions, typically ranging between $100,000 and $200,000. This is not a new phenomenon. Retired military executives have been taking positions with defense contractors for decades, following retirement from the military. However, recently, there has been a very large increase in the numbers of individuals doing so and it is creating significant controversy since these individuals are being compensated both by taxpayers and by industry, with very little if any oversight to prevent their private industry employers from making use of acquired knowledge to secure government contracts. This is not, however, illegal. There is nothing that prohibits retired personnel from engaging in such events.

According to the *USA Today* article, based on interviews and public records:

80 percent of the 158 retired generals and admirals had ties to defense contractors, including earning salaries, stock options, and/or serving as employees or board members.

The individuals were hired as independent contractors and, thus, are not subject to government ethics regulations that would otherwise apply if they were serving in the capacity of a federal employee.

Mentors are compensated at between $200 and $340 an hour for their time.

The concern is not with the amount of money that these individuals are making, but rather with the information that they are exposed to and how they and their private employers may profit from access to such information. For instance, if a retired marine general is hired as a private contractor to oversee war games and offer advice on deployment strategies and technology to employ, then he or she will undoubtedly have access to the latest in military strategies and hardware. This contractor can then go back to his or her company and divulge such information, which could benefit the private company with regard to future government contracts. A retired senior air force official was quoted as saying, "I am sure that I am getting current information and updates that could make me 'useful' to some aerospace contractor." The question isn't so much if senior mentors have access to such information, but rather what they choose to do with it.

Marine General James Mattis, commander of Norfolk-based Joint Forces Command, was quoted as saying, "if your concern is that we're exposing them to things that would allow them to have an advantage for their company, I doubt if that can be refuted.... The only way to not have that would be to have either amateurs on their boards of directors, or amateurs in our thing." Therein lies the problem. Neither industry nor the military benefits from having amateurs in either position. And yet, with knowledgeable professionals, there appears to be the potential for ethically muddy waters. Representative Edolphus Towns (D-NY), chairman of the House Committee on Oversight and Government Reform, released a statement pertaining to the situation, saying that "government ethics laws are in place for a reason. These laws require that any potential conflicts of interest be disclosed, evaluated, and managed. I would expect the Pentagon to fully comply with both the letter and spirit of these requirements. The invaluable expertise of retired military officers should be utilized without sacrificing transparency and accountability."

Private defense companies have long sought retired military personnel to act as advisors, as has the government sought retirees to offer insight. The ethical matter of concern isn't the paycheck (or paychecks, in some cases) associated with such insight, but rather the perception (or actuality) of insider knowledge being used to secure future government contracts. Access and insider knowledge continue to be prized, and as a result, there will need to be continued concern and oversight with regards to the ethics and legality of this practice.

BRIBERY IN CONTRACTING

DEPARTMENT OF JUSTICE
Office of Public Affairs
FOR IMMEDIATE RELEASE

Tuesday, January 19, 2010

TWENTY-TWO EXECUTIVES AND EMPLOYEES OF MILITARY AND LAW ENFORCEMENT PRODUCTS COMPANIES CHARGED IN FOREIGN BRIBERY SCHEME

Defendants Arrested in Las Vegas and Miami; 21 Search Warrants Executed in United States and United Kingdom

Twenty-two executives and employees of companies in the military and law enforcement products industry have been indicted for engaging in schemes to bribe foreign government officials to obtain and retain business, announced Assistant Attorney General Lanny A. Breuer of the Criminal Division; U.S. Attorney Channing Phillips for the District of Columbia; and Assistant Director Kevin Perkins of the FBI's Criminal Investigative Division. Twenty-one defendants were arrested in Las Vegas yesterday. One defendant was arrested in Miami. The indictments stem from an FBI undercover operation that focused on allegations of foreign bribery in the military and law enforcement products industry.

The 16 indictments unsealed today represent the largest single investigation and prosecution against individuals in the history of DOJ's enforcement of the Foreign Corrupt Practices Act (FCPA), a law that prohibits U.S. persons and companies, and foreign persons and companies acting in the United States, from bribing foreign government officials for the purpose of obtaining or retaining business. The indictments unsealed today were returned on Dec. 11, 2009, by a grand jury in Washington, D.C.

In connection with these indictments, approximately 150 FBI agents executed fourteen search warrants in locations across the country, including Bull Shoals, Arkansas; San Francisco; Miami; Ponte Vedra Beach, Florida; Sarasota, Florida; St. Petersburg, Florida; Sunrise, Florida; University Park, Florida; Decatur, Georgia; Stearns, Kentucky; Upper Darby, Pennsylvania; and Woodbridge, Virginia. Additionally, the United Kingdom's City of London Police executed seven search warrants in connection with their own investigations into companies involved in the foreign bribery conduct that formed the basis for the indictments.

"This ongoing investigation is the first large-scale use of undercover law enforcement techniques to uncover FCPA violations and the largest action ever undertaken by the Justice Department against individuals for FCPA violations," said Assistant Attorney General Lanny A. Breuer. "The fight to erase foreign bribery from the corporate playbook will not be won overnight, but these actions are a turning point. From now on, would-be FCPA violators should stop and ponder whether the person they are trying to bribe might really be a federal agent."

"Corrupt payments to foreign officials to obtain or retain business erode public confidence in our free market system and threaten to undermine foreign governments," said U.S. Attorney Channing Phillips. "These indictments set forth serious allegations and reflect the department's commitment to aggressively investigate and prosecute those who try to advance their businesses through foreign bribery."

"Investigating corruption at all levels is the number one priority of the FBI's Criminal Division," said Assistant Director Kevin Perkins of the FBI's Criminal Investigative Division. "In this era of global commerce, the FBI is committed to curbing corruption at home or overseas. Companies should prosper through honest business practices, not the practice of backroom deals and bribery."

The indictments allege that the defendants engaged in a scheme to pay bribes to the minister of defense for a country in Africa. In fact, the scheme was part of the undercover operation, with no actual involvement from any minister of defense. As part of the undercover operation, the defendants allegedly agreed to pay a 20 percent "commission" to a sales agent who the defendants believed represented the minister of defense for a country in Africa in order to win a portion of a $15 million deal to outfit the country's presidential guard. In reality, the "sales agent" was an undercover FBI agent. The defendants were told that half of that "commission" would be paid directly to the minister of defense. The defendants allegedly agreed to create two price quotations in connection with the deals, with one quote representing the true cost of the goods and the second quote representing the true cost, plus the 20 percent "commission." The defendants also allegedly agreed to engage in a small "test" deal to show the minister of defense that he would personally receive the 10 percent bribe.

The indictments charge the following executives and employees of the various companies in the military and law enforcement product industries:

Daniel Alvirez, 32, and Lee Allen Tolleson, 25, the president and director of acquisitions and logistics at a company in Bull Shoals, Arkansas, that manufactures and sells law enforcement and military equipment.

Helmie Ashiblie, 44, the vice president and founder of a company in Woodbridge, Virginia, that supplies tactical bags and other security-related articles for law enforcement agencies and governments worldwide.

Andrew Bigelow, 40, the managing partner and director of government programs for a Sarasota, Florida, company that sells machine guns, grenade launchers, and other small arms and accessories.

R. Patrick Caldwell, 61, and Stephen Gerard Giordanella, 50, the current and former chief executive officers of a Sunrise, Florida, company that designs and manufactures concealable and tactical body armor.

Yochanan R. Cohen, aka Yochi Cohen, 47, the chief executive officer of a San Francisco company that manufactures security equipment, including body armor and ballistic plates.

Haim Geri, 50, the president of a North Miami Beach, Florida, company that serves as a sales agent for companies in the law enforcement and military products industries.

Amaro Goncalves, 49, the vice president of sales for a Springfield, Massachusetts, company that designs and manufactures firearms, firearm safety/security products, rifles, firearms systems, and accessories.

John Gregory Godsey, aka Greg Godsey, 37, and Mark Frederick Morales, 37, the owner and agent of a Decatur, Georgia, company that sells ammunition and other law enforcement and military equipment.

Saul Mishkin, 38, the owner and chief executive officer of an Aventura, Florida, company that sells law enforcement and military equipment.

John M. Mushriqui, 28, and Jeana Mushriqui, 30, the director of international development and general counsel/U.S. manager of an Upper Darby, Pennsylvania, company that manufactures and exports bulletproof vests and other law enforcement and military equipment.

David R. Painter, 56, and Lee M. Wares, 43, the chairman and director of a United Kingdom company that markets armored vehicles.

Pankesh Patel, 43, the managing director of a United Kingdom company that acts as sales agent for companies in the law enforcement and military products industries.

Ofer Paz, 50, the president and chief executive officer of an Israeli company that acts as sales agent for companies in the law enforcement and military products industries.

Jonathan M. Spiller, 58, the owner and president of a Ponte Vedra Beach, Florida, company that markets and sells law enforcement and military equipment.

Israel Weisler, aka Wayne Weisler, 63, and Michael Sacks, 66, owners and co-chief executive officers of a Stearns, Kentucky, company that designs, manufactures, and sells armor products, including body armor.

John Benson Wier III, 46, the president of a St. Petersburg, Florida, company that sells tactical and ballistic equipment.

All of the defendants except Giordanella were arrested yesterday by FBI agents in Las Vegas. Giordanella was arrested in Miami, also by FBI agents.

Each of the indictments allege that the defendants conspired to violate the FCPA, conspired to engage in money laundering, and engaged in substantive violations of the FCPA. The indictments also seek criminal forfeiture of the defendants' ill-gotten gains.

The maximum prison sentence for the conspiracy count and for each FCPA count is five years. The maximum sentence for the money laundering conspiracy charge is 20 years in prison.

These cases are being prosecuted by Assistant Chief Hank Bond Walther and Trial Attorney Laura N. Perkins of the Criminal Division's Fraud Section, and Matthew C. Solomon of the U.S. Attorney's Office for the District of Columbia. The cases were investigated by the FBI Washington Field Office squad that specializes in investigations into FCPA violations (http://www.justice.gov/opa/pr/2010/January/10-crm-048 .html).

regards to contractual relationships in public service can be a good contract, which can lead to productive future relationships between the contractor and the involved government agency.

Legislation Regarding Ethics in Public Service

As government contracts become potentially more lucrative, there is an increased probability for corruptness and ethical violations associated with such matters. Recent historical events have resulted in legislation to combat this potential, and, in some cases, this reality. Following the Hurricane

Katrina tragedy, which struck the United State's southern coast, there was widespread abuse of federal resources that had been earmarked for disaster assistance to the stricken regions. Fraudulent companies, contractors, and individuals came out of the woodwork to "assist" with disaster relief efforts, but who ultimately made off with millions of federal aid dollars. The result was a country shocked and an industry mistrusted. This was the impetus for the 2007 Emergency and Disaster Assistance Fraud Penalty Enhancement Act.

H.R. 846—EMERGENCY AND DISASTER ASSISTANCE FRAUD PENALTY ENHANCEMENT ACT OF 2007 (INTRODUCED IN HOUSE – IH) HR 846 IH

110TH CONGRESS
1st Session
H. R. 846

To amend title 18, United States Code, with respect to fraud in connection with major disaster or emergency funds.

IN THE HOUSE OF REPRESENTATIVES
February 6, 2007

Mr. CHABOT (for himself, Mr. SMITH of Texas, Mr. GALLEGLY, Mr. COBLE, Mr. FRANKS of Arizona, and Mr. PENCE) introduced the following bill; which was referred to the Committee on the Judiciary.

A BILL

To amend title 18, United States Code, with respect to fraud in connection with major disaster or emergency funds.

Be it enacted by the Senate and House of Representatives of the United States of America in Congress assembled

SECTION 1. SHORT TITLE.

This Act may be cited as the "Emergency and Disaster Assistance Fraud Penalty Enhancement Act of 2007."

SEC. 2. FRAUD IN CONNECTION WITH MAJOR DISASTER OR EMERGENCY BENEFITS.

(a) In General—Chapter 47 of title 18, United States Code, is amended by adding at the end the following:

Sec. 1039. Fraud in connection with major disaster or emergency benefits

(a) Whoever, in a circumstance described in subsection (b) of this section, knowingly

    (1) falsifies, conceals, or covers up by any trick, scheme, or device any material fact; or

    (2) makes any materially false, fictitious, or fraudulent statement or representation, or makes or uses any false writing or document knowing the same to contain any materially false, fictitious, or fraudulent statement or representation, in any matter involving any benefit authorized, transported, transmitted, transferred, disbursed, or paid in connection with a major disaster declaration under section 401 of the Disaster Relief Act of 1974, or an emergency declaration under section 501 of the Disaster Relief Act of 1974, or in connection with any procurement of property or services related to any emergency or disaster declaration as a prime contractor with the United States or as a subcontractor or supplier on a contract in which there is a prime contract with the United States, shall be fined under this title, imprisoned for not more than 30 years, or both.

(b) The circumstance to which subsection (a) of this section refers is that—

    (1) the authorization, transportation, transmission, transfer, disbursement, or payment of the benefit is in or affects interstate or foreign commerce;

    (2) the benefit is transported in the mail at any point in the authorization, transportation, transmission, transfer, disbursement, or payment of that benefit; or

    (3) the benefit is a record, voucher, payment, money, or thing of value of the United States, or of any department or agency thereof.

(c) In this section, the term 'benefit' means any record, voucher, payment, money or thing of value, good, service, right, or privilege provided by the United States, State or local government, or other entity.

(b) Clerical Amendment: The table of sections for chapter 47 of title 18, United States Code, is amended by inserting at the end the following new item:

> 1039. Fraud in connection with major disaster or emergency benefits.

SEC. 3. INCREASED CRIMINAL PENALTIES FOR ENGAGING IN WIRE, RADIO, AND TELEVISION FRAUD DURING AND RELATION TO A PRESIDENTIALLY DECLARED MAJOR DISASTER OR EMERGENCY.

Section 1343 of title 18, United States Code, is amended by inserting: 'occurs in relation to, or involving any benefit authorized, transported, transmitted, transferred, disbursed, or paid in connection with, a presidentially declared major disaster or emergency, or' after 'If the violation.'

SEC. 4. INCREASED CRIMINAL PENALTIES FOR ENGAGING IN MAIL FRAUD DURING AND RELATION TO A PRESIDENTIALLY DECLARED MAJOR DISASTER OR EMERGENCY.

Section 1341 of title 18, United States Code, is amended by inserting: 'occurs in relation to, or involving any benefit authorized, transported, transmitted, transferred, disbursed, or paid in connection with, a presidentially declared major disaster or emergency, or' after 'If the violation.'

SEC. 5. DIRECTIVE TO SENTENCING COMMISSION.

(a) In General: Pursuant to its authority under section 994(p) of title 28, United States Code, and in accordance with this section, the United States Sentencing Commission forthwith shall—

(1) promulgate sentencing guidelines or amend existing sentencing guidelines to provide for increased penalties for persons convicted of fraud or theft offenses in connection with a major disaster declaration under section 5170 of title 42, United States Code, or an emergency declaration under section 5191 of title 42, United States Code; and

(2) submit to the Committees on the Judiciary of the United States Congress an explanation of actions taken by the Commission pursuant to paragraph (1) and any additional policy recommendations the Commission may have for combating offenses described in that paragraph.

(b) Requirements: In carrying out this section, the Sentencing Commission shall—
  (1) ensure that the sentencing guidelines and policy statements reflect the serious nature of the offenses described in subsection (a) and the need for aggressive and appropriate law enforcement action to prevent such offenses;
  (2) assure reasonable consistency with other relevant directives and with other guidelines;
  (3) account for any aggravating or mitigating circumstances that might justify exceptions, including circumstances for which the sentencing guidelines currently provide sentencing enhancements;
  (4) make any necessary conforming changes to the sentencing guidelines; and
  (5) assure that the guidelines adequately meet the purposes of sentencing as set forth in section 3553(a)(2) of title 18, United States Code.
(c) Emergency Authority and Deadline for Commission Action: The Commission shall promulgate the guidelines or amendments provided for under this section as soon as practicable, and in any event not later than the 30 days after the date of the enactment of this Act, in accordance with the procedures set forth in section 21(a) of the Sentencing Reform Act of 1987, as though the authority under that Act had not expired (http://thomas.loc.gov/cgi-bin/query/z?c110:H.R.846:).

Conclusion

Regardless of the area of public service where one finds oneself employed, a foundation in ethical decision making is of paramount importance. As has been shown repeatedly throughout this text, there are numerous obstacles along the way and difficult circumstances in which one may be confronted. Perception can oftentimes be the reality that we live and work by, and so it is necessary that one stops to consider the perception, as well as the impact of the decisions that he or she makes through the course of his/her work in public service.

Questions for Review

1. True or false: When looking at ethics in the military, unethical decisions have no consequences on the battlefield.

2. The seven army values include _____, _____, _____, _____, _____, _____, and _____.

3. What is integrity?

4. There are _____ or field _____ for every aspect of the army.

5. It is the responsibility of every supervisor and every soldier to do what is _____, _____, and _____ right.

6. What is the primary obligation of the social work profession?

7. The specific areas of ethical concern for emergency medical services include _____, _____, _____, _____, and _____.

8. Federal Acquisition Regulations were enacted that now require a code of business ethics be a component of many government contracts.

References

Hersh, S. E. 1970. *My Lai 4: A report on the massacre and its aftermath*. New York: Random House.

Higham, S., and Stephens, J. 2004. New details of prison abuse emerge. *The Washington Post*, May 21, p. A01, www.washingtonpost.com.

http://www.gallup.com/poll/1654/Honesty-Ethics-Professions.aspx, accessed August 29, 2010.

http://www.jswvearchives.com/, accessed October 11, 2017.

http://www.usoge.gov/, accessed October 12, 2017.

ICMA 2017. International City/County Management Association. (http://icma.org /en/icma/about/organization_overview) (Accessed May 22, 2017).

Jones, A. R., and Fay, G. R. 2004. AR 15-6 investigation of the Abu Ghraib Prison and 205th Military Intelligence Brigade. Department of Defense Report, August 23, Washington, DC.

Kern, P., Jones, A. R., and Fay, G. R. 2004. Defense Department Briefing on Results of Investigation of Military Intelligence Activities at Abu Ghraib Prison Facility, Wednesday, August 25, Washington, DC.

National Association of Social Workers. 2010. Practice. From www.naswdc.org /practice/default.asp (accessed August 2, 2010).

Newell, Terry. 2017. *Failure in Flint: The Moral Responsibility of Public Servants*, Huffington Post, February 23, 2017.

Taguba, A. M. 2004. AR 15-6 Investigation of the 800th Military Police Brigade. Department of Defense Report, June 4, Washington, DC.

Tucker, B., and Triantafyllos, S. 2008. Lynndie England, Abu Ghraib, and the new Imperialism. *Canadian Journal of American Studies* 38: 83–100.

www.ama-assn.org/ama/pub/physician-resources/medical-ethics/code-medical-ethics .shtml.

Ethics Training and Education

12

To educate a man in mind but not in morals is to create a menace to society.

Theodore Roosevelt

A man is ethical only when life, as such, is sacred to him... truth has no special time of its own. Its hour is now—always.

Albert Schweitzer

Key Terms

Culturalization   Socialization

Learning Objectives

1. Define and explain the concept of **culturalization**.
2. Define and explain the concept of **socialization**.
3. Be able to explain the impact of failing to monitor and regulate ethics within a department.
4. Define and differentiate between the ethical systems that are a component of ethics-based training.
5. Define the components of successful leadership training.

Introduction

There are two primary methods of education that are used within the majority of criminal justice agencies within the United States. These educational methods can be categorized as being either socializational (learned) or culturalizational (adopted) in nature (Bowen, 2010).

Education by **socialization** is a practice whereby individuals acquire ethical knowledge and principles through training and experiential education. With regards to ethical education, this method is oftentimes utilized within the medical and legal fields. Typical coursework is made up of a blend of philosophy and logic, and centers around discussions relating to specific ethical challenges relevant to employment. The training is typically led by experts within the appropriate field or veteran employees of the agency or

RIPPED FROM THE HEADLINES

FIRED FOR ETHICS VIOLATION

A sheriff deputy from Heber Springs, Arkansas was fired in February of 2017 when he passed a stationary school bus. In an internal investigation it was determined the deputy committed a traffic violation by passing the school bus. The deputy was then terminated when he violated the Law Enforcement Code of Ethics by providing contradicting information about the incident (McMahon, 2017).

organization. Employees also are provided with instruction relating to reasonable expectations of their field of employment.

Culturalization refers to the informal method of education whereby new employees learn values and ethics-based decision-making skills based on personal experiences, typically from instructors or mentors who were also taught ethics-based skills informally. As this pattern of informal training advances, individual interpretation of the agency, organization, or overall professions' ethical principles can become confused or muddied. Instructor or mentor bias also strongly influences this method of education. If a mentor has negative values that conflict with organizational, societal, or even legal values, the student receives improper information and, thus, the educational process has done them a tremendous disservice.

There is no way to ensure that an agency's or organization's policies and procedures are detailed enough to regulate every situation that an individual may encounter during the course of his/her employment. These unregulated or uninstructed "gray areas" are where an individual is required to make a discretionary decision. It is an individual's training and experience with regards to ethical decision making that will result in the "best" outcome with regards to discretionary decisions. In situations that necessitate the individual to make a discretionary decision, they must "rely on her inherent, learned, and adopted values that may present the opportunities for unethical behavior" (Bowen, 2010).

Ethics-Based Training

Ethics-based training is invaluable to the public service profession. As outlined throughout this book, no one who is employed by the public is free from scrutiny. Headlines are not made when a machinist commits an unethical act, the headline is made when that machinist works for the government. Public servants, both on and off duty, should exemplify the highest ethical and moral standards.

INFLUENCE ON CULTURE

The 2005 National Business Ethics Survey found the ethical culture of an organization influences people's perceptions and actions: ethical behaviors on the part of top management is associated with employees observing less misconduct; ethical actions by coworkers is associated with employees having an increased willingness to report misconduct; and employees' overall satisfaction increases when they perceive that organizational members are held accountable for their actions (Johannesen, Valde, and Whedbee, 2008).

When considering training for the public service professional, five areas of importance must be addressed:

- Statutory regulations and requirements
- Organizational policies and procedures
- Best interests of the public
- Best interests of the organization
- Best interests of those victimized by unethical behavior

Ethics is law enforcement's greatest training and leadership need for several crucial reasons. Most law enforcement agencies neglect to conduct annual internal ethics training and many never provide this type of instruction even though nothing is more devastating to the agencies and profession than police misbehavior (Prevost and Trautman, n.d.). The fallout from this devastation includes the following:

1. Large-scale civil suits with substantial settlements or judgments.
2. Misconduct is fully publicized and sometimes exaggerated by the media.
3. Community relations and respect from the public is damaged.
4. Supervisors may be fired or demoted; others are more fortunate, but may never be promoted again.
5. Individual officers and their families face overwhelming public humiliation.
6. Each year, two to three times the number of officers who die in the line of duty commit suicide. Some of them do so as the result of their misconduct, believing they have lost both their career and cannot face their loved ones (p. 1).

In recent years, ethics training has become a prominent component of police academies. Generally, the topic of these courses consist of one

ETHICAL CONSIDERATIONS

Stemming from President Obama's task force for 21st Century policing, the term "guardian" was coined. The 70-page report from the task force provided insight into training police personnel in the art of community policing and emphasized eliminating a warrior mindset. The task force identified best practices and offered recommendations on building public trust. The task force also offered two recommendations to the President. They suggested the president support the creation of a National Crime and Justice Task Force to examine areas of criminal justice and propose reforms and that he support programs that take a comprehensive and inclusive look at community-based initiatives addressing core community issues including poverty, education, health, and safety (policemag.com).

philosophical framework and then discussion of hypothetical or researched ethical dilemmas that are evaluated using that one philosophy.

Students are educated on a variety of ethical issues and asked to constructively determine their ethical fiber based on issues such as gratuities, corruption, bribery, whistle-blowing, loyalty, undercover tactics, use of deception, discretion, sex on duty, using deadly force, and brutality. Many of these issues involve officer deviance and are easy for students to determine their responses while sitting in a classroom. In some situations, however, any decision that an officer makes is not clearly wrong (Pollock and Becker, 1996).

Williamson et al. (2007) discuss partial dilemmas that face officers outside of the classroom that depend on police discretion and border, or cross the line of, officer misconduct. Police officers function as the constituted authority charged with enforcing laws that society deems immoral. An example of this dilemma would be the street officer who knows that a woman is a prostitute, but does not actively pursue an investigation against her because he knows prostitution is the only method she has to support her family.

Development of Ethical Systems

Ethics-based training consists of the development of ethical systems to help identify and apply procedural framework (Pollock and Becker, 1996):

1. **Religious ethics:** What is good conforms to a deity's will. Religious ethics borrows moral concepts from religious teachings and draws on the participants' various religious beliefs. Discussions lead students to recognize that religious philosophies are ethical systems based on absolute concepts of good, evil, right, and wrong.

2. **Natural law:** What is good is what conforms to nature. If what is natural is good, then students easily can appreciate the constraints of a natural law ethical system within the artificial constructs of modern society. It becomes clear that natural law theory offers only limited assistance when students compare peoples' most basic, natural inclination with their motivations in resolving complex dilemmas.

3. **Ethical formalism:** What is good is what is pure in motive. When discussing ethical formalism, students are asked to resolve a specific dilemma by selecting a resolution that is pure and unblemished in motive, regardless of the consequences. Discussions within this framework present almost absolute answers to ethical dilemmas and show that some actions have little or no ethical support.

4. **Utilitarianism:** What is good is what results in the greatest number. Students who find the consequences of resolving a dilemma more ethically significant than the motive behind the decision-making process will resolve a dilemma with what they perceive to be an acceptable consequence. Yet, in most instances, predicting the consequences is virtually impossible. This results in discussions that become simply a means to project the most likely effects of choices.

5. **Ethics of care:** What is good is that which meets the needs of those involved and does not hurt relationships. Police agency mottoes often reflect a philosophy based on the ethics of care, such as "to protect and serve." The ethics of care is founded in the natural human response to provide for the needs of children, the sick, and the injured. Many police officers operate under the ethics of care when they attempt to solve problems rather than rigidly enforce the law (p. 7).

Successfully completing a course in ethics-based training does not necessarily provide students an advantage in decision making. It helps stimulate an understanding of the rationale used for making ethical decisions. Such training can increase understanding of the potential antecedents to ethical decision making in general, and the interplay between religion, spirituality, self-control, and moral identity (Vitell et al., 2009).

Law enforcement agencies promote ethical behavior based on their culture and paramilitary structure. Police administrators attempt to regulate their

A QUESTION OF ETHICS

Aristotle suggested that morality cannot be learned simply by reading a treatise on virtue. The spirit of morality, said Aristotle, is awakened in the individual only though the witness and conduct of a moral person (Ciulla, 2004).

personnel's behavior through written policies and procedures. Detailed and numerous policies fail to provide a workable guide for action through their cumbersome guidelines, while general and vague policies are functionally useless.

In addition to the academy training for law enforcement, two other areas are important for training personnel; they are the field training officer (FTO) programs and leadership training. FTO programs should be an extension of an agency's culture. Generally, institutionalized scandals are related in some way to ineffective FTO programs. FTOs need to play a vital role in the training of rookie to senior officers in the perspectives of ethical issues and ethics-based training.

Leadership Training

Top police agency leaders have the best opportunity to influence the culture of their agencies. They need to include themselves in opportunities to increase their knowledge in ethics training. Decision makers often fail to take advantage of learning about issues and solutions. When chiefs and sheriffs choose not to attend ethics training, they send a message that the training is not important. Most corruption prevention solutions fail because decision makers have little knowledge about them (Prevost and Trautman, n.d.).

Administrators must address ethical problems before ethics-based training is administered. When personnel are ordered to ethics-based training and a glaring unethical situation within an agency is not addressed, administrators are viewed as hypocrites. Nearly every significant case of employee misconduct has had warning signs that leaders either ignored or failed to recognize. Lack of training does not reduce leaders' responsibility. Leadership training should consist of the following areas (Prevost and Trautman, p. 2):

1. *Quality FTO Program*: Placing an emphasis on an FTO program and rewarding quality officers to conduct training increases the likelihood of maintaining a positive organizational culture. FTOs should be taught how to teach ethics/career survival to new and veteran officers.
2. *Fight Political Interference*: Political interference is a detriment to law enforcement. Typically it attacks five aspects of an agency by lowering hiring standards, interfering with promotions, interfering with

"CODE OF SILENCE"

It is the description of the real or perceived practice whereby individuals within a profession remain conspicuously quiet about the unethical or unlawful actions of coworkers. The contributing factors that cause moral silence, deafness, and blindness are cultural, individual, and organizational in nature (Johannesen, Valde, and Whedbee, 2008).

transfers, failing to provide needed resources, and interfering with discipline. The best solution is usually to educate local officials about the consequences of their actions.

3. *Ensuring Consistent, Fair Accountability*: The lack of accountability is extremely destructive to the culture of an organization. Accountability must start at the top and run solidly through an organization. Administrators must set an example by holding themselves accountable toward integrity issues.

4. *Officers' Anger and Frustration*: Bad morale is a particularly significant contributor to misconduct. Unhappy officers rationalize their misconduct, feeling they have been mistreated by their department.

5. *Employee Intervention Process*: Intervention programs are valuable when implemented with the objective of assisting officers to survive in their career. Programs can track statistical data related to behaviors and training can help build a culture that has an understanding that when misconduct is first exhibited, fellow officers are the first to have an opportunity to intervene and prevent the personnel from destroying their career.

6. *Make Character the Highest Consideration for Promotion*: First-line supervisors are the best defense against wrongdoing because they have the option and are in a position to either condone or ignore minor transgressions. Failing to address minor issues promotes a culture that is accepting of major misconduct. Drug agents, evidence custodians, school resource officers, SWAT team members, and those assigned to work in high crime areas usually face additional temptations and dilemmas.

7. *Demand Positive Leadership Role Models*: Role modeling is the single greatest source for developing traits, such as sincerity, loyalty, honesty, respect, and dedication. It is impossible for an agency to have a culture of integrity if line supervisors are unethical, for role modeling also can be used to instill corrupt behavior.

An officer's integrity is possibly the single most important asset they have as a keeper of the peace. They deal with the worst society has to offer and temptations are continuous. Corruption destroys public confidence and devastates the fiber of the profession. Ethics-based training is not given the priority it deserves by most departments. This results in misbehavior perpetuating itself.

Conclusion

Ethics-based training is currently provided to most agencies in the United States. However, most of those agencies only provide the basic training necessary to stay in compliance with essential rules and regulations. This includes profile stops, sexual harassment, and biased-based policing. Little more is provided by police administrators to curtail police misbehavior. This needs to be addressed. Ethics-based training should not be centered around accreditation or compliance with rules and regulations; it should be centered around the foundation of proper values and operational strategies of an agency or organization, and the ethical decision making of its employees. This cannot be addressed simply in a one or two hour annual in-service training. This must be a commitment to longevity. A commitment to institutional ethics will result in better public perception and confidence as well as better internal operation and a reduction of detrimental incidents. Hiring cannot solve all ethical challenges, and although a person without proper moral or ethical grounding cannot be trained to be "good," continued training in ethics and ethical decision making can assist those with a firm foundation in making the "best" choices, and in ensuring the integrity of themselves and their agency.

Questions for Review

1. _____ is a practice whereby individuals acquire ethical knowledge and principles through training and experiential education.
2. The informal method by which new employees learn values and ethics-based decision-making skills based on personal experiences is known as _____.
3. True or false: There is no way to ensure that an agency's or organization's policies and procedures are detailed enough to regulate every situation that an individual may encounter during the course of his employment.
4. _____ is law enforcement's greatest training and leadership need.
5. What does ethics-based training consist of?
6. Ethics-based training helps stimulate an understanding of the rationale used for making _____ decisions.
7. How do police administrators attempt to regulate their personnel's behavior?
8. True or false: Administrators must address ethical problems before ethics-based training is administered.

References

Bowen, R.T. 2010. *Ethics and the practice of forensic science*. Boca Raton, FL: Taylor & Francis Group.
Ciulla, J.B., ed. 2004. *Ethics, the heart of leadership* (2nd ed.). Westport, CT: Praeger.

Final Report of The President's Task Force on 21st Century Policing (2015, May). Retrieved from http://files.policemag.com/documents/21stcpolicingtaskforce-finalreport.pdf

Johannesen, R.L., Valde, K.S., and Whedbee, K.E. 2008. *Ethics in human communication* (8th ed.). Long Grove, IL: Waveland Press.

McMahon, T. 2017. *Deputy Cited for Passing School Bus, Fired for Ethics Violation* Retrieved June 15, 2017 from http://www.schoolbusfleet.com/news/720015/deputy-cited-for-passing-stopped-school-bus-fired-for-ethics-violation.

Pollock, J., and Becker, R. 1996. Ethics training. *FBI Law Enforcement Bulletin* 65(11), 20. Retrieved from Master FILE Premier database.

Prevost, A., and Trautman, N. n.d. *Police ethics training's state-of-the-art now more effective and comprehensive* (accessed July 28, 2010 from www.ethicsinstitute.com).

Vitell, S., Bing, M., Davison, H., Ammeter, A., Garner, B., and Novicevic, M. 2009. Religiosity and moral identity: The mediating role of self-control. *Journal of Business Ethics* 88(4), 601–613.

Williamson, C., Baker, L., Jenkins, M., and Cluse-Tolor, T. 2007. Police-prostitute interactions: Sometimes discretion, sometimes misconduct. *Journal of Progressive Human Resources* 18(2), 15–37. doi: 10.1300/JO59v18n0203

The Future of Public Service Ethics

13

We drive into the future using only our rear view mirror.

(Herbert) Marshall McLuhan
Canadian educator and media philosopher (1911–1980)

Learning Objectives

1. Identify areas of future research need with regards to ethics.
2. Explain how technology will impact the future of public service ethics.

Introduction

The past two decades have seen profound changes in management style, recruiting methods, and the delivery of public services throughout the world. These changes have had an impact upon public service ethics and will continue to do so. We live and work in a dynamic world. As such, our ethical foundation and ethics-based decision making must continue to evolve to adapt and stay current with the world around us. This does not imply that ethics should be compromised in an effort to evolve or become modern. In fact, quite the opposite is the case. One must constantly assess his/her changing environment and stay current with his/her ability to perceive the changes and implement sound, ethics-based decisions.

Future Research Needs

Training

More research needs to be conducted on the influences of unethical behavior to identify key target areas for training. In 2016, Dr. Leslie Palmer conducted research on several variables and their influence on unethical behavior. While her research was limited to correctional professionals, this type of research can help identify key influential variables that influence unethical behavior. Her research attempted to identify a possible correlation between personnel

189

with and without degrees, length of employment, employee misconduct, and career advancement.

Many of the factors researched are applicable to a variety of professions in the public service industry. This study showed no set correlations between the factors examined. However, when considering the magnitude of the differences, or effect size, correctional officers without college degrees tended to have longer length of employment and those with degrees tended to have fewer infractions (Palmer, 2016).

In the future, it will become necessary to place more emphasis on the relationship between unethical behavior and the individuals and organizations involved in unethical behavior. There is a necessity for further research on the topic of public service and organizational ethics. Specifically, there needs to be research dedicated to the voids in public safety training. There has not been any considerable, unbiased, scholarly research, that has been conducted that attempts to identify the training currently offered within the various categories of public service, and the relationship of this training (or lack thereof) to the ethical violations found within each category. The questions that require answering if there is to be a significant shift in how training is given, and what the content of ethics-based training consists of, are, at minimum, the following:

Questions Regarding Ethics Training

- What training is currently offered to the agency/organization/employees relating to ethics?
- Is the above training lecture-based? Computer-based? Decision/scenario-based? Q & A?
- How often is training conducted? How many hours per quarter/year?
- Is the training given as some sort of mandatory requirement for accreditation?

Questions Regarding Ethics Violations

- Are ethics violations tracked within the agency/organization?
- Who/what department is responsible for tracking these violations?
- How many incidents of ethical violations have there been during the past quarter/year?
- What was the most common violation?
- How many persons were responsible for the violations noted?
- What was the most common reason listed as the reason/justification for why the violation was committed?
- Did the size of the agency/organization impact the number of violations?

Relationship between Training and Violations

- Does there appear to be a relationship between the types of ethics violations and the type of training given?
- Did individuals/agencies/organizations with certain training have less/more ethics violations?
- Was there a type of training that appeared to work better for certain sections of public service, but not as well in other sections?
- Did individuals/agencies/organizations receiving training have less/more violations than those not receiving training?

With in-depth research related to the above, it would be possible to identify voids in training within sectors of public service and, once identified, train to fill these voids and, thus, reduce the number of incidents of unethical behavior. It will never be possible to completely avoid instances of unethical behavior; however, it is possible to reduce the occurrences.

Recruiting

There also is further need to explore the relationship between recruiting efforts and ethics violations within departments, agencies, and organizations.

- How are new recruits/employees tested to ensure a proper foundation in ethics-based decision making?
- If testing is conducted, is it oral in nature? Computer-based? Written?
- Does there appear to be a relationship between the age of recruits/new employees and ethics violations?
- What was the size of the agency/organization?
- Are new recruits/employees assigned a mentor? If yes, did these employees display any incident of less/more ethics-based violations?

Overall, there continues to be a void between ascertaining the relationship between what training and education is being given and where the greatest number of violations is occurring. Any research that has been conducted (and referred to within this text) has largely been conducted on an inappropriate sample size (too small), was not conducted within areas across the wide range of public service professions, did not include scholarly or appropriate survey instruments or questionnaires, or were incomplete. However, if such research is eventually and consistently conducted, it could have a profound impact on the future of public service ethics.

A QUESTION OF ETHICS

At a time when police officers and fire personnel are retiring at an accelerated rate, departments across the country are scrambling to find qualified people to fill those positions. Many municipalities have experienced a decrease as much as 75 percent in applications for open positions (Cooper, 2017).

Over the past several years, the interest in law enforcement as a career has experienced a dramatic decrease. Public criticism of law enforcement in recent years has drawn increased scrutiny of officers and their profession, making the job less desirable. The result has been a need for agencies to reevaluate their hiring standards. Age old, automatic disqualifiers no longer disqualify a candidate. Today, it can be very difficult to find, hire, and retain people with a strong root of honesty and integrity. When candidates are identified, multiple agencies fight to hire them (Simmons, 2016).

Reducing hiring standards may solve issues of staffing initially, but what unintended consequences will this produce? Most agencies require written exams, physical fitness testing, oral boards, background checks, and polygraphs. Reducing any of these standards will undoubtedly affect the profession. At a time when the public is crying for police reform, should departments be reducing their hiring standards? Are there other options?

Organizational Ethics

Just as it is wise to look at the impact of the individual and his or her ethical foundation on the organization, it is wise to research further how the organization structure, hierarchy, policies, etc. impact the individual and his/her ethics-based decisions. This text has only briefly covered this topic, and it is one that has a profound impact on all areas of public service ethics. Further research relating to this relationship would do wonders for public service management structure and for future design of ethics-based training.

The Impact of Technology on Ethics Training

After nearly three decades of using technology to provide realistic scenario-based training for use of force, the industry is finally realizing that such technology can be applied to other areas. In the future, there will be increased use of distance learning and web-based simulation training relating to ethics-based decisions. This will allow organizational leadership to provide exceptional training and instruction to employees at tremendous cost savings and in an extraordinarily efficient manner. Currently, there are already courses via distance education from the Federal Law Enforcement Training Center (FLETC) that cater to such needs. The continued development of such applications will undoubtedly save the lives of public service professionals and those who they are obligated with serving.

Pendulum Swinging

On December 18, 2014, President Barack Obama signed an Executive Order establishing the Presidents Task Force on 21st Century Policing. The task force members sought expertise from stakeholders and input from the public as they worked to identify best practices and make recommendations for the future of the police profession. Proponents of the task force recommendations believe the work produced solid guidelines for law enforcement to follow. Adversaries believe the foundation of the formation of the task force was flawed and therefore the recommendations were biased and duplicitous. The final report was published in May 2015.

The recommendations of the Task Force were predicated on six pillars for promoting effective crime reduction while building public trust.

- Pillar One: Building Trust and Legitimacy
  - A primary component to this pillar was for law enforcement to embrace a guardian, rather than a warrior mindset, to build trust and legitimacy both within agencies and with the public. Law enforcement should also establish a culture of transparency and accountability and adopt procedural justice as the guiding principle for internal and external policies.
- Pillar Two: Policy and Oversight
  - A primary component to this pillar is for law enforcement to adopt policies that reflect community values. Essential to this pillar is the training of officers in de-escalation.
- Pillar Three: Technology and Social Media
  - This pillar guides the implementation, use, and evaluation of technology and social media by law enforcement agencies.
- Pillar Four: Community Policing and Crime Reduction
  - Pillar four focuses on the importance of community policing as a guiding philosophy for all stakeholders. Specifically, law enforcement agencies should develop and adopt policies and strategies that reinforce the importance of community engagement and managing public safety.

- Pillar Five: Training and Education
  - Pillar five focuses on the training and education needs of law enforcement. To ensure the high quality and effectiveness of training and education, law enforcement agencies should engage community members, particularly those with special expertise, in the training process and provide leadership training to all personnel throughout their careers.
- Pillar Six: Officer Wellness and Safety
  - Pillar six emphasizes the support and proper implementation of officer wellness and safety as a multi-partner effort. It recommended Congress to develop and enact peer review error management legislation (policemag.com, 2017).

During the tenure of President Obama, this report became a basis for law enforcement to follow, especially when applying for federal grants. In 2017, when President Trump took office, Attorney General Jeff Sessions swiftly moved to freeze or cancel police training and oversight programs developed under the Obama administration. Sessions ordered his top deputies to review the police reform agreements and consent decrees being enforced in various cities.

Consent decrees, over the last few years, have been filed by the Federal Department of Justice and once approved by a judge is a binding order directing police agencies to take measures to correct certain behaviors. Proponents to the consent decrees see them as very dangerous because they interfere with the judgment and independence of officers on the ground. Sessions asserted the federal government should not have the responsibility to manage non-federal law enforcement agencies (nbcnews).

Over the course of Trump's presidency, many interesting changes are in store regarding the reform for government agencies. President Trump supports reducing federal government's role in state and local policy making. He has not wasted time signing new executive orders that have changed the strategic planning of both private and government organizations (*The Bond Buyer*, 2017). Regardless of how history will be written, this is an interesting time for ethics and the public service professional.

Conclusion

As has been addressed throughout the confines of this text, the topic of ethics is one that is best addressed through a continual dialog and with continued emphasis. No text or individual can provide an organization with all of the tools necessary to ensure a complete understanding or foundation in ethics. The field of ethics is incredibly detailed and expansive. What is necessary is that an organization recognize that instilling sound ethics-based decision making within its employees is of paramount concern, and then find a way to effectively do it. This has been the case for hundreds of years and will continue to be the case for hundreds more, within the area of public service. A utopian society is an impossibility and, thus, public service professions continue to be areas with great job security and areas that will continue to be impacted by violations of poor ethics-based decision making. No measure of research or training will eliminate all ethics violations; however, a reduction of incidents remains a constant possibility.

Questions for Review

1. In the future, it will become necessary to place more emphasis on the relationship between _____ behavior and the individuals and organizations involved in unethical behavior.
2. There needs to be research dedicated to the voids of _____ training.
3. True or false: It will be possible to completely avoid instances of unethical behavior with more effective training.
4. There is a need to explore the relationship between _____ efforts and ethics _____ within departments/agencies/organizations.
5. What are the benefits of utilizing technology, such as distance learning and web-based simulation training relating to ethic-based decisions?

References

Cooper, M. 2017. Springfield police, fire struggling to recruit, retain employees. *TCA Regional News*.

http://files.policemag.com/documents/21stcpolicingtaskforce-finalreport.pdf (accessed June 15, 2017).

http://www.nbcnews.com/storyline/president-trumps-first-100-days/100-days -trump-police-n752281 (accessed May 3, 2017).

Kleiser, G. 2003. *Training for Power and Leadership,* Kessinger Pub Co.

Palmer, L. K. (2016). *The relationship between education level and Minnesota correctional officers' retention, advancement, and employee misconduct.*

Simmons, T. (2016, Dec 03). Greeley, weld county law enforcement officials: Changes in country, candidates forcing a new definition of qualified police. *TCA Regional News*. Retrieved from https://search.proquest.com/docview/1845405 474?accountid=35812

Trump's turn to private jails boosts their bonds. 2017. *The Bond Buyer, 1* (34671).

Appendix A

U.S. Government Entities with Ethics/ Conduct-Related Authority

This chart provides an informal reference for agency ethics officials to the subject matter areas most frequently addressed to the Office of Government Ethics (OGE). The Department of Justice (DOJ) (including U.S. Attorneys' Offices), and agency Inspectors General also handle enforcement matters in a number of these areas, even where not specifically listed. Of course, individual executive branch agencies have responsibility in many of these areas as well, including their own statutory authority and supplemental regulations.

Topic	Federal Entity Concerned
Standards of Ethical Conduct for Employees of the Executive Branch (5 C.F.R. part 2635) (Standards of Ethical Conduct)	OGE
Executive branch-wide regulations on public and confidential financial disclosure, outside employment limitations, ethics training, certain financial interests, and post-government employment (5 C.F.R. parts 2634, 2636, 2637, 2638, 2640, and 2641)	
Conflict of Interest statutes (18 U.S.C. §§ 202, 203, 205, 207, 208, and 209)—interpretations	OGE DOJ, Office of Legal Counsel
Hatch Act provisions (5 U.S.C. § 7321 et seq.) Whistleblower Protection Act Complaints of prohibited personnel practices	Office of Special Counsel Office of Personnel Management (OPM) (certain Hatch Act regulations)
Criminal political contribution/activity restrictions (18 U.S.C. §§ 602, 603, 606, 607, and 610)	DOJ Individual U.S. Attorneys' Offices
Appropriations law and contract protests "Frequent flyer miles"	Comptroller General (General Accounting Office (GAO)) GSA (regulations on frequent flyer benefits)
Ethics audit reports	GAO OGE
Prosecution of violations of criminal conflict of interest statutes (information about a violation of the statutes must be referred to DOJ (28 U.S.C. § 535))	DOJ, incl. Public Integrity Section Individual U.S. Attorneys' Offices

(Continued)

197

Topic	Federal Entity Concerned
Restrictions against gambling on government property, conduct "prejudicial to the government" (i.e., criminal, infamous, or notoriously disgraceful conduct) and special preparation of persons for civil and foreign service examinations (5 C.F.R. part 735)	OPM General Services Administration (GSA) (restrictions on gambling on federal property)
General personnel/federal employment matters	OPM
Government Employees Training Act (see 5 U.S.C. § 4111 in particular)	OPM OGE (ethics aspects)
Use of government-owned property and equipment, e.g., phones, photocopying equipment (41 C.F.R.) Official travel	GSA OGE (ethics aspects and agency § 1353 reports)
Use of government vehicles (31 U.S.C. § 1344)	
Gifts of travel from nonfederal sources (31 U.S.C. § 1353)	
Procurement integrity restrictions (41 U.S.C. § 423)	Office of Management and Budget (OMB), Office of Federal Procurement Policy (OFPP), Federal Acquisition Regulatory (FAR) Council (DoD, GSA, NASA, and OFPP) OGE (ethics-related provisions)
Lobbying restrictions on recipients of federal contracts, grants, loans, etc. (Byrd Amendment)	OMB Clerk of the House of Representatives Secretary of the Senate
Lobbyist registration, reporting lobbying activities (Lobbying Disclosure Act of 1995—P.L. 104-65)	Clerk of the House of Representatives Secretary of the Senate
Restrictions against lobbying with appropriated funds (18 U.S.C. § 1913)	DOJ, Public Integrity Section
Appeals from disciplinary actions for violations of the Standards of Ethical Conduct	Merit Systems Protection Board
Fraud, waste, mismanagement, and abuse in individual agencies	Agency Inspectors General
Prosecutions of violations of the restrictions on outside earned income and outside employment for certain non-career employees (5 U.S.C. app. §§ 501–502)	DOJ, Civil Division Individual U.S. Attorneys' Offices
Prosecutions of failure to file or false filings of public financial disclosure reports	DOJ, Civil and Criminal Divisions Individual U.S. Attorneys' Offices
Foreign Agents Registration Act (22 U.S.C. § 611 et seq.; see also 18 U.S.C. § 219)	DOJ, Internal Security Section
Nepotism (5 U.S.C. § 3110)	OPM

(Continued)

Topic	Federal Entity Concerned
Gifts and decorations from foreign governments	Department of State, Office of Protocol GSA (regulations on disposal/ minimal value)
Coordination of governmental efforts to promote integrity and efficiency and to prevent fraud, waste, and abuse in federal programs (Executive Order 12805)	President's Council on Integrity and Efficiency (PCIE) Executive Council on Integrity and Efficiency (ECIE)
Federal advisory committees (5 U.S.C. app.)	GSA, Committee Management Secretariat
President Clinton's Ethics Pledges for top executive-branch officials (Executive Order 12834)	White House Counsel's Office DOJ (enforcement, statement of covered activities/foreign agents) OGE (forms)

Appendix B

Examples of Codes of Conduct

ICMA Code of Ethics with Guidelines

The ICMA Code of Ethics was adopted by the ICMA membership in 1924, and most recently amended by the membership in April 2015. The Guidelines for the Code were adopted by the ICMA Executive Board in 1972, and most recently revised in June 2015.

The mission of ICMA is to create excellence in local governance by developing and fostering professional local government management worldwide. To further this mission, certain principles, as enforced by the Rules of Procedure, shall govern the conduct of every member of ICMA, who shall:

Tenet 1. Be dedicated to the concepts of effective and democratic local government by responsible elected officials and believe that professional general management is essential to the achievement of this objective.

Tenet 2. Affirm the dignity and worth of the services rendered by government and maintain a constructive, creative, and practical attitude toward local government affairs and a deep sense of social responsibility as a trusted public servant.

GUIDELINE
Advice to Officials of Other Local Governments. When members advise and respond to inquiries from elected or appointed officials of other local governments, they should inform the administrators of those communities.

Tenet 3. Be dedicated to the highest ideals of honor and integrity in all public and personal relationships in order that the member may merit the respect and confidence of the elected officials, of other officials and employees, and of the public.

GUIDELINES
Public Confidence. Members should conduct themselves so as to maintain public confidence in their profession, their local government, and in their performance of the public trust.

Impression of Influence. Members should conduct their official and personal affairs in such a manner as to give the clear impression that they cannot be improperly influenced in the performance of their official duties.

Appointment Commitment. Members who accept an appointment to a position should not fail to report for that position. This does not preclude the possibility of a member considering several offers or seeking several positions at the same time, but once a bona fide offer of a position has been accepted, that commitment should be honored. Oral acceptance of an employment offer is considered binding unless the employer makes fundamental changes in terms of employment.

Credentials. An application for employment or for ICMA's Voluntary Credentialing Program should be complete and accurate as to all pertinent details of education, experience, and personal history. Members should recognize that both omissions and inaccuracies must be avoided.

Professional Respect. Members seeking a management position should show professional respect for persons formerly holding the position or for others who might be applying for the same position. Professional respect does not preclude honest differences of opinion; it does preclude attacking a person's motives or integrity in order to be appointed to a position.

Reporting Ethics Violations. When becoming aware of a possible violation of the ICMA Code of Ethics, members are encouraged to report the matter to ICMA. In reporting the matter, members may choose to go on record as the complainant or report the matter on a confidential basis.

Confidentiality. Members should not discuss or divulge information with anyone about pending or completed ethics cases, except as specifically authorized by the Rules of Procedure for Enforcement of the Code of Ethics.

Seeking Employment. Members should not seek employment for a position having an incumbent administrator who has not resigned or been officially informed that his or her services are to be terminated.

Tenet 4. Recognize that the chief function of local government at all times is to serve the best interests of all of the people.

GUIDELINE
Length of Service. A minimum of two years generally is considered necessary in order to render a professional service to the local government. A short tenure should be the exception rather than a recurring experience. However, under special circumstances, it may be in the best interests of the local government and the member to separate in a shorter time. Examples of such circumstances would include refusal of the appointing authority to honor commitments concerning conditions of employment, a vote of no confidence in the member, or severe personal problems. It is the responsibility of an applicant for a position to ascertain conditions of employment. Inadequately determining terms of employment prior to arrival does not justify premature termination.

Tenet 5. Submit policy proposals to elected officials; provide them with facts and advice on matters of policy as a basis for making decisions and setting community goals; and uphold and implement local government policies adopted by elected officials.

GUIDELINE
Conflicting Roles. Members who serve multiple roles – working as both city attorney and city manager for the same community, for example – should avoid participating in matters that create the appearance of a conflict of interest. They should disclose the potential conflict to the governing body so that other opinions may be solicited.

Tenet 6. Recognize that elected representatives of the people are entitled to the credit for the establishment of local government policies; responsibility for policy execution rests with the members.

Tenet 7. Refrain from all political activities which undermine public confidence in professional administrators. Refrain from participation in the election of the members of the employing legislative body.

GUIDELINES

Elections of the Governing Body. Members should maintain a reputation for serving equally and impartially all members of the governing body of the local government they serve, regardless of party. To this end, they should not participate in an election campaign on behalf of or in opposition to candidates for the governing body.

Elections of Elected Executives. Members shall not participate in the election campaign of any candidate for mayor or elected county executive.

Running for Office. Members shall not run for elected office or become involved in political activities related to running for elected office, or accept appointment to an elected office. They shall not seek political endorsements, financial contributions or engage in other campaign activities.

Elections. Members share with their fellow citizens the right and responsibility to vote. However, in order not to impair their effectiveness on behalf of the local governments they serve, they shall not participate in political activities to support the candidacy of individuals running for any city, county, special district, school, state or federal offices. Specifically, they shall not endorse candidates, make financial contributions, sign or circulate petitions, or participate in fund-raising activities for individuals seeking or holding elected office

Elections relating to the Form of Government. Members may assist in preparing and presenting materials that explain the form of government to the public prior to a form of government election. If assistance is required by another community, members may respond.

Presentation of Issues. Members may assist their governing body in the presentation of issues involved in referenda such as bond issues, annexations, and other matters that affect the government entity's operations and/or fiscal capacity.

Personal Advocacy of Issues. Members share with their fellow citizens the right and responsibility to voice their opinion on public issues. Members may advocate for issues of personal interest only when doing so does not conflict with the performance of their official duties.

Tenet 8. Make it a duty continually to improve the member's professional ability and to develop the competence of associates in the use of management techniques.

GUIDELINES

Self-Assessment. Each member should assess his or her professional skills and abilities on a periodic basis.

Professional Development. Each member should commit at least 40 hours per year to professional development activities that are based on the practices identified by the members of ICMA.

Tenet 9. Keep the community informed on local government affairs; encourage communication between the citizens and all local government officers; emphasize friendly and courteous service to the public; and seek to improve the quality and image of public service.

Tenet 10. Resist any encroachment on professional responsibilities, believing the member should be free to carry out official policies without interference, and handle each problem without discrimination on the basis of principle and justice.

GUIDELINE

Information Sharing. The member should openly share information with the governing body while diligently carrying out the member's responsibilities as set forth in the charter or enabling legislation.

Tenet 11. Handle all matters of personnel on the basis of merit so that fairness and impartiality govern a member's decisions, pertaining to appointments, pay adjustments, promotions, and discipline.

GUIDELINE

Equal Opportunity. All decisions pertaining to appointments, pay adjustments, promotions, and discipline should prohibit discrimination because of race, color, religion, sex, national origin, sexual orientation, political affiliation, disability, age, or marital status.

It should be the members' personal and professional responsibility to actively recruit and hire a diverse staff throughout their organizations.

Tenet 12. Public office is a public trust. A member shall not leverage his or her position for personal gain or benefit.

GUIDELINES

Gifts. Members shall not directly or indirectly solicit, accept or receive any gift if it could reasonably be perceived or inferred that the gift was intended to influence them in the performance of their official duties; or if the gift was intended to serve as a reward for any official action on their part.

The term "Gift" includes but is not limited to services, travel, meals, gift cards, tickets, or other entertainment or hospitality. Gifts of money or loans from persons other than the local government jurisdiction pursuant to normal employment practices are not acceptable.

Members should not accept any gift that could undermine public confidence. De minimus gifts may be accepted in circumstances that support the execution of the member's official duties or serve a legitimate public purpose. In those cases, the member should determine a modest maximum dollar value based on guidance from the governing body or any applicable state or local law.

The guideline is not intended to apply to normal social practices, not associated with the member's official duties, where gifts are exchanged among friends, associates and relatives.

Investments in Conflict with Official Duties. Members should refrain from any investment activity which would compromise the impartial and objective performance of their duties. Members should not invest or hold any investment, directly or indirectly, in any financial business, commercial, or other private transaction that creates a conflict of interest, in fact or appearance, with their official duties.

In the case of real estate, the use of confidential information and knowledge to further a member's personal interest is not permitted. Purchases and sales which might be interpreted as speculation for quick profit should be avoided (see the guideline on "Confidential Information"). Because personal investments may appear to influence official actions and decisions, or create the appearance of impropriety, members should disclose or dispose of such investments prior to accepting a position in a local government. Should the conflict of interest arise during employment, the member should make full disclosure and/or recuse themselves prior to any official action by the governing body that may affect such investments.

This guideline is not intended to prohibit a member from having or acquiring an interest in, or deriving a benefit from any investment when the interest or benefit is due to ownership by the member or the member's family of a de minimus percentage of a corporation traded on a recognized stock exchange even though the corporation or its subsidiaries may do business with the local government.

Personal Relationships. Member should disclose any personal relationship to the governing body in any instance where there could be the appearance of a conflict of interest. For example, if the manager's spouse works for a developer doing business with the local government, that fact should be disclosed.

Confidential Information. Members shall not disclose to others, or use to advance their personal interest, intellectual property, confidential information, or information that is not yet public knowledge, that has been acquired by them in the course of their official duties.

Information that may be in the public domain or accessible by means of an open records request, is not confidential.

Private Employment. Members should not engage in, solicit, negotiate for, or promise to accept private employment, nor should they render services for private interests or conduct a private business when such employment, service, or business creates a conflict with or impairs the proper discharge of their official duties.

Teaching, lecturing, writing, or consulting are typical activities that may not involve conflict of interest, or impair the proper discharge of their official duties. Prior notification of the appointing authority is appropriate in all cases of outside employment.

Representation. Members should not represent any outside interest before any agency, whether public or private, except with the authorization of or at the direction of the appointing authority they serve.

Endorsements. Members should not endorse commercial products or services by agreeing to use their photograph, endorsement, or quotation in paid or other commercial advertisements, marketing materials, social media, or other documents, whether the member is compensated or not for the member's support. Members may, however, provide verbal professional references as part of the due diligence phase of competitive process or in response to a direct inquiry.

Members may agree to endorse the following, provided they do not receive any compensation: (1) books or other publications; (2) professional development or educational services provided by nonprofit membership organizations or recognized educational institutions; (3) products and/or services in which the local government has a direct economic interest.

Members' observations, opinions, and analyses of commercial products used or tested by their local governments are appropriate and useful to the profession when included as part of professional articles and reports.

International Association for Identification
Code of Ethics and Standards of Professional Conduct

The ethical and professionally responsible International Association for Identification (IAI) member or certificant:

Professionalism

1.01   Is unbiased, and objective, approaching all assignments and examinations with due diligence and an open mind.

1.02   Conducts full and fair examinations in which conclusions are based on the evidence and reference material relevant to the evidence, not on extraneous information, political pressure, or other outside influences.

1.03   Is aware of his/her limitations and only renders conclusions that are within his/her area of expertise and about matters for which he/she has given careful consideration.

1.04   Truthfully communicates with all parties (i.e., the investigator, prosecutor, defense, and other expert witnesses) about information related to his/her analyses, when communications are permitted by law and agency practice.

1.05   Maintains confidentiality of restricted information obtained in the course of professional endeavors.

1.06   Reports to appropriate officials any conflicts between his/her ethical/professional responsibilities and applicable agency policy, law, regulation, or other legal authority.

1.07   Does not accept or participate in any case in which he/she has any personal interest or the appearance of such an interest and shall not be compensated based upon the results of the proceeding.

1.08   Conducts oneself personally and professionally within the laws of his/her respective jurisdiction and in a manner that does not violate public trust.

1.09   Reports to the appropriate legal or administrative authorities unethical, illegal, or scientifically questionable conduct of other practitioners of which he/she has knowledge.

1.10   Does not knowingly make, promote, or tolerate false accusations of a professional or criminal nature.

1.11   Supports sound scientific techniques and practices and does not use his/her position to pressure a practitioner to arrive at conclusions or results that are not supported by reliable scientific data.

Competency and Proficiency

2.01   Is committed to career-long learning in the forensic disciplines in which he/she practices, and stays abreast of new technology and techniques while guarding against the misuse of methods that have not been validated.

2.02   Expresses conclusions and opinions that are based on generally accepted protocols and procedures. New and novel techniques must be validated prior to implementation in case work.

2.03   Is properly trained and determined to be competent through relevant testing prior to undertaking the examination of the evidence.

2.04   Gives utmost care to the treatment of any samples or items of potential evidentiary value to avoid tampering, adulteration, loss or unnecessary consumption.

2.05   Uses controls and standards, including reviews and verifications appropriate to his/her discipline, when conducting examinations and analyses.

Clear Communications

3.01   Accurately represents his/her education, training, experience, and area of expertise.

3.02   Presents accurate and complete data in reports, testimony, publications and oral presentations.

3.03   Makes and retains full, contemporaneous, clear and accurate records of all examinations and tests conducted, and conclusions drawn, in sufficient detail to allow meaningful review and assessment of the conclusions by an independent person competent in the field.

3.04   Does not falsify or alter reports or other records, or withhold relevant information from reports for strategic or tactical litigation advantage.

3.05   Testifies to results obtained and conclusions reached only when he/she has confidence that the opinions are based on good scientific principles and methods. Opinions are to be stated so as to be clear in their meaning.

3.06   Attempts to qualify his/her responses while testifying when asked a question with the requirement that a simple "yes" or "no" answer be given, if answering "yes" or "no" would be misleading to the judge or the jury.

The ethical and professionally responsible International Association for Identification (IAI) member:

Organizational Responsibility

4.01   Does not misrepresent his/her affiliation with the IAI.

4.02   Does not issue any misleading or inaccurate statement that gives the appearance of representing the official position of the IAI.

4.03   Reports violations of this code of which he/she knows to the President of the IAI.

4.04   Cooperate fully with any official investigation by the IAI.

Law Enforcement Code of Ethics

As a law enforcement officer, my fundamental duty is to serve the community; to safeguard lives and property; to protect the innocent against deception, the weak against oppression or intimidation and the peaceful against violence or disorder; and to respect the constitutional rights of all to liberty, equality and justice.

I will keep my private life unsullied as an example to all and will behave in a manner that does not bring discredit to me or to my agency. I will maintain courageous calm in the face of danger, scorn or ridicule; develop self-restraint; and be constantly mindful of the welfare of others. Honest in thought and deed both in my personal and official life, I will be exemplary in obeying the law and the regulations of my department. Whatever I see or hear of a confidential nature or that is confided to me in my official capacity will be kept ever secret unless revelation is necessary in the performance of my duty.

I will never act officiously or permit personal feelings, prejudices, political beliefs, aspirations, animosities or friendships to influence my decisions. With no compromise for crime and with relentless prosecution of criminals, I will enforce the law courteously and appropriately without fear or favor, malice or ill will, never employing unnecessary force or violence and never accepting gratuities.

I recognize the badge of my office as a symbol of public faith, and I accept it as a public trust to be held so long as I am true to the ethics of police service. I will never engage in acts of corruption or bribery, nor will I condone such acts by other police officers. I will cooperate with all legally authorized agencies and their representatives in the pursuit of justice.

I know that I alone am responsible for my own standard of professional performance and will take every reasonable opportunity to enhance and improve my level of knowledge and competence.

I will constantly strive to achieve these objectives and ideals, dedicating myself before God to my chosen profession... law enforcement.

Law Enforcement Code of Ethics
(http://www.theiacp.org/codeofethics)

The IACP adopted the Law Enforcement Code of Ethics at the 64th Annual IACP Conference and Exposition in October 1957. The Code of Ethics stands as a preface to the mission and commitment law enforcement agencies make to the public they serve.

Appendix C

National Code of Professional Responsibility for Forensic Science and Forensic Medicine Service Professionals

NATIONAL COMMISSION ON FORENSIC SCIENCE

National Institute of
Standards and Technology
U.S. Department of Commerce

Recommendation to the Attorney General
National Code of Professional Responsibility for Forensic
Science and Forensic Medicine Service Providers

Subcommittee		Date of Current Version	22/03/16
Interim Solutions		Approved by Subcommittee	29/02/16
Status		Approved by Commission	22/03/16
Adopted by the Commission		Action by Attorney General	[dd/mm/yy]

Commission Action
On March 22, 2016, the Commission voted to adopt this Recommendation by a more than two-thirds majority affirmative vote (77% yes, 20% no, 3% abstain)

Overview
The US Attorney General should require the forensic science service providers within the Department of Justice to adopt the National Code of Professional Responsibility for Forensic Science and Forensic Medicine Service Providers[1], that the Code be annually reviewed and signed by all forensic science service providers, and that steps be defined to address violations.

The US Attorney General should strongly urge <u>all</u> forensic science and forensic medicine service providers, associated certification and accreditation bodies, and professional societies to adopt the National Code of Professional Responsibility for Forensic Science and Forensic Medicine Service Providers, and for their management systems to develop policies and procedures to enforce the standards embodied in this code.

Statement of Issue
The 2009 National Research Council of the National Academies report entitled *Strengthening Forensic Science in the United States: A Path Forward* ("NAS Report") recommended a national code of ethics for all forensic science disciplines and encouraged professional forensic science societies to incorporate the national code into their own codes of professional responsibility and code of ethics. The NAS Report also recommended exploring mechanisms to enforce serious ethical violations.

---

[1] A forensic science service provider is defined by the NCFS as any forensic science agency or forensic science practitioner providing forensic science services. A forensic medicine service provider is any forensic medicine agency or forensic medicine practitioner providing forensic medicine services.

In 2010, the Education, Ethics, and Terminology Inter-Agency Working Group (EETIWG) of the National Science and Technology Council's Subcommittee on Forensic Science developed a National Code of Ethics and Professional Responsibility for the Forensic Sciences (NCEPRFS). Further, the EETIWG recommended that all practitioners "who provide reports and expert opinion testimony with respect to forensic evidence in United States courts of law, adopt the NCEPRFS." Unfortunately, this recommendation was not acted upon and no NCEPRFS exists today.

Background

The EETIWG reviewed codes of ethics in use by forensic science organizations. While it noted the lack of a single code of ethics that covered all forensic disciplines, the working group identified four major categories addressed by every code of ethics it reviewed: 1) working within professional competence, 2) providing clear and objective testimony, 3) avoiding conflicts of interest, and 4) avoiding bias and influence, real or perceived.

The EETIWG found that the most broadly applicable code of ethics that would best serve as the NCEPRFS was the *ASCLD/LAB Guiding Principles of Professional Responsibility for Crime Laboratories and Forensic Scientists*. The working group found that the principles in this document were appropriate to the work conducted in the federal forensic laboratories, and ultimately proposed that the ASCLD/LAB document be adopted as the NCEPRFS. The Interim Solutions Subcommittee of the National Commission on Forensic Sciences utilized this code as its starting point for a National Code of Professional Responsibility ("Code") for all forensic science and forensic medicine service providers. The subcommittee chose professional responsibility rather than ethics as the title because ethics is a much broader term referring to many issues beyond those directly associated with forensic science and forensic medicine service providers' professional responsibilities.

Perhaps the key element lacking from the proposed NCEPRFS was the acknowledgement and address of serious violations of professional conduct, as recommended in the NAS Report. Oversight and enforcement are critical to compliance.

Most practitioners in forensic science and forensic medicine are committed, hard-working, ethical professionals; however, education and guidance on professional responsibility is uneven and there is no enforceable universal code of professional responsibility. In addition, when nonconformities or breaches of law or professional standards that adversely affects a previously issued report or testimony occur, there must be a process in place for reporting and remediation.

THE CODE

The National Code of Professional Responsibility for Forensic Science and Forensic Medicine Service Providers

The National Code of Professional Responsibility ("Code") defines a framework for promoting integrity and respect for the scientific process among forensic science and forensic medicine service providers, both practitioners and agencies, including its managers, must meet requirements 1-15 enumerated below. Requirement 16 specifically refers to the responsibility of forensic science and forensic medicine management rather than individual practitioners.

1. Accurately represent relevant education, training, experience, and areas of expertise

2. Be honest and truthful in all professional affairs including not representing the work of others as one's own

3. Foster and pursue professional competency through such activities as training, proficiency testing, certification, and presentation and publication of research findings

4. Commit to continuous learning in relevant forensic disciplines and stay abreast of new findings, equipment, and techniques

5. Utilize scientifically validated methods and new technologies, while guarding against the use of unproven methods in casework and the misapplication of generally-accepted standards

6. Handle evidentiary materials to prevent tampering, adulteration, loss, or nonessential consumption of evidentiary materials

7. Participation in any case in which there is a conflict of interest shall be avoided

8. Conduct independent, impartial, and objective examinations that are fair, unbiased, and fit-for-purpose

9. Make and retain contemporaneous, clear, complete, and accurate records of all examinations, tests, measurements, and conclusions, in sufficient detail to allow meaningful review and assessment by an independent professional proficient in the discipline

10. Ensure interpretations, opinions, and conclusions are supported by sufficient data and minimize influences and biases for or against any party

11. Render interpretations, opinions, or conclusions only when within the practitioner's proficiency or expertise

12. Prepare reports and testify using clear and straightforward terminology, clearly distinguishing data from interpretations, opinions, and conclusions and disclosing known limitations that are necessary to understand the significance of the findings

13. Reports and other records shall not be altered and information shall not be withheld for strategic or tactical advantage

14. Document and, if appropriate, inform management or quality assurance personnel of nonconformities[2] and breaches of law or professional standards

---

[2] Nonconformities are any aspect of laboratory work that does not conform to its established procedures. An evaluation of the nonconformity risk is appropriate to deciding whether or not reporting is necessary.

15. Once a report is issued and the adjudicative process has commenced, communicate fully when requested with the parties through their investigators, attorneys, and experts, except when instructed that a legal privilege, protective order or law prevents disclosure.

16. Appropriately inform affected recipients (either directly or through proper management channels) of all nonconformities or breaches of law or professional standards that adversely affect a previously issued report or testimony and make reasonable efforts to inform all relevant stakeholders, including affected professional and legal parties, victim(s) and defendant(s).

Recommendations

The National Commission on Forensic Science recommends that the Attorney General take the following action(s):

- **Recommendation #1: The Attorney General should require all DOJ forensic science service providers to adopt the Code and for their management systems to develop policies and procedures to enforce the standards embodied in this code.**

Policies and procedures should describe or define a system where by individuals are protected when reporting suspicious, unscrupulous, unethical, or criminal actions without punitive concerns. The Code must be annually reviewed and signed by all DOJ forensic science service providers. In addition, there must be an effective process to report and correct nonconformities or breaches of law or professional standards that adversely affects a previously issued report or testimony.

- **Recommendation #2: The Attorney General should strongly urge all forensic science and medicine service providers, associated certification and accreditation bodies, and professional societies to adopt the Code, and for their management systems to develop policies and procedures to enforce the standards embodied in this code.**

Policies and procedures should describe or define a system where by individuals are protected when reporting suspicious, unscrupulous, unethical, or criminal actions without punitive concerns. The Code should be annually reviewed and signed by all forensic science and forensic medicine service providers. In addition, there should be an effective process to report and correct nonconformities or breaches of law or professional standards that adversely affects a previously issued report or testimony.

Appendix D

Office of Government Ethics Standards of Ethical Conduct

This booklet contains summaries of the
Standards of Ethical Conduct for Employees
of the Executive Branch, 5 C.F.R. Part 2635.
These summaries are not a substitute for actual
ethics advice. You should consult your agency
ethics official for specific **guidance about** the
application of these rules to your situation.

USE OF GOVERNMENT
POSITION AND RESOURCES

In order to ensure that your public office is not used for private gain, there are restrictions on your use of the authority associated with your Government position:

- **Inducement or coercion of benefits.** You may not use your Government position to induce or coerce anyone to provide a benefit to you or to another.

- **Endorsement.** You may not use your Government position to suggest that your agency or any part of the executive branch endorses organizations (including nonprofits), products, services, or people.

- **Use of title or agency's name.** Except in limited circumstances (see box), you may not use your Government title or agency's name to suggest that the agency or any part of the executive branch endorses your personal activities or the activities of another.

Likewise, there are also restrictions on the use of resources you have access to while performing your Government duties:

- **Use of Government information.** You may not use or allow the use of nonpublic Government information to further your own private interests or the private interests of others. If information has not been made known to the public and is not authorized to be made known upon request, then it is nonpublic information and cannot be disclosed.

- **Use of Government property.** You have a duty to protect and conserve Government property and may not use Government property, or allow its use, for purposes that aren't authorized.

- **Use of official time.** Except as otherwise authorized, you must use official time in an honest effort to perform your Government duties. Additionally, you may not ask or direct subordinates to perform activities other than those required in the performance of their Government duties.

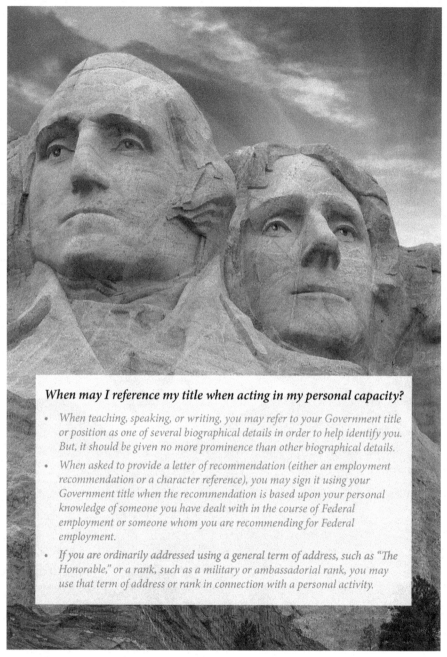

When may I reference my title when acting in my personal capacity?

- When teaching, speaking, or writing, you may refer to your Government title or position as one of several biographical details in order to help identify you. But, it should be given no more prominence than other biographical details.

- When asked to provide a letter of recommendation (either an employment recommendation or a character reference), you may sign it using your Government title when the recommendation is based upon your personal knowledge of someone you have dealt with in the course of Federal employment or someone whom you are recommending for Federal employment.

- If you are ordinarily addressed using a general term of address, such as "The Honorable," or a rank, such as a military or ambassadorial rank, you may use that term of address or rank in connection with a personal activity.

ETHICAL CONDUCT · 7 · STANDARDS

CONFLICTING
FINANCIAL INTEREST

In addition to the Standards of Ethical Conduct, a criminal statute (18 U.S.C. section 208) prohibits you from working on Government matters that will affect your own personal financial interest, or the financial interests of certain other people, including:

- your spouse, minor child, or general partner;

- any organization in which you are serving as an officer, director, trustee, general partner or employee; and

- any person or organization with whom you are negotiating or have an arrangement for future employment.

There are various ways you could experience a conflict of interest between the work you perform and a financial interest you or others hold. Stock ownership is one example. If you or your spouse or minor child owned $30,000 of stock in a company that would be affected by your job duties, you would not be able to perform those duties until certain measures are taken to resolve the conflict. This would be true even if the extent of the gain or loss is small or isn't known.

Keep in mind, however, that conflicts can arise from interests other than stock. For example, if you are on the board of directors of an organization, you could not act on a grant or contract that would benefit that organization.

In some cases, the law recognizes that your financial interest may be so remote or inconsequential that the interest should not prevent you from being involved in a particular assignment. However, your agency may also have additional restrictions that prohibit you from holding certain interests or outside positions.

If you think you might have a conflicting financial interest, you should discuss it with your supervisor or your ethics official. They can provide you with guidance to address the conflict. This might include not working on the Government matter, selling stocks, or resigning from an outside position. Your ethics official will be able to assist you with your particular circumstances.

Examples of conflicting financial interests:

- Rachel's husband works for a contractor that has a contract with her agency. He is eligible to receive a bonus based on the contract's success. She may not participate in the evaluation of that contractor's performance under the contract.

- Carlo is the president of a neighborhood improvement organization that has applied to his agency for a rehab loan. As part of his Government duties, he may not work on the review of the organization's application.

- Helen's husband owns a janitorial service company that does business with the Government. Helen cannot recommend that the agency hire her husband's company nor can she review and comment on a proposal from his company to provide services to her agency.

ETHICAL CONDUCT ⁓ 11 ⁓ STANDARDS

IMPARTIALITY

First, and perhaps most intuitively, your impartiality could be questioned if the Government matter on which you are working is likely to affect the financial interests of a member of your household.

However, your impartiality could also be questioned if you were to work on a Government matter where someone with whom you have a "covered relationship" is involved—they are a party or represent a party to the Government matter.

The rule lists a number of "covered relationships" with people and organizations that could create an improper appearance. These "covered relationships" include:

- a person with whom you have or seek to have a business, contractual, or other financial relationship;

- a person who is a member of your household or a relative with whom you have a close personal relationship;

- a person or organization for whom your spouse, parent, or dependent child serves or seeks to serve as an officer, director, trustee, general partner, agent, attorney, consultant, contractor, or employee;

- any person or organization for whom you have, within the last year, served as an officer, director, trustee, general partner, agent, attorney, consultant, contractor, or employee; and

- any organization, other than a political party, in which you are an active participant.

Finally, there may be circumstances other than those described here that would raise a question regarding your impartiality.

If you have a situation that you think might raise such a concern, then you should immediately talk to an ethics official at your agency. He or she will be able to tell you whether or not there is an appearance problem and give you advice on how to deal with it.

Note: Additional restrictions may apply, if you received from your prior employer an extraordinary payment or other item worth more than $10,000. Such a payment may bar you from participating, for two years, in Government matters in which your former employer is a party or represents a party.

Examples of situations where your impartiality might be questioned:

- If Marvin handled a consumer complaint that was submitted to his agency by his business associate, or by a close friend, his impartiality could be questioned.

- Roy's work on an investigation in which his brother is representing the company under investigation would raise a question about his impartiality.

- Susan should have concerns about reviewing grant applications to her agency if one of the applicants is an organization where her father serves on the board of directors.

SEEKING OTHER
EMPLOYMENT

Before you begin seeking employment, you need to know whether the person or organization that you are thinking about working for could be affected by projects and other matters you work on for the Government. If the project could affect your prospective employer, then you may need to stop working on that project before you make any employment-related contacts.

These rules may apply to you sooner than you think. You are considered to be "seeking employment" (and therefore may **not** work on Government matters affecting the future employer's financial interest) if any of the following occurs:

- you contact a prospective employer about possible employment (unless you are merely requesting a job application),

- a prospective employer contacts you about possible employment and you make a response other than rejection, or

- you are engaged in actual negotiations for employment.

Talk with an ethics official before you look for a job, whether full-time or part-time. He or she can advise you about the rules on seeking employment. Also contact an ethics official immediately if you receive an unsolicited offer or inquiry from a prospective employer who may have a financial interest in matters that cross your desk.

If you are thinking about looking for part-time work, your ethics official can also tell you whether your agency has specific rules that apply to certain kinds of outside employment or that require you to obtain permission before you take a part-time job. The ethics official can also tell you about things you will not be able to do for your new employer.

A note about resumes—there is no "mass mailing" exception to the seeking employment restrictions. However, you are not considered to be seeking employment with anyone if you merely post a resume to your personal social media account.

When am I no longer considered to be "seeking employment?"

- *If you sent an unsolicited resume, and two months have passed without having received any expression of interest, the seeking employment restrictions no longer apply to you with respect to that employer.*

- *If either you or the prospective employer rejects the possibility of employment and all discussions of possible employment have ended.*

- *If you merely defer employment discussions until the foreseeable future, you have not rejected the possibility of employment.*

Example: *An official of a State Health Department compliments Karen on her work and asks her to call if she is ever interested in leaving her agency. Karen replies that she cannot discuss future employment while working on a project that affects the State's health care funding, but would like to once the project is finished. Because she merely deferred the discussion until the foreseeable future, she is "seeking employment."*

OUTSIDE ACTIVITIES

An outside activity could be prohibited by a law or regulation that applies to your agency, or it might present a conflict of interest or raise a question of impartiality in the performance of your duties.

Several laws and regulations restrict specific types of outside activities. These restrictions include:

- a prohibition against receiving compensation for teaching, speaking, or writing related to your Government duties;

- a prohibition on personally representing others (or sharing in compensation for another's representation) before any court, Federal agency, or certain other entities concerning matters of interest to the United States (subject to certain exceptions);

- limitations on fundraising in a personal capacity; and

- a prohibition against serving as an expert witness, other than on behalf of the United States, in certain proceedings in which the United States is a party or has a direct and substantial interest.

Additionally, there are outside income limitations and other special rules that apply to high-ranking noncareer employees and Presidential appointees.

Keep in mind that some agencies have rules that require their employees to obtain prior approval before engaging in specified outside activities. However, even if prior approval is not required, you are strongly encouraged to seek advice from an agency ethics official, particularly if it's possible that the activity could conflict with your Government duties or is otherwise restricted. Your ethics official can provide you with guidance tailored to your specific situation.

Examples of things that may or may not be done as outside activities:

- Victoria **may** work as a part-time salesperson with a clothing store as long as her Government duties do not affect the company that owns the chain of clothing stores.

- Carter's agency has a prior-approval requirement for certain outside activities. Having received approval, Carter serves as a board member for a local nonprofit organization. Carter **may not** work on Government matters that could affect the organization.

- George, who processes Medicare claims, **may not** be paid for teaching a one-day seminar for senior citizens on the Medicare program and how to fill out Medicare claims.

- Val **may not** use her job title or position with a Federal law enforcement agency-nor could she wear her uniform-when she raises funds for her county's police officers' association as an outside activity.

GIFTS
FROM OUTSIDE SOURCES

Generally, anything that has monetary value is considered a gift.

Ask yourself if the gift would have been offered if you were not working for the Government. If the answer is no, then the gift is being offered because of your Government position and, as a general rule, you cannot accept it.

Also, you may not accept a gift from people or organizations who are "prohibited sources"—those who do business with, or seek to do business with your agency, who seek some official action by your agency, or who have activities regulated by your agency. Gifts from these people or groups are prohibited, whether or not you deal with them when doing your job. You must also turn down a gift from those who have interests that may be significantly affected by your Government duties, as they are also considered "prohibited sources."

There are a few exceptions to the prohibition on gifts from outside sources.

- Items valued at $20 or less (other than cash), provided that the total value of gifts from the same person is not more than $50 in a calendar year.

- Gifts motivated solely by a family relationship or personal friendship.

- Gifts based on an employee's or his spouse's outside business or employment relationships.

- Meals, lodging, and transportation customarily provided by a prospective employer as part of bona fide employment discussions.

- Benefits provided in connection with certain political activities.

- Free attendance at certain widely attended gatherings, provided that the agency has determined that attendance is in the interest of the agency.

What about a cup of coffee?

A cup of coffee is alright. It is such a modest refreshment that it is not considered a gift. So you may accept it without worrying about who is giving it or why. Inexpensive food and refreshment items such as donuts or soda may also be accepted. Other items are not considered gifts, such as greeting cards, bank loans at commercial rates, publicly available discounts, certain contest prizes, and things for which you pay fair value.

But remember, the definition of a gift is very broad. If you have a question about a gift, ask your ethics official.

ETHICAL CONDUCT · 27 · STANDARDS

GIFTS BETWEEN EMPLOYEES

Employees are generally prohibited from giving gifts to their official superiors, or from making or soliciting donations for such gifts. An official superior includes your immediate boss and anyone above your boss in the chain of command in your agency. An employee also cannot accept a gift from another employee who earns less pay, unless the person giving the gift is not a subordinate and the gift is based on a personal relationship.

There are several exceptions that would allow you to give your official superior a gift, or that would allow you to accept a gift from another employee who earns less pay. These include:

- gifts valued at $10 or less (other than cash), on an occasion when gifts are traditionally given or exchanged. These occasions could include, for example, the holidays, a birthday, or a return from an out-of-town vacation;

- food, or nominal contributions for food, that will be shared in the office among several employees; and

- personal hospitality. This would include inviting your boss to your home for a meal or party, or conversely, being invited to the home of an employee who earns less pay. If your boss invites you to his or her home, you can take the same type of gift for your boss that you would normally take to anyone else's home for a similar occasion.

You may also give your boss a gift on a special, infrequent occasion of personal significance. Similarly, on these types of occasions, you could accept a gift from another employee who earns less pay. These occasions include:

- marriage;

- illness;

- birth or adoption; or

- occasions that end the employee-superior relationship, such as retirement, resignation, or transfer.

Examples of permissible gifts between employees:

- *Clarissa may participate in the office's holiday "grab bag" gift exchange by buying and contributing a store gift card worth $10.*

- *Ralph may bring his boss a jar of macadamia nuts when he returns from his Hawaiian vacation.*

- *Kailash may collect contributions to purchase a fishing rod and tackle box for his boss when his boss retires. He may suggest a specific but nominal amount, provided that he makes it clear to his coworkers that they are free to contribute less or nothing at all.*

Note: A birthday, even a milestone birthday, is never a "special, infrequent occasion."

For special, infrequent occasions, employees are allowed to ask for contributions of nominal amounts from fellow employees on a strictly voluntary basis for a group gift.

Remember that gift giving is strictly voluntary.

No one may ever pressure you to give a gift or contribute to a group gift.

ETHICAL CONDUCT   · 31 ·   STANDARDS

Appendix E

Office of Government Ethics 14 General Principles for Public Service Conduct

- ETHICS -

GENERAL PRINCIPLES

The following general principles apply to every employee and may form the basis for the standards contained in this part. Where a situation is not covered by the standards set forth in this part, employees shall apply the principles set forth in this section in determining whether their conduct is proper.

1. Public service is a public trust, requiring employees to place loyalty to the Constitution, the laws and ethical principles above private gain.

2. Employees shall not hold financial interests that conflict with the conscientious performance of duty.

3. Employees shall not engage in financial transactions using nonpublic Government information or allow the improper use of such information to further any private interest.

4. An employee shall not, except as permitted by subpart B of this part, solicit or accept any gift or other item of monetary value from any person or entity seeking official action from, doing business with, or conducting activities regulated by the employee's agency, or whose interests may be substantially affected by the performance or nonperformance of the employee's duties.

5. Employees shall put forth honest effort in the performance of their duties.

6. Employees shall not knowingly make unauthorized commitments or promises of any kind purporting to bind the Government.

7. Employees shall not use public office for private gain.

8. Employees shall act impartially and not give preferential treatment to any private organization or individual.

9. Employees shall protect and conserve Federal property and shall not use it for other than authorized activities.

10. Employees shall not engage in outside employment or activities, including seeking or negotiating for employment, that conflict with official Government duties and responsibilities.

11. Employees shall disclose waste, fraud, abuse, and corruption to appropriate authorities.

12. Employees shall satisfy in good faith their obligations as citizens, including all just financial obligations, especially those—such as Federal, State, or local taxes—that are imposed by law.

13. Employees shall adhere to all laws and regulations that provide equal opportunity for all Americans regardless of race, color, religion, sex, national origin, age, or handicap.

14. Employees shall endeavor to avoid any actions creating the appearance that they are violating the law or the ethical standards set forth in this part. Whether particular circumstances create an appearance that the law or these standards have been violated shall be determined from the perspective of a reasonable person with knowledge of the relevant facts.

Appendix F

Useful Links Pertaining to Public Service Ethics

Ethics in Government

United States Office of Government Ethics: http://www.usoge.gov
/home.html
Center for Ethics in Government: http://www.ncsl.org/Ethics/
Center for Campaign Leadership: http://campaigns.berkeley.edu/
House Committee on Standards of Official Conduct: http://www.house
.gov/ethics
City Ethics: http://www.cityethics.org/
Center for Public Integrity: http://www.publicintegrity.org
Council on Governmental Ethics Laws: http://www.cogel.org/
Senate Select Committee on Ethics: http://ethics.senate.gov

Ethics in Law

American Bar Association: http://www.abanet.org
State Ethics Links (legal): http://www.hricik.com/StateEthics.html
Code of Conduct for United States Judges: http://www.uscourts.gov
/guide/vol2/ch1.html
Code of Conduct for Judicial Employees: http://www.uscourts.gov
/guide/vol2/ch2.html

Ethics Research and Education

Josephson Institute for Business Ethics: http://josephsoninstitute.org
/business/resources/links.html
Center for the Study of Ethics in the Professions: http://www.iit.edu
/departments/csep/
International Institute for Public Ethics: http://www.iipe.org/
Harvard University Center for Ethics and the Professions: http://ethics
.harvard.edu/
Institute for Global Ethics: http://www.globalethics.org
Association for Practical and Professional Ethics: http://www.indiana
.edu/~appe/

Center for Applied Ethics: http://www.ethics.ubc.ca/
Ethics Resource Center: http://www.ethics.org/

Ethics in Law Enforcement

International Association of Chiefs of Police: http://www.theiacp.org/
Ethics in Policing: http://www.ethicsinpolicing.com/

Ethics in Forensic Science

American Academy of Forensic Sciences: http://www.aafs.org
American Board of Criminalists: www.abc.org
International Association of Identification: http://theiai.org

Glossary

Absolutists: Grounded in the belief that the best outcome to any situation can be obtained by following absolute universal moral principles.

Altruism: Unselfish concern for the welfare of others.

Argument: Any number of sentences that claim to prove one another.

Authority: The power to determine or otherwise settle issues or disputes; the right to control, command, or determine something or someone.

Bad argument: Exists when a premise is false, a premise is irrelevant to the conclusion, or a premise simply restates the conclusion.

Blue wall: An unauthorized and unwritten rule where officers do not give negative information about any other officers to anyone.

Canons: The principles or rules listed in the "Model Code of Judicial Conduct."

Categorical imperative: The theory of eighteenth-century philosopher Immanuel Kant that individuals have certain obligations regardless of the consequences they evoke.

Code of ethics: An assembly of institutional guidelines used to reduce ethical vagueness within an organization and serve as a means of reinforcing ethical conduct.

Code of silence: An unauthorized and unwritten rule where officers do not give negative information about any other officers to anyone.

Conclusion: Sentence that an argument claims to prove.

Conflict of interest: This exists when an individual tasked with a decision can be influenced by a relationship with another person or group or has a special interest that can affect the decision maker's judgment.

Credentials: A term generally referring to a certificate, letter, experience, or the like, to authenticate the quality of someone or something.

CSI effect: A general acceptance by society that television drama is exactly how cases can be handled by law enforcement, regardless of reality, including limitations in technology.

Culturalization: The informal method of education whereby learned values and ethics-based decision-making skills are based on personal experiences.

Descriptive ethics: The study of an individual's beliefs relating to morality.

Determinism: The premise that all occurrences, thoughts, and actions are beyond the control of an individual.

Deterrence: A punishment viewpoint that focuses on future outcomes rather than past misconduct.

Discretionary authority: The power to decide whether or not to exercise influence is a given situation.

Drylabbing: The reporting of results based on forensic analysis when no test or analysis was ever performed.

Economic corruption: Refers to the gain of some type of economic benefit received when one does not enforce the law.

Effectiveness model: One of the three domains that public officials use in decision making as outlined by Patrick Dobel; this domain incorporates the concept of prudence and effectiveness.

Empathy: As described in the text, it is the ability to understand or feel a person's viewpoint.

Esprit de corps: A sense of common purpose with respect to a group.

Ethical culture: A movement started by Felix Adler in 1876, based on the premise that living with and honoring ethical principles is at the heart of what it takes to live a fulfilling and meaningful life, while helping to create a good and positive world for all individuals.

Ethical dilemma: A situation in which one is faced with choosing between competing virtues that are considered equally important, but which cannot be simultaneously honored.

Ethics: The study of moral standards and how they affect conduct.

Ethics triangle: The process of considering the three different approaches of principle, consequence, and virtue to ethical reasoning.

Exceptionists: Follows the same theory as an absolutist by believing that the best outcome to any situation can be obtained by following absolute universal moral principles; however, they acknowledge that certain situations may require a deviation or exception to those ideals.

Existentialism: Refers to an individual's freedom to make decisions free of influence from others.

Expert witness: Someone who is called upon to answer questions within a court of law in order to provide specialized information relative to a case.

Fair: Being free from dishonesty or injustice and being consistent with regard to dispensing discipline or justice.

Federal Rules of Evidence, (FRE) 702: A legal check on experts who are expected to be rendering opinion in a trial.

Fiduciary relationship: A relation between two or more persons, a person in authority and a person or persons to whom the authority is directed.

Forensic science: The application of science to civil and criminal law.

Fruit of the poisonous tree doctrine: A legal metaphor used to describe evidence that is obtained illegally, the terminology suggests that anything connected to illegal evidence is not admissible in court.

Frye test/rule: A rule established through a Supreme Court decision in Frye v. United States in 1923 that directly affected the admissibility of evidence for 70 years, determining that scientific evidence must be generally accepted by the relevant scientific community in order to be admitted into court.

General codes: These codes provide minimal guidance in specific circumstances.

Good argument: Exists if the premises are true, the premises are relevant to the conclusion, and no premise simply restates the conclusion.

Good faith doctrine: Refers to the exception that evidence obtained in violation of a person's rights will not be excluded from trial if the law enforcement officer, though mistaken, acted reasonably.

Government transparency: The release of information that is relevant for evaluating institutions.

Hearsay: Unfounded information or opinions.

Idealism: A principle anchored in the belief that a desirable outcome is always obtained by using the right or correct action.

Impartial: Being free from bias and having the ability to be fair.

Integrity: Behavior that is above question.

Intentionalism: A term given to the premise that individuals have free will and are accountable for their actions and the results of their decisions.

Invalid: Refers to a bad argument where even if the premises were true, they do not demonstrate the truth or probability of the conclusion.

Just desserts: A term that reflects the retribution viewpoint and provides a justifiable rationale for support of the death penalty, it is rooted in the belief of society's need for vengeance.

Leadership: As defined by Richard Brookhiser, is knowing yourself, knowing where you want to go, and then taking others to that new place.

Legal institutional model: Is designed to limit discretion in public office by making sure that a public official's decisions are capable of being traced back to either clear lines of authority or clearly defined mandates.

Meta-ethics: The fundamental nature of ethics, including whether or not such ethics have an objective justification. This is how individuals determine for themselves what societal norms to follow.

Morale: The mental and emotional condition of an individual or group with regard to the function or tasks at hand.

Morals: A set of rules defining what is considered to be right or wrong as accepted by a group or society.

Noble cause corruption: The act of officers justifying doing what it takes to get criminals off of the street, even if that means breaking the law.

Normative ethics values: The universally shared standards used to determine the rightness or wrongness of a person's actions.

Perjury: Telling a lie within a court of law by somebody who has taken an oath to tell the truth.

Personal codes: Based on personal ethics, they assist in the development and implementation of more formalized organizational codes of ethics.

Personal responsibility model: One of the three domains that public officials use in decision making as outlined by Patrick Dobel; this domain is founded on the premise that an individual's commitments, abilities, and character are what form the heart of their integrity.

Premises: Any sentence that an argument offers as proof or evidence of the conclusion.

Relativism: A principle anchored in the belief that everything is relative to a given circumstance and, therefore, undesirable outcomes will be a fact of life.

Retribution: An ideology that the criminal is an enemy of society and deserves severe punishment for willfully breaking its rules.

Sanctions: Jeremy Bentham's belief that man and society co-exist on physical, political, moral, and religious motivators.

Scientific determinism: An individual's actions, character, and decisions as results associated with genetics or one's surroundings.

Scope of authority: Refers to authority over only a certain group of persons or matters, and this authority does not translate to other persons or matters.

Situationists: Individuals who believe that everything is relative and tend to reject any type of universal moral rule or code.

Social contract theory: The authority of the state to provide protection and to punish offenders.

Socialization: A practice whereby individuals acquire ethical knowledge and principles through training and experiential education.

Sound: Refers to an argument where all stated premises are true.

Specific codes: These codes help to establish guidelines and define a profession or organization for the first time.

Subjectivist: Follows the same theory as a situationist by believing that everything is relative; however, they subject each event to a personal assessment based solely upon his or her own moral principles.

Trier of fact: Refers to a judge or jury.

Unsound: Refers to an argument where at least one stated premise is false.

Utilitarianism: The philosophical belief of actions that produce the greatest good for the greatest number of persons are "good" actions. The principle that human beings judge morality of actions in terms of the consequences or results of those actions.

Whistle-blower: A person who informs on another or makes public disclosure of corruption or wrongdoing.

References

Alexander, M. http://www.goodreads.com/quotes/tag/incarceration (accessed June 12, 2017).

Ambika, G. 2015. Ed Lorenz: Father of the 'Butterfly effect.' *Resonance*, 20 (3), 198–205. doi:10.1007/s12045-015-0170-y

American Academy of Forensic Sciences. www.aafs.org (accessed January 23, 2017).

American Board of Criminalists. 2017. Code of Ethics, www.abc.org (accessed January 23, 2017).

Apple, R. W. Jr. 1993. Note left by White House aide: Accusation, despair and anger. *New York Times*, August 11.

Ariel, B., W. A. Farrar, and A. Sutherland. 2015. The effect of police body-worn cameras on use of force and citizens' complaints against the police: A randomized controlled trial. *Journal of Quantitative Criminology*, 31 (3), 509–535. doi:10.1007/s10940-014-9236-3

Barker, T. 1996. *Police ethics crisis in law enforcement.* Springfield, IL: Charles C. Thomas.

Barnett, P. D. 2001. *Ethics in forensic science: Professional standards for the practice of criminalistics.* Boca Raton, FL: CRC Press.

Bauhr, M., and M. Grimes. 2012. What is Government Transparency? New Measures and Relevance for Quality of Government, *2012:16 QOG The Quality of Government Institute. ISSN 1653-8919.*

Bauhr, M., and N. Nasiritousi. 2012. Linköpings universitet, Institutionen för tema, Tema vatten i natur och samhälle, Centrum för klimatpolitisk forskning, & Filosofiska fakulteten. Resisting transparency: Corruption, legitimacy, and the quality of global environmental policies. *Global Environmental Politics,* 12 (4), 9–29. doi:10.1162/GLEP_a_00137

Bayley, B. 2009. Improving ethics training for the 21st century. From www.policeone.com (accessed February 12, 2010).

Beccaria, C. 1774. *Essay on crimes and punishment.* Trans. by Henry Paolucci. New York: Bobbs–Merrill, 1963.

Bennis, W., and J. Goldsmith. 1997. *Learning to lead.* Boston: Addison Wesley.

Bentham, J. 1789. *An introduction to the principles of morals and legislation.* Chap. 1. London: B. Hensley.

Berger, W., and C. Peed. 2010. Introduction to ethics toolkit. *International Association of Chiefs of Police global leadership in policing.* Advance online publication: www.theiacp.org (accessed July 28, 2010).

Bowen, R. T. 2010. *Ethics and the practice of forensic science.* Boca Raton, FL: Taylor & Francis Group.

Brooker, P. 2003. *A glossary of cultural theory,* 2nd ed. London: Arnold.

Brookhiser, R. 2008. *George Washington on leadership.* New York: Basic Books.

Calvert, S. Philadelphia district attorney indicted on federal corruption charges; R. Seth Williams accused of doling out favors in exchange for bribes. *Wall*

Street Journal (Online) https://search.proquest.com/docview/1879382429?account id=35812 (accessed March 21, 2017).

Capitol hill: IRS scandal update: 'Smoking-gun proof' of harassment. 2015. Chatham: Newstex. Retrieved from https://search.proquest.com/docview/1699708299 ?accountid=35812.

Christopher, W. 1991. *Report of the independent commission on the Los Angeles Police Department.* Los Angeles.

Ciulla, J. B., ed. 2004. *Ethics, the heart of leadership,* 2nd ed. Westport, CT: Praeger.

Colson, C. W. 2000. The problem of ethics. *Christian Ethics Today: Journal of Christian Ethics,* 031, 6 (6). http://www.christianethicstoday.com/Issue/031/The%20 Problem%20of%20Ethics%20By%20Charles%20W%20Colson_031_6_.htm (accessed March 21, 2017).

Considering Police Body Cameras. 2015. *Harvard Law Review,* 128 (6), 1794–1817.

Cooper, M. 2017. Springfield police, fire struggling to recruit, retain employees. *TCA Regional News.*

Correctional officer and two others plead guilty to racketeering conspiracy at eastern correctional institution. 2016. Lanham: Federal Information & News Dispatch, Inc.

Cortrite, M. D. 2007. Servant leadership for law enforcement. PhD diss. Los Angeles: University of California.

Crank, J. P., and M. A. Caldero. 2000. *Police ethics: The corruption of noble cause.* Cincinnati, OH: Anderson Publishing Co.

Daubert v. Merrell Dow Pharmaceuticals, 509 U.S. 579 (1993).

Dimitrov, D. 2006. Cultural differences in motivation for organizational learning and training. *International Journal of Diversity in Organisations, Communities & Nations,* 5 (4), 37–48.

Dobel, J. P. 1999. *Public integrity.* Baltimore, MD: The Johns Hopkins University Press.

Dreisbach, C. 2009. *Ethics in criminal justice.* New York: McGraw-Hill.

Drug Reform Coordination Network. 2000. *A barrel full of bad apples: Police corruption and the war on drugs.* From http://stopthedrugwar.org (accessed July 25, 2010).

Dutelle, A. W. 2017. *An introduction to crime scene investigation,* 3rd ed. Burlington, MA: Jones and Bartlett Learning.

Exclusionary Rule and the Fruit of the Poisonous Tree... (n.d.). Retrieved June 25, 2017 from Legal-dictionary.threfreedictionary.com/The+Exclusionary+Rule+and +the+Poisonous+Tree=Doctrine

Final Report of The President's Task Force on 21st Century Policing (2015, May). Retrieved from http://files.policemag.com/documents/21stcpolicingtaskforce -finalreport.pdf.

Fish, J. T., L. S. Miller, and M. C. Braswell. 2007. *Crime scene investigation.* Newark, NJ: LexisNexis Group.

Fish, J. T., L. S. Miller, and M. C. Braswell. 2014. *Crime scene investigation,* 3rd ed. Newark, NJ: LexisNexis Group.

Fisher, B. A. J. 2000. *Techniques of crime scene investigation,* 6th ed. Boca Raton, FL: CRC Press.

Former polk correctional officer sentenced for corruption. 2016. Lanham: Federal Information & News Dispatch, Inc. Retrieved from https://search.proquest .com/docview/1783946610?accountid=458.

Foster, G. D. 2003. Ethics: Time to revisit the basics. In *The ethics edge,* 2nd ed., eds. J. P. West, and E. M. Berman. Washington, D.C.: International City/County

Management Association. (Originally published in *The Humanist*, March–April 63(2).)

Friedman, C. A. 2005. *Spiritual survival for law enforcement*. Linden, NJ: Compass.

Frye v. U.S., 293 F. 1013 (D.C. Cir. 1923).

Garrett, B. L., and P. J. Neufeld. 2009. Invalid forensic science testimony and wrongful convictions. *Virginia Law Review*, 95(1). www.virginialawreview.org (accessed June 5, 2017).

Garrison, D. 2004. Precision without accuracy in the cruel world of crime scene work. *Midwestern Association of Forensic Sciences Newsletter*. April.

Goodman, D. 2010. Detroit mayor: Ousted chief 'blindsided' him. *Officer.com*. From http://www.officer.com (accessed July 23, 2010).

Heinzmann, D. (2009, October). Police misconduct allegations up almost 19%. *Chicago Tribune*. From http://articles.chicagotribune.com (accessed July 25, 2010).

Hersh, S. E. 1970. *My Lai 4: A report on the massacre and its aftermath*. New York: Random House.

Higham, S., and J. Stephens. 2004. New details of prison abuse emerge. *The Washington Post*, May 21, p. A01, www.washingtonpost.com.

Hobbes, T. 1985. *Leviathan*. ed. C. B. Macpherson. London: Penguin Books. (Original work published in 1691.)

Holeman, B., and J. Ziedenberg. n.d. *The Dangers of Detention: The Impact of Incarcerating Youth in Detention and Other Secure Facilities*, A Justice Policy Institute Report.

http://files.policemag.com/documents/21stcpolicingtaskforce-finalreport.pdf (accessed June 15, 2017).

http://www.coloradoforethics.org/about (accessed July 14, 2010).

http://www.concordmonitor.com/print/208122 (accessed July 14, 2010).

http://www.gallup.com/poll/1654/Honesty-Ethics-Professions.aspx (accessed August 29, 2010).

http://www.jswvearchives.com/ (accessed October 11, 2017).

http://www.nbcnews.com/storyline/president-trumps-first-100-days/100-days -trump-police-n752281 (accessed May 3, 2017).

http://www.ppic.org/main/publication_show.asp?i=1036 (accessed April 12, 2017).

http://www.usoge.gov/ (accessed October 12, 2017).

ICMA 2017. International City/County Management Association. http://icma.org/en /icma/about/organization_overview (accessed May 22, 2017).

Johannesen, R., K. Valde, and K. Whedbee. 2008. *Ethics in human communication*, 6th ed. Long Grove, IL: Waveland Press, Inc.

Johnson, C. 2005. *Meeting the ethical challenges of leadership*, 2nd ed. Thousand Oaks, CA: Sage.

Johnson, V. 1974. *Crime correction, and society*. Homewood, IL: Dorsey Press.

Jones, A. R., and G. R. Fay. 2004. AR 15-6 investigation of the Abu Ghraib Prison and 205th Military Intelligence Brigade. Department of Defense Report, August 23, Washington, DC.

Justnews.com. 2010. *Ex Fla. trooper pleads no contest in fake tickets case*. From http://www.officer.com (accessed July 23, 2010).

Kambic, R., and P. Press. (2015, February 19). Mundelein police eye body cameras. *Chicago Tribune*. Retrieved from https://search.proquest.com/docview/165597 1921?accountid=35812.

Kant, I. 1785. *Groundwork on the metaphysics of morals.* (Trans. in 1964 by H. J. Paton. New York: Harper & Row.)

Kant, I. 1964. *The metaphysical principles of virtue: Part II of The metaphysics of morals.* University of Michigan: Bobbs-Merrill Co.

Kardasz, F. 2008. *Ethics training for law enforcement: Practices and trends.* Saarbrücken, Germany: VDM Verlag.

Kathleen Kane – Former Pennsylvania Attorney General Sentenced to Prison. 2016. https://www.nytimes.com/2016/10/25/us/kathleen-kane-former-pennsylvania -attorney-general-is-sentenced-to-prison.html?_r=0 (accessed June, 25, 2017).

Kauffman, K. 1988. *Prison officers and their world.* Cambridge, MA: Harvard University Press.

Kem, J. D. 2006. Ethical decision making: Using the "ethical triangle" in military ethical decision making. *Public Administration and Management,* 11.1 (2006), 22.

Kern, P., A. R. Jones, and G. R. Fay. 2004. Defense Department Briefing on Results of Investigation of Military Intelligence Activities at Abu Ghraib Prison Facility, Wednesday, August 25, Washington, DC.

Kidder, R. M. 1995. *How good people make tough choices.* New York: William Morrow and Company, Inc.

Kirk, P. L. 1953. *Crime investigation: Physical evidence and the police laboratory.* New York: Interscience.

Kleiser, G. 2003. *Training for power and leadership.* Kessinger Pub Co.

Klockars, C. B., S. K. Ivkovich, W. E. Harver, and M. R. Haberfeld. 2000. *The measurement of police integrity.* Washington, D.C.: National Institute of Justice.

Lander, E. S. 1989. DNA fingerprinting on trial. *Nature* 339 (501), 505.

Legal Information Institute. 2009. *Federal Rules of Evidence.* Ithaca, NY: Cornell Law School. From www.law.cornell.edu/rules/fre/rules.htm (accessed June 6, 2017).

Lowenkamp, C. T., E. J. Latessa, and A. M. Holsinger. 2006. The risk principle in action: What have we learned from 13,676 offenders and 97 correctional programs? *Crime & Delinquency,* 52 (1), 77–93. doi:10.1177/0011128705281747

Maher, T. 2008. Police chiefs' views on police sexual misconduct. *Police Practice & Research,* 9 (3), 239–250.

Marche, G. E. 2009. Integrity, culture, and scale: An empirical test of the big bad police agency. *Crime, Law and Social Change,* 51 (5), 463.

McMahon, T. 2017. *Deputy Cited for Passing School Bus, Fired for Ethics Violation.* Retrieved June 15, 2017 from http://www.schoolbusfleet.com/news/720015 /deputy-cited-for-passing-stopped-school-bus-fired-for-ethics-violation.

Mill, J. S. 1861. *Utilitarianism. Fraser's Magazine.* Reprinted in book form in 1963, London: Parker, Son, and Bourn. From http://www.utilitarianism.com/mill1 .htm (accessed May 20, 2017).

Mill, J. S. 1869. *On Liberty.* London: Longman, Roberts, and Green; New York: Bartleby.com, 1999. www.bartleby.com/130/.

Miller, S., J. Blackler, and A. Alexandra. 2006. *Police ethics.* Crows Nest NSW, Australia: Allen & Unwin.

Muraskin, R., and M. Muraskin. 2001. *Morality and the law.* Upper Saddle River, NJ: Prentice Hall.

Murphy, M. 2008. The role of emotions and transformational leadership on police culture: An autoethnographic account. *International Journal of Police Science and Management,* 10 (2), 165–178.

National Academy of Science. 2009. Strengthening forensic sciences in the United States: A path forward. From www.ncjrs.gov/pdffiles1/nij/grants/228091.pdf (accessed June 6, 2017).

National Association of Social Workers. 2010. Practice. From www.naswdc.org/practice/default.asp (accessed August 2, 2010).

National Commission on Forensic Science. http://www.justice.gov/ncfs (accessed February 15, 2017).

National Criminal Justice Reference Service. *Frye v. United States* 54 App. D.C., at 47, 293F., at 1014; *Daubert v. Merrell Dow Pharmaceuticals Inc.* 509 U.S 579; *Kumho Tire Co. v. Carmichael*, 119 S. Ct. 1167. http://www.ncjrs.gov/spotlight/forensic/legislation.html (accessed June 9, 2017).

National Institute of Ethics. www.ethicsinstitute.com/ (accessed September 24, 2016).

Newburn, T. 1999. *Understanding and Preventing Police Corruption: Lessons from the Literature.* London: Research, Development and Statistics Directorate.

Newell, T. 2017. *Failure in Flint: The Moral Responsibility of Public Servants.* Huffington Post, February 23, 2017.

Packer, H. L. 1968. *The limits of criminal sanction.* Stanford, CA: Stanford University Press.

Palmer, L. K. 2016. *The relationship between education level and Minnesota correctional officers' retention, advancement, and employee misconduct.*

Paoline III, E. A., ed. 2001. *Rethinking police culture: Officers' occupational attitudes.* New York: LFB Scholarly Publishing LLC.

Police Corruption. 2004. *Issues & controversies on file.* From Issues & Controversies database: www.2facts.com/article/i0400270 (accessed February 16, 2010).

Pollock, J. M. 2006. *Ethics in crime and justice: Ethical dilemmas and decisions in criminal justice*, 5th ed. Belmont, CA: Wadsworth.

Pollock, J., and R. Becker. 1996. Ethics training. *FBI Law Enforcement Bulletin*, 65 (11), 20. Retrieved from Master FILE Premier database.

Preston, N. 2001. *Understanding ethics*, 2nd ed. Annandale, NSW, Australia: Federation Press.

Prevost, A., and N. Trautman. n.d. *Police ethics training's state-of-the-art now more effective and comprehensive.* From www.ethicsinstitute.com (accessed July 28, 2010).

Quintilian, M. F. 2006. *Institutio oratoria.* From http://penelope.uchicago.edu?Thayer/E/Roman/Texts/Quintilian/Institutio_Oratoria/home.html (accessed July 20, 2009).

Robbins, R., and Phoenix Pulmonary and Critical Care Research and Education Foundation, Gilbert, AZ. 2014. VA scandal widens. *Southwest Journal of Pulmonary and Critical Care*, 8 (5), 288–289. doi:10.13175/swjpcc070-14

Roberson, C. and S. Mire. 2010. *Ethics for criminal justice professionals.* Boca Raton, FL: CRC Press.

Roberson, C., and H. Wallace. 1998. *Introduction to criminology.* Incline Village, NV: Copperhouse.

Roetzel, R. 2003. *Towards the Army's Ethical System.* U.S. Army Command and General Staff College Leadership Instruction Division, Leadership Course Materials.

Rothwell, G., and J. Baldwin. 2007. Ethical climate theory, whistle-blowing, and the code of silence in police agencies in the State of Georgia. *Journal of Business Ethics*, 70 (4), 341–361.

Rubio, M. 2010. *COPS ethics and integrity training*. From International Association of Chiefs of Police Global Leadership in Policing: www.theiacrg (accessed February 10, 2010).

Schafer, S. 1969. *Theories in criminology*. New York: Random House.

Schafer, J. A., and T. J. Martinelli. 2008. First-line supervisor's perceptions of police integrity: The measurement of police integrity revisited. *Policing*, 31 (2), 306–323.

Second Pennsylvania Supreme Court justice resigns over pornographic email scandal. (2016, March 16). Associated Press. Retrieved from http://www.fox news.com/politics/2016/03/16/second-pennsylvania-supreme-court-justice -resigns-over-pornographic-email-scandal.html

Shafritz, J. M., E. W. Russell, and C. P. Borick. 2007. *Introducing public administra- tion*, 5th ed. New York: Pearson Longman, Inc.

Silva, S., and G. Brown. 2017. *Repairing the Harm with 'VOD' High-Risk Victim Offender Dialogue*. PP presentation, Denver, Colorado.

Simmons, T. (2016, Dec 03). Greeley, weld county law enforcement officials: Changes in country, candidates forcing a new definition of qualified police. *TCA Regional News*. Retrieved from https://search.proquest.com/docview/1845405 474?accountid=35812.

Taguba, A. M. 2004. AR 15-6 Investigation of the 800th Military Police Brigade. Department of Defense Report, June 4, Washington, DC.

Thompson, C. (2015, December 8) PA. Supreme Court justice charged in email scandal. Retrieved from http://www.pennlive.com/midstate/index.ssf/2015/12 /judicial_conduct_board_files_c.html

Trump's turn to private jails boosts their bonds. 2017. *The Bond Buyer*, 1 (34671).

Tucker, B., and S. Triantafyllos. 2008. Lynndie England, Abu Ghraib, and the newImperialism. *Canadian Journal of American Studies*, 38, 83–100.

U.S. Military Academy. 2016. *Building the Capacity to Lead*. West Point, NY.

United States Department of Justice (September 12, 2016). "Justice Department Announces New Steps to Advance and Strengthen Forensic Science." https:// www.justice.gov/opa/pr/justice-department-announces-new-steps-advance -and-strengthen-forensic-science (accessed May 3, 2017).

United States v. Olsen (2013 December 10) Retrieved June 26, 2017 from http://cdn .ca9.uscourts.gov/datastore/opinions/2013/12/10/10-36063%20web.pdf

Vitell, S., M. Bing, H. Davison, A. Ammeter, B. Garner, and M. Novicevic. 2009. Religiosity and moral identity: The mediating role of self-control. *Journal of Business Ethics*, 88 (4), 601–613.

Von Hirsch, A. 1976. *Doing justice*. New York: Hill and Wang.

Watson, A. 2010. Clean as a hound's tooth: The origin of the military police creed. *Military Police*, 43–44. (Retrieved from International Security & Counter Terrorism Reference Center database.)

Wedge, D., and O. Johnson. 2010. *Cop quits after on-duty viewing of midget stripper show*. From www.policeone.com (accessed July 23, 2010).

Weitzer, R. 2015. American policing under fire: Misconduct and reform. *Society*, 52 (5), 475–480. doi:http://dx.doi.org/10.1007/s12115-015-9931-1

West, J. P., and E. M. German, eds. 2006. *The ethics edge*, 2nd ed. Washington, DC: International City/County Management Association. www.merriam-webster .com (accessed June 10, 2017).

Williamson, C., L. Baker, M. Jenkins, and T. Cluse-Tolor. 2007. Police-prostitute interactions: Sometimes discretion, sometimes misconduct. *Journal of Progressive Human Resources* 18 (2), 15–37. doi:10.1300/JO59v18n0203

wlwt.com. 2010. *Ohio officer suspended for on-duty affair with mayor.* From www .officer.com (accessed May 15, 2010).

Wright, A. L. 2008. *Spirituality-centered leadership: Perceptions of law enforcement leaders.* Huntsville, TX: Sam Houston State University.

www.ama-assn.org/ama/pub/physician-resources/medical-ethics/code-medical -ethics.shtml.

www.dictionary.com (accessed December 26, 2010).

www.ethical-perspectives.be/page.php?LAN=E&FILE=subject&ID=119&PAGE=1 (accessed February 15, 2017).

www.expertpages.com (accessed August 20, 2010).

www.merriam-webster.com (accessed May 10, 2016).

www.newworldencyclopedia.org/entry/Ethical_Culture (accessed December 21, 2016).

Zehr, H. 2015. Reflections on lenses. *Restorative Justice*, 3 (3), 460–467. doi:10.1080 /20504721.2015.1109370

Index